How to Sell Out

A Manual to Becoming the Hottest Ticket in Town

by Joe Shellard

First Edition
Published in London, 2024

ISBN: 9798876060006

Written by Joe Shellard
Editorial consultant Andrew Ladd
Cover design by Studio Doug
Author's photograph by Ivan Weiss

For more information, visit www.joeshellard.co.uk

Dedicated to my grandparents.

Introduction

The Coliseum in Rome is a magnificent amphitheatre with capacity for fifty thousand spectators. Above each limestone entrance archway is carved a Roman numeral corresponding to the seating position of incoming audience members — emperors, senators, noble knights and plebeians. For over two millennia, humankind has been engraving numbers into stone and telling people where to sit for a show. Box office managers today, with their perforated stock, Excel spreadsheets and dynamic pricing matrices can trace their professional lineage back to 80 AD and beyond.

We sell more than tickets; we sell experiences, possibilities, and travel into imaginary worlds. We are in the business of memory-making. Tickets are a passport into some of the most pleasurable, joyous, cathartic, and thought-provoking hours in someone's life, and we have the privilege of getting to sell tickets every day. I can't think of many jobs which deliver as much delight as ours.

I got started in ticketing as a teenager by consigning a wad of printed tickets and approaching strangers in city pubs, unsuccessfully asking them if they'd like to buy a ticket for a show I was producing. The endeavour was a failure in every conceivable sense and the show was my first flop. For the first time I felt how painful it is to see an empty auditorium, and how much effort it takes to sell one ticket, let alone ten thousand. That's when I began my obsession with selling out.

In my early twenties I took jobs in box offices at various theatres as a way to watch as many shows as I could, learning about what tickets audiences wanted to buy and how much they'd pay. In the play *Privacy*, a data scientist character called Clive Humby exposes how much theatres can know about their audiences, how they can use it to grow ticket sales, and paints a vision of the future where theatres use big data to produce shows which audiences want to see. Inspired by the futuristic opportunity which the play imagined, I wrote to the real-life Clive Humby and got a job working for him, gathering data from hundreds of theatres around the country, finding trends in how audiences behaved, analysing what caused some performances to sell out whilst others didn't, and tapping the vast potential of data which ticketing organisations sit upon. Clive sold the business after three years and I went on to take roles as head of data for a theatre advertising agency and most recently at an international ticket agency.

Throughout all that, I've seen ticket sales from every side: at the booth, in the auditorium as audiences take their seats, on my phone with the rise of apps and e-tickets, in producer meetings during big on-sales and early closures and tens of millions of pounds of Covid refunds, and into the post-pandemic years as the industry has rebuilt itself into something bigger and better. Along the way, I've seen what works and what doesn't, and I've advised shows of all shapes, sizes and genres about one thing: how to sell tickets.

I will draw on all of these experiences throughout the book, as we discuss how to find an audience for a dud, and how to have your hits earn enough to pay a year of salaries; as we learn what language is most likely to make audiences buy, the optimum day to go on sale, the right discount to offer, the best price for a premium ticket to maximise income, and much more.

This book is split into two halves. The first part will walk you through the lifecycle of setting up a new show, getting it live, selling the tickets, making optimisations and closing the show. We will dive deep into the world of pricing, look at example seating plans, model prices, and discuss mechanics for optimising revenue like premium tickets and subscriptions. We'll consider how long shows should run for and how to optimise towards different lengths of run, before laying out some common problems and how to tackle them.

In part two I'll share my toolkit for selling out, starting with consumer psychology and how to take advantage of the heuristics which are at play when consumers are browsing for tickets to increase your conversion rates and average ticket price. We'll explore measurement in depth, empowering you with total visibility about what state your show is in, and where to look for opportunities and risks within your sales data. I'll lay out which KPIs matter, and which you should ignore. Finally, I'll show you visual examples of the fourteen most important charts and graphs for reaching sell-out success.

I don't claim that the ideas in this book are my own. I have learned a great deal from working with talented clients and colleagues, and this book is my attempt to formalise and consolidate that thinking into a structure which can be applied to shows more broadly. My examples will range from one-night concerts, to studio comedy, to sports nights, to musicals that have run for decades. If you follow the framework suggested in this book from start to finish, it will expose the strengths of your sales, the weaknesses in your potential, and aspects of the ticketing strategy which need to be adjusted.

This framework is bespoke to the business of ticket selling, as opposed to general retail or sales strategy. Ticketing is a deceptively unique sales proposition, because customers often purchase your product weeks or even months before they intend to "use" it, and because there are thousands of slightly-different iterations of the product on different days and with different sight lines. Yet the framework I suggest is nevertheless suitable for events anywhere in the world, large or small, and for events that run for a night or for decades.

This book will offer advice whether you're a marketing professional, a producer, a ticketing manager, or an audience insight specialist. If you are interested in a career in the box office or theatre management, if you want to analyse data about live entertainment, or become an inventory manager, or producer — then the lessons of my experiences can guide your own. Learning from your mistakes is good practice, but learn from someone else's mistakes and you'll find success much quicker. I hope the insights in these pages will inspire your own ticketing endeavours so that shows may continue playing in sold-out houses for thousands of years to come.

Three goals

"Friday and Saturday — that will take care of itself naturally. If you can fill Monday, Tuesday, Wednesday then you're 90% of the way there."
- Gordon Ramsay[1]

It's easy to sell out a show; you spend a lot on marketing and make the tickets cheap. The art — and the subject of this book — will be selling out smart, so that advertising expenditure is in line with income, and tickets are sold at the correct market value. As in Chef Ramsay's quote above, it is about balancing demand for the show with your available inventory.

Consider, as a first question: when do you want to sell out? Selling out too early will leave money on the table from customers who would have bought last minute, while selling out late isn't an option because no one will buy a ticket once the show is over. We need to sell out like Goldilocks: not too early, not too late, not too cheap, not too expensive.

For a second question, consider what you should be charging per seat. In a thousand-seat auditorium, increasing ticket prices from £100 to £105 might cause 20 people not to attend, but still increases revenues by £2,900. So perhaps it's not as simple as just selling out.

Every event has three goals it can chase:

- High occupancy (filling every seat)
- High yield (maximising revenue)
- Longevity (keeping the show running a long time)

Most professionals can achieve any one of these in isolation, and an intelligent ticketing manager can create strategies and compromises which achieve two. Reaching all three is near impossible, so we'll work on strategies to meet the bespoke brief of each show.

To glibly answer the question of this book's title, the fastest way to sell out is to disregard either yield or longevity. But the shrewd move is to balance all three objectives at different points in an event's lifecycle, which will make for higher attendance and revenue in the long run.

---

[1] Hot Ones. https://www.youtube.com/watch?v=U9DyHthJ6LA

Ground rules

"The play's the thing"
- William Shakespeare [2]

This book is preoccupied with the optimum ways to sell tickets from a practical perspective. But I also have my own sentiments about how best to sell tickets from a philosophical perspective, and naturally those inform my practical recommendations. Before we launch into the fine details of ticketing strategy, we must touch on that bigger picture. Otherwise, I fear, if you are reading this book hoping you will be able to better hoodwink audiences into padding your bank balance with a show worse than Max Bialystock's, then you will be very disappointed.

Whatever our role — be it actor, set designer, or ticket-seller — we are all in service of the show. We got into this industry because we love what happens on stage, the buzz of an incoming audience, the thrill of an ephemeral performance, and the electricity of a standing ovation.

So while this book will deal with optimising the minutiae of selling tickets, it will always be in service of the show and is an expression of our love for live entertainment. We have no misapprehension that we are the main reason for a show's success. The show is the thing.

The role of a ticketing manager is a commercial position, but we are a representative of the art. It isn't becoming of us to use underhand tactics to prise money from our audiences. If the purpose of a show is to move an audience emotionally, then the emotions shouldn't be humiliation or resentment. The musical might be *Oliver*, but we are not Fagin.

Our work will not just have good ends but also good means, so treat audiences and customers with respect. They are not to be conned or fleeced. We value their custom, and they need to make informed consent with each purchase — which means giving them all of the relevant information up front and not covertly charging them for something they don't need, or conspicuously steering them to a premium ticket whilst concealing that lower prices are available.

Not only is this the right thing to do, but the nature of having a thousand customers pass through the doors each day means that bad word will soon

[2] Shakespeare, W. (1601) Hamlet, act two, scene two.

get around the community about anything underhand and, as we shall see, loyalty is the lifeblood of successful ticket-selling. Cheating someone from an extra dollar now will lose us ten in the long run.

Our tactics should be that of a jeweller or a wedding planner, making highly valued, customer-centric recommendations, rather than those of a second-hand car salesperson who seeks only to make a quick buck. I implore the reader to reject the magnetic temptations of the dark side of ticketing and instead use the tactics outlined in this book to achieve sell-out auditoriums of satisfied audiences, who are happy with their purchase and enthusiastic about returning.

So we have our rules of the road - the play is the thing, we will be Oliver but not Fagin, and there are only three possible objectives we can chase. Now we are ready to start selling some tickets.

Part one: pricing, promotions and problem-solving

2022 was an awful year for theatre in London, and should have been amongst the worst on record. Brexit had dented inbound tourism almost 25% percent[3], anxiety raged about new Covid variants, and no A-list American stars crossed the Atlantic to grace our stages. The hospitality, airline and hotel sectors were struggling all around us, and there was little to protect the theatre sector from deflating.

But in spite of those challenges, there were more tickets sold for West End theatre in 2022 than pre-pandemic in 2019. Despite Brexit, coronavirus and massive decline to tourist visitors: box office receipts were up. There were no extra seats installed or venues built, just the same thirty nine Victorian-era playhouses which had existed for a century. And yet attendances were increased 7% on 2019 and revenue jumped 12%[4].

How could this be?

One answer is optimisation of inventory: a focused effort to be hyper-targeted about who we are trying to sell a ticket to, which performance we want audiences to see, and where we want them to sit.

This precise strategy is how London theatre was able to take extraordinarily difficult circumstances and still come out on top. In terms of a marketing funnel, fewer potential customers came in the top, but ticketing managers and producers were exceptionally successful at converting more of them into buying a ticket.

Admittedly, London had an advantage and inadvertently drew some audiences away from regional theatres. These local theatres were grappling with their own set of challenges, including severe cuts to arts funding and the difficulties in securing touring productions from producers who were increasingly risk-averse.

---

3 https://www.visitbritain.org/research-insights/inbound-visits-and-spend-annual-uk

4 Society of London Theatre (2023) The Box Office Data Report 2022

The West End came out of the pandemic with an unfair advantage over the regions, but that doesn’t mean its ticketing managers weren’t working harder than ever in 2022 to squeeze more from less. This book is all about learning from that example. It's a guide on how to do more with less — to make a sale from more of your potential customers and to optimise every single piece of the finite inventory which you have available. By exploring the strategies employed by London's theatres, we uncover insights into making the most of challenging situations, demonstrating how focused effort and precise strategy can lead to success even under extraordinary circumstances.

Establishing your ticketing strategy

"Someone is sitting in the shade today because someone planted a tree a long time ago."
- Warren Buffett[5]

Your ticketing strategy will be your roadmap to success. Every show needs a strategy, from the smallest one-nighter to a Vegas spectacular which runs for decades. Strategies align everyone around the same expectations, ensure that diverse efforts pursue the same goals, and ultimately form your competitive advantage against fate.

We need to define and write down the strategy early on so it is clear to everyone involved, because it will soon get tested, and we can't be thrown off course by third parties who have their own incentives. Having a written strategy can also help to codify your objectives so that you can remind yourselves why it is is or isn't right to take a particular decision much later in the show's lifetime.

One of the ways that show business is different from other industries is that the product and target customer vary from one project to the next. A small change in the venue, capacity, or actors can make for a huge contrast between two productions, even if you've put the same show on sale in previous years. Therefore we cannot rely on doing the same thing we did on the last show, or assuming that our team knows which levers to pull. A ticketing strategy is required for every show to get clarity on what the product is and how it will sell out.

A common failure when selling shows occurs when colleagues have different ideas about what the show is trying to do, and unintentionally pursue contrary strategies. This leads to undermining the product, customer confusion, and selling fewer tickets than you otherwise could have.

---

[5] Kilpatrick, A. (1996) Of permanent value: The story of Warren Buffett. Birmingham, AL: AKPE.

Realism

Most producers think that their show is better than average.

That simply can't be true. It is a mathematical impossibility for most to be better than average and is an example of illusory superiority, a cognitive bias where people overestimate themselves in relation to others. Many producers I've met think that their script is better written, their set better designed, and their actors better performers, so their tickets should be priced higher than the competition.

Many producers think that their show is *Hamilton*.

Well, not even *Hamilton* is *Hamilton*.

Looking at *Hamilton's* box office receipts, they have softer weeks just like everyone else, and need a well-capitalised advertising campaign to keep sales buoyant. At the time of writing, grosses for *Hamilton* on Broadway are down 20% year-on-year.[6]

It is easy in the early days of a show for a hype-fever to circulate within the team. So it's important to stay level-headed with an eye on what is actually achievable rather than fooling yourself that you have the next *Hamilton*. Unless you are exceptionally lucky, you probably don't.

---

[6] https://www.broadwayleague.com/research/grosses-broadway-nyc/ Hamilton July 2023 versus July 2022

Objectives

Decide and agree on what your objectives are for sales. Make sure that these are realistic and formulated to maximise the success of the show, rather than driven by ego. For example, it may sound ambitious to want to have 'sold all of the tickets before the first performance', but this is foolish if you stand a better chance of selling them for a higher price once reviews are out.

Don't set objectives for the sake of it, either; you should only need two or three from the list above, and if you try to set more you will only confuse your strategy. The leadership team needs to align around two to three high-level objectives, which you will focus on at the cost of anything else.

This is a good time for your team to debate what success looks like for you. Can it be artistically successful with a packed audience, even if it doesn't break even? If the average ticket price is high, does it matter that the auditorium is half-empty? Is it necessary to have built up a large advance by the first performance, or can you afford to wait for word to get around once you've opened, if that means you finish with higher sales in total? Would discounting damage your brand value, or would it be worth it for the increased tickets?

Revenue is easy to quantify, but there may be other softer objectives like diversity, accessibility, community engagement, and so on, which also need consideration. With some thought, you should be able to quantify these as well. For example, "We are prepared to accept that we lose income on 100 seats if we can get young people to fill these. But 100 empty seats or an auditorium without any young people would be a failure". You could consider giving yourself goals in these areas:

- Revenue by the end of the run
- Tickets sold by the end of the run, or proportion of total tickets sold vs unsold
- Advance sold by the first performance
- Average ticket price
- Diversity / accessibility quotas.

Once you have decided on your objective(s), you can set about a strategy to get there.

Understand the product

Evaluate the nature of your product (for example the show's title and pedigree, any star casting), along with the capacity and location of the venue, and the number of planned performances.

An unknown title or new play may mean you need to rely on word-of-mouth once performances have started to really maximise your sales. A short-run may force you to sell most tickets ahead of time because there will be no time for people to buy tickets once opening night has happened. If the location is unusual or far away from a population centre, then it may be a considered purchase for consumers, something where they will need to plan travel and accommodation ahead of time. If that's the case, you won't be able to rely on same-day sales and must fill seats weeks ahead of each performance.

It's also important to consider the competitive landscape in which you'll be selling your product. If your show will be in a crowded field of similar alternatives, you will require a very different approach than if you have a unique format or proposition that nobody in your market has experienced before.

Only once you understand the product can you make informed decisions about how to sell it.

Fireworks and hot water bottles

If there is one problem with the way that live entertainment often sells tickets, it is that they treat shows like fireworks. Shows can be given a minute to burn brightly before they quickly fizzle out and are forgotten. Well, the light that burns twice as bright burns half as long. Instead, longevity should be the name of the game, because it is what keeps theatres full, actors on stage, and all of us in gainful employment. Fireworks are the antithesis of longevity.

Ticketing managers could learn a lot from the humble hot water bottle. The rubber vessel gets filled with boiling water in the late evening and manages to preserve its heat for twelve hours, dissipating it gently overnight and keeping its guardian toasty warm through the chills of winter.

The challenge faced by good shows is that they are only 'hot' for a short moment. I was once involved in 'the must-see show-of-the-year'. It opened to great fanfare because its lead star, fresh from Hollywood, appeared on primetime national television to promote the show. Visits to the website went up 10,000%. We were sold out for months ahead, and tickets got resold at astronomical prices. The problem came only weeks later when the celebrity left the cast, and suddenly, we were just like all of the other shows, vying for attention. It had all been a sugar high, and the coming months were much more challenging than they needed to be because people either mistakenly thought we were sold out or were disappointed because the Sexiest Man of the Year was no longer appearing. Instead of paying a star for six weeks, we should have used the money to create a sustainable hit which would be hot year-round.

The economics of showbiz is that production (development, building, rehearsal, etc.) is expensive, and roll-out (performances) is the profit centre. So we want to stay within the world of roll-out, if we can, to avoid the costs of producing a new show. For that reason, we should avoid our shows being hot for a day and then fading from everyone's memories. Consider the hot water bottle and how we can preserve heat so that it dissipates over time and gives us months or years of roll-out.

A theme of this book will be about balancing supply and demand. Our supply is fixed; for example the show might have a thousand tickets to sell per night, eight times a week. When supply is a constant, demand needs to be manipulated. We will need to put in place thoughtful strategies which siphon demand in the right quantities so that there are always enough customers coming through the funnel to justify ticket prices, whilst not having too many potential customers that it overwhelms us and we have no tickets to sell them. There are macro tactics for moving supply, such as advertising "tickets from £20" on television, but these sometimes serve to be so broad that they overwhelm the show with lots of demand at one price point or particular performance dates, and leave holes elsewhere.

We should aim to utilise tactics which disrupt the fewest possible prospects, whilst steering them into the inventory which we need to move. The more precise that our tactics can be, the better that we can optimise sales. When you are presented with a potential tactic to drive sales, consider how precisely it addresses your specific problem in terms of the number of prospects who will be exposed to it, the amount of targeted inventory which it will sell, and the collateral damage of either selling inventory which you weren't targeting, or disappointed prospects who are unable to buy the inventory being advertised.

By way of example, say you were struggling to sell midweek tickets and were offered the opportunity to sell half-price tickets to teachers at nearby schools. On the one hand, this sounds like a good opportunity as teachers seem deserving of a discount, they can fill seats which would otherwise go empty, and its better to earn some money from these tickets than to give them away for free.

However, the discount is being offered on all performances, when in fact only the midweek performances need the help, and so isn't tackling the precise problem. It is targeting a very large pool of prospects (teachers at a several local schools), which might create wide awareness that there are discounts around, thereby devaluing the show. It's reasonable that some of those teachers might have been planning to buy full-priced tickets anyway, and so it creates collateral damage by handing them a discount unnecessarily.

This scenario could be improved by doing a price-sensitivity analysis to understand what is the minimum discount required to increase ticket sales for the midweek performances, by tightening the group of people who the promotion is advertised to (such as only one school), or keeping ticket prices as-is but offering a free third ticket to midweek performances so that the midweeks reach higher capacity but without devaluing the show and undercutting your own ticket price.

Example ticketing strategy

Show
Hamlet by William Shakespeare

Casting
Major Hollywood star

Venue
London, West End theatre, 800 seats

Performances
December - January next year

Background
Hollywood star wants to be seen as a serious actor so is doing a very short theatre run.

Objectives
Tickets sold by the end of the run: 100%.
Important not to embarrass the star by having any empty seats, especially early in the run or in conspicuous front rows.

Advance sold by the first performance: 80% of ticket potential

Average ticket price: Aiming for £80 based on last year's show, but comfortable with less if demand doesn't materialise.

Competitive landscape
Hamlet is a perennial favourite, frequently staged in London, and audiences have appetite for new stagings and fresh casting of this title.
There are no other celebrities doing Shakespeare in the city next Winter, and the season is dominated by family-orientated Christmas shows, as well as three productions of *A Christmas Carol* starring celebrities of lesser calibre.
The Royal Shakespeare Company is performing a high-profile *Macbeth,* but we feel that Stratford-Upon-Avon is sufficiently distant from London to not be a risk for our production.

Insights

The product is strong but the timing is difficult. December may be challenging as there is so much festive entertainment competing for consumers' attention around Christmastime, which may be more appealing to audiences than this dark Shakespeare. January is always difficult to sell because audiences' budgets are tight post-holidays. Therefore we'll try to secure bookings early, before advertising for the festive entertainment starts. Christmas shows have a lot of inventory at cheap prices, so we'll avoid a race to the bottom by focusing marketing efforts on attracting culture-vulture, high-ATP bookers, supplemented by an accessibility scheme to encourage young and diverse audiences.

The auditorium has many restricted view seats, and so we will need to maximise use of premium inventory to reach the required revenue targets. Performances start next year so our targets should reflect slow sales until much closer, given that the marketing budget will need to stretch over a long period and audiences will be choosing to tickets for shows which are currently playing. The run is short so we won't have much time for word-of-mouth or reviews to create sales once performances have begun, so will need to be close to sold out by first performance.

Strategy

Put all performances on sale at once so that January gets the best possible chance at selling. Don't discount any weeks as the run is so short and appeal of the star is so high that customers should cascade into the off-peak January weeks naturally once December has sold. Promote the restricted-view seats with an accessible entry price, and clearly label them as restricted view. Hold back some of the premium tickets so that the plan doesn't look overly expensive, and trickle them on each time that a pair sells, so that there are always a handful of prime seats at top price available.

Anticipating high demand, have a 'ticketing availability' page on the website with a clear calendar showing which performances have the most inventory left available, and where to look for the cheapest tickets. We'll give clear messaging that no additional performances will be added so that customers feel urgency to book now, or risk not getting a ticket. Place an exit-intent popup for anyone who goes to leave the site without buying, and prompt them to leave their email address in case more tickets become available later. Use this email list in case of any last-minute returns, so that every seat is filled.

Put in place a strict policy of releasing holds four weeks before performance, to ensure that every seat goes sold. For any tickets returned by customers, put them on sale at the higher dynamic price. Make a 10% allocation available for subscribers to the Hollywood star's fan club, so that there is a supportive audience. Put this on sale at the same time as the general onsale to maximise PR around the event.

Onsale will be our opportunity to gauge latent demand for this star. If page views are high but conversions are low, then we will look at reducing ticket prices. If page views are low then the marketing team will encourage the star to do more PR appearances to promote the project. If conversion rate remains low, then we will place holds on many of the tickets so that the seating plans look more occupied and therefore encourage browsing customers to book. We have no requirement to create a brand as the show will only run for two months, and so we will utilise discounting as means to fill the top of funnel if required. We will utilise a ticket agent for this as it brings in a new potential audience and still allows us to sell at full-price through our main website.

The week before performances begin, announce an on-the-day rush. Important not to announce sooner, as we don't want this to cannibalise our full price tickets. Tickets will be £50, which is higher than rush tickets usually sell for, but we believe still competitive given the calibre of our star and the fact that we should be largely sold out by this point. Rush tickets will be the first row of the stalls, to create a supportive and youthful audience, and also used to fill any gaps in the premium section which have gone unsold by day-of-performance. This will balance our desire for accessibility and sell out with the ambition to reach high ticket yields in a small auditorium.

Sales targets

	Tickets	Gross	Average ticket price (ATP)
Potential	50,000 (100%)	£4.35m (100%)	£85
By first week of onsale	16,650 (33%)	£1.3m (30%)	£80
By 12 weeks out	33,300 (66%)	£2.6m (61%)	£80
By first performance	40,000 (80%)	£3.2m (74%)	£80
By end of the run	50,000 (100%)	£4m (92%)	£80

Targets or forecasts?

"It is often possible to make a profit by being pretty good at prediction in fields where the competition succumbs to poor incentives, bad habits, or blind adherence to tradition—or because you have better data or technology than they do."
- Nate Silver[7]

Ticket sales is an industry which statistician Nate Silver would recognise as having been poor at prediction in the past and ripe for someone to profit by doing it better. In my previous role as a ticketing manager, my forecasts could transform the production's level of success by how I chose to alter the course — or not — dependent on how those forecasts compared to the production's targets.

These estimates help dictate whether prices should go up or down, they inform decisions of whether or not to increase investments, they determine which shows and campaigns require more significant advertising efforts, they define how staff are resourced, and most crucially they are the final backstop in mitigating a commercial failure before it happens.

It's important to be clear on the difference between objectives, targets and forecasts. Objectives are the realm of the futurist, who is looking ahead and anticipating what could happen in months or years' time, and quantifying what it means for ticket sales to have been a success. If the organisation fails to meet the objective, the show has failed. This could be not earning enough revenue to cover the costs, or getting lower audience numbers than are required for future funding. Objectives tend to be focused around the end of a show's run the end of a season, or a year's performances for a long-running title, such as to have played to an average 80% attendance.

Targets are a more practical short-term way of thinking about objectives. They help align and motivate a marketing team around a common sales goal. Targets can be modest, ambitious or pragmatic. In any case, their purpose is to orient everyone about what success looks like on a daily, weekly or monthly basis. An example of a target is to sell 300 tickets per week; an easily-understood, short-term goal which everyone can monitor

---

[7] Silver, N. (2015) The signal and the noise: The art and science of prediction. London: Penguin Group.

and focus their actions towards. Objectives, which may be years away, can feel impossible to control as the numbers are massive, but staff can and should feel capable of reaching targets.

Forecasts are the realm of the realist and detail what one believes will actually happen. They are grounded in hard data about how previous shows have performed, how the current show is performing, and the quantifiable state of the entertainment market and macro consumer trends. Forecasts should have absolutely no bias whatsoever. Unlike targets, which are determined by the particular subjective needs of the people and organisations setting them, anyone looking at all of the data should in theory reach a similar forecast.

Forecasts leverage datasets like hourly sales figures, website visits, footfall statistics and industry reports. Forecasts can be used for the most delicate decision-making around production viability and cash flow. They are often kept secretive because the sensitivity around their implications can be significant for all working on the show.

Unfortunately, there is often a significant lack of precision when discussing these various numbers that are so vital to guiding a show's success. Targets are often shared as if they are forecasts, even though the two numbers serve very different purposes. To use an analogy, a fisherman may have a target of catching ten lobsters today, but if he checks the sonar that shows inclement conditions are imminent, their forecast may be to only catch five lobsters today. His objective of catching 3,000 lobster this year is unchanged.

Note that targets and forecasts don't necessarily bear resemblance to one another. Targets are often spoken about as if they were forecasts because it provides a helpful fiction for shareholders and staff alike to remain optimistically focused on where they hope to get to. If someone shares their "forecast" with you, hold some healthy scepticism that it may, in fact, be a target.

Setting targets

> **"In God we trust. Others must bring data."**
> **— Professor Edwin R. Fisher[8]**

Some of the best targets in life are curiously simple: 10,000 steps to stay fit, five fruit and vegetables for a healthy diet, and eight hours of sleep a night to stay alert. These targets have caught hold with the general public because they favour memorability over precision.

Human beings struggle to remember multiple data points, so it is wise to avoid burdening your team with too many numbers. Instead, one or two well-considered targets which are very memorable will become much more helpful because they are easy to recall.

Call on all data which you can possibly claim access to when setting targets. Look to historical sales from your own company, other shows that have played at this venue or similar ones, digital data about search trends and consumer interests, and industry reports about footfall, retail, restaurants, or hotels. Often, there will be shortcomings in a particular data source, whether it is historical, about a different production, or concerning another type of customer. This is why a patchwork is needed to view the entire picture.

Targets and forecasts are established using similar methodologies. However, a key distinction lies in their adaptability to changing circumstances. Targets, in an ideal scenario, remain constant, serving as steadfast goals to strive towards. In contrast, forecasts are dynamic and should be adjusted as conditions evolve.

In its most basic form, we can set targets by dividing up the total objective (e.g. 10,000 sold tickets) by the number of weeks until the end of the run (e.g. 10) and arrive at a target (the need to sell 1,000 tickets every week), though I propose some nuances.

There are three points in the lifecycle of a limited-run event where it is helpful to have a target: on-sale, or the couple of days immediately following when tickets initially go on sale; the first performance, or gala night if you have one; and the end of the run. (Obviously, for some shows,

---

[8] Effect of smoking on nonsmokers hearing before the Subcommittee on Tobacco of the Committee on Agriculture, House of Representatives, Ninety-fifth Congress, second session, September 7, 1978.

the first performance and the end of the run may be the same date.) Each of these points should have a target, which can be in tickets and/or revenue. The numbers should be framed as cumulative sales to date for the entire run/season. I call these "season totals" since they describe the total sales made to date for all performances in the entire season.

Example targets are:

Bookings by the end of the first day of sales: 100 tickets | £2,000

Bookings by the first performance: 2,000 tickets | £40,000

Bookings by the end of the run: 6,000 tickets | £120,000

I suggest it's counter-productive to have more than three or four sales targets when shows run for less than six months of performances because colleagues struggle to meaningfully focus on them, and they start to describe quite small periods of time and rely on individual marketing tactics, rather than the trajectory of the campaign as a whole.

I prefer the cumulative season totals rather than wrap figures, because it means that if you miss your first target, you can still aim to make the second target by unweighting the campaign. If we only used wrap targets, then the second target would need to be adjusted to take into account the shortfall.

If setting a revenue target, pick net or gross revenue, but don't confuse things by having a target for both. Attempting to increase your gross-to-net ratio is not a sensible target. This is a substantial strategic exercise which involves renegotiating ticketing contracts or applying for tax exemptions, so is not within the realm of what the ticketing team could reasonably expect to achieve on a week-by-week basis.

Average ticket price (ATP) could be a secondary target, but in reality, it is a very difficult metric to move because it is an average of thousands of ticket sales, and is determined by your goals for tickets and revenue.

For a long-running show, a valuable additional target is the weekly wrap, i.e. all the transactions made within a week for all performances. The weekly wrap is usually quite sensitive to marketing activity, so it is a particularly useful target when you're considering new sales initiatives or reducing advertising spend.

I recommend weekly wraps because figures for daily wraps tend to be small and subject to external interference, such as consumers generally preferring to buy more tickets on a Monday and fewer on a Sunday. As such, they are not a meaningful target and are too granular for marketing teams to learn anything from. However, if the pace of your sales is slower or more consistent, then monthly wrap targets could be more appropriate than weekly ones.

On a long-running title, it can be helpful to set targets for how you expect each week of performances to mature, and then some milestones for how these sales will build in the weeks leading up to performance. (We will discuss this in more detail later, in the chapter on Measurement and Optimisation.) The benefit of this is that it acknowledges there will be peaks and troughs to the year, so all performances will not sell equally, and also that there is an expected trajectory to sales. Measuring whether sales are tracking above or behind this trajectory helps a marketing and sales team to define which performances need attention with extra promotion or discounting and where yield should be maximised. My advice to only use these latter targets on long-running shows and not limited-run events is because the data can be quite noisy, subject to large fluctuations on short-run events and not predictable without several months of historical data to call upon.

When sharing your targets, present your thinking clearly, re-draft in response to collegial feedback, and deliver the signed-off targets in an evident form to the whole marketing and sales team so that they have an obvious record to which they can refer back later. Clearly lay out your rationale for why you have set the targets that you have.

Often, you will be unsure of what targets you should set because there are so many uncertainties, so make explicit the assumptions which you have made. List out every piece of promotional activity and PR which you are aware of and its anticipated timings alongside the respective target. The purpose here is not to nickel-and-dime each part of marketing activity, but instead as a way for you to justify and comment on any deviation from the targets.

For example, suppose some anticipated advertising did not happen, and targets were unmet. In that case, there is a helpful cause-and-effect to point to, which justifies increasing targets later in the sales cycle and doing more promotion. Because you have so little data to call upon in the target setting, it is all the more important to make clear what you know and the assumptions you are making.

Plotting sales trajectories

"People notice one type of mistake—the failure to predict rain —more than another kind, false alarms. If it rains when it isn't supposed to, they curse the weatherman for ruining their picnic, whereas an unexpectedly sunny day is taken as a serendipitous bonus." - Nate Silver[9]

When setting targets, consider your show's likely sales trajectory and give yourself an easier time at first. Few things are more demoralising for a sales team than to produce a set of targets and immediately fall short of the first. It casts doubt on the sales manager's skill for target-setting and whether or not the production will reach its overall objective. On the other hand, narrowly reaching your day-one target gives everyone confidence that sales are where they should be, and that they are being led by a competent sales manager.

In turn, this does mean that targets will have to be slightly higher later on in the sales cycle, but by this point, collective attention will have moved on from the accuracy of targets, and you'll have appreciated enough goodwill to see you through a week or two of missed targets if needed. This is a benevolent deception where targets are made slightly lower than they could be in order to benefit the entire team's morale.

On longer running shows where you're tracking weekly wraps, don't make the common pitfall of setting a record-breaking wrap target during your final weeks, because there is an oft-forgotten existential limitation. Your target for tickets wrapped during your last weeks of performances should always be less than those wrapped during the early weeks of performances, because there is much less inventory available. Consumers who purchase during your opening week can choose to book a performance from opening week or any other week in the run. In contrast, consumers booking on the final week are limited to only a handful of performances. Even though you are riding high, your wraps should always take a dip towards the end because there are fewer performances, and you hopefully have better advance sales into the remaining performances.

---

[9] Silver, N. (2015) The signal and the noise: The art and science of prediction. London: Penguin Group.

Measuring against targets

Only set targets you can easily measure, like those listed on the preceding pages. Whilst there may be particular interest in tracking some specific metric, it will prove more burdensome and unhelpful if it is not a figure easily found in real-time.

For example, data points like the number of distinct people who have viewed all of your adverts within a week are near-impossible to ascertain, because you can't avoid double-counting between advertising platforms. It's tempting to measure the number of people who have never been to a theatre before, but this relies on patchy self-reporting at the time of booking and omits the 50% or more of your audience who are "ghosts" — that is, the companions of the ticket purchaser whom you have no way of measuring.

Even something as seemingly simple as the proportion of the audience who are under the age of 18 is challenging to measure due to data protection regulations around minors. Hence, think carefully about what metrics you will use as targets and ensure you can confidently access accurate figures on an ongoing basis.

I advise against modifying targets once they have been set because the psychology of moving the goalposts makes teams think that the targets have become less relevant. If you are continually tracking behind the targets, preserving this truth is important so the team can recognise how much distance they have to make up. Conversely, tracking ahead of target gives you some buffer in case past performance does not predict future success.

The main time when adjusting targets is acceptable is if the fundamental objective has changed, and this will either be a reduction of production costs (I live to see the day) or an increase in inventory (extra performances being added). In these cases, your targets should change so substantially that the old ones are redundant. That said, if the modification is within 10%, then I suggest it is best to keep the existing targets because the confusion and fragmentation will do more harm than good.

As with the original target setting, ensure that version two is fully signed off and agreed upon by all stakeholders, because there are few things more confusing than tracking actual numbers concurrently against two sets of targets. As I mentioned earlier, the team must be able to agree on what success looks like.

Consider your marketing options if you fall behind targets. What levers can you pull to set sales back on course? Consider how drastic these levers are and the order in which you would want to pull them.

For example, if sales are only slightly behind for one week, then maybe an extra social media post would suffice, whereas three consecutive weeks would require you to bring forward a planned e-shot to local businesses. How bad would sales need to be before you activate above-the-line discounting?

It is sensible to consider all of these questions collectively before going on sale, because you can see things with a clearer view than during the panicked melee which takes hold when sales fall behind. It gives you a reference point to work from rather than making rushed judgements in the heat of things.

Marketing funnel

The marketing funnel is a concept that describes the journey a customer takes from the first interaction with a brand to the final purchase or conversion. It's visualised as a funnel because it starts with a very broad pool of people with many potential customers (the "top" of the funnel), and then narrows down through various stages to the few who eventually make a purchase (the "bottom" of the funnel). Post-purchase stages can also be included, such as customer retention, loyalty, and advocacy, which can lead to repeat purchases, season tickets and referrals.

The goal of a marketer is to guide as many customers as possible through the funnel, passing through each of the following stages. Ticketing professionals are concentrated with the bottom of the funnel whilst advertisers and media-buyers focus on the top of the funnel.

Awareness

At this first stage, the customer first becomes aware of a a show. Perhaps they come across an advertisement while scrolling through their social media feed, see a video trailer on YouTube, or receive an email from a ticket agent newsletter they subscribe to. This digital content aims to not only inform them about the show but also entice them to learn more.

Consideration

Now intrigued, the customer actively seeks more information about the show. They might visit the theatre's website to read about the show in detail, watch interviews with the cast, or check out audience reviews. They could also compare it with other shows using online entertainment guides or discussion forums. The theatre's digital strategy at this stage might involve providing comprehensive and engaging content on their website, optimising for search engines (SEO) so that their show comes up early on results pages, and encouraging positive online reviews.

Conversion

Finally, the customer decides to purchase the ticket. They return to the theatre or ticket agent website, choose their preferred date and seat, and complete the payment. The goal is to make this process as easy and frictionless as possible, by providing clearly presented instructions and ticket options, a secure and user-friendly payment system, and immediate confirmation of their purchased seats.

The conversion rate is the number of people who buy tickets divided by the total number of prospects who were advertised to; anywhere from 2% to 5% is common. The unit of measurement is customers, not tickets. One of the most valuable targets you can set yourself is to increase the proportion of customers who move from awareness to consideration, and consideration to conversion. Conversion rates are usually so low that optimisation for these two metrics will have an oversized benefit at the box office. A one-percentage-point increase in conversion rate can be responsible for a 10% increase in ticket sales.

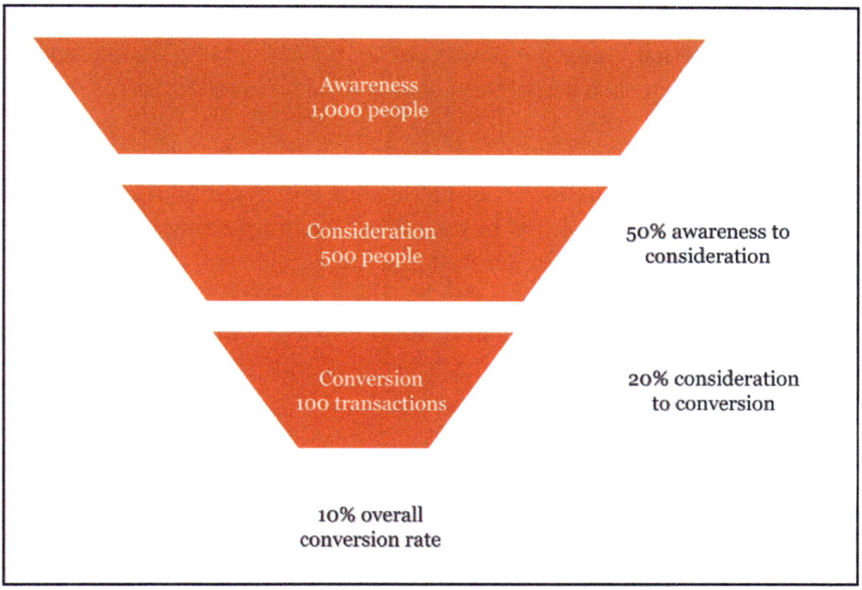

Ticketing

Many great books have been written about arts marketing in the context of awareness and consideration. Much of what this book covers is the last stage of the funnel: conversion. This is the portion which we can most confidently measure as ticketing managers, and which will lead to the most immediate results on your bottom line. However, there are times when the ticketing manager also needs to consider what's happening further up the funnel.

Our tactics must be contextual to the stage of the funnel which we are trying to improve. For example, if a show wanted to increase the top of the funnel, then announcing star casting or buying outdoor advertisements would be suitable. If the show wanted to increase the number of tickets sold on Tuesday evenings, then it'd be better to put messaging on the website's calendar page saying “best tickets at the best price on Tuesdays”.

Where shows come unstuck is where they try to solve one part of the funnel with a tactic for a different part. For example, outdoor adverts which say "best prices on Tuesdays" is jarring to a customer who is learning about the show for the first time, and is a poor use of prime space which should be giving high-level brand messaging about why someone should see the show at all. Generally, messaging at the top of the funnel should be about the show's brand and themes, the consideration period should be used for sharing social proof, developing FOMO and any required education (such as the show being in two parts, or in an unusual location), and the conversion stage is the point for any ticketing signposting such as performance days, parts of the house, group sizes. Each stage of the funnel addresses a reducing number of prospects and so the tactics should become more specific with each stage, but avoid getting too specific too early.

Inevitably, even after a long period of successful sales, your good fortune will come to an end and the ticketing revenue will begin to dry up. It is easy for naive fingers to be pointed in your direction, suggesting that ticket prices need to be reduced unilaterally. In my experience, this is rarely the right course of action. I suggest that by this point in the sales cycle, your conversion machine is running at its most efficient; you have settled on a range of prices which the market can bear and optimised a booking flow which makes checkout straightforward.

Most likely, the reason for your recent decline in sales on a long-runner is because the number of people coming down the funnel from awareness and consideration has dropped. That is to say, the marketing team are running dry of prospects and they aren't finding people who are interested in your product in the same volume as before. Or perhaps your product has changed; the lead star has left, it's no longer the hot ticket, you've saturated the available market. Whatever the cause might be of the marketing funnel getting narrower, it isn't pricing — because pricing only has an impact right at the bottom. So before leaping to reduce all of your prices, think first about what levers can be pulled higher up the funnel to actually increase your number of prospects, rather than handing out bargains to your dwindling pool of hot leads.

That's not to say that discounts are *never* a meaningful way to widen the funnel, because ticket agents can use them to reach more people (awareness), and they act as a compelling hook (consideration). However, simply reducing your prices across the board — without shouting about it — is no good without accompanying marketing action.

Pricing

Pricing directly influences consumer behaviour in many respects, including their product selection, attendance frequency, and willingness to pay.

By now, you will have outlined a ticketing strategy with goals for occupancy, revenue, and longevity. Your next task is to determine the range of prices that you will offer, in the correct volumes, to help you reach your aims. Consider how your goals for pricing relate to your overall sales objectives. Are you seeking to achieve profitability, increase audience attendance, attract new customers, or foster customer loyalty? What influence will the forces of pricing have on those objectives?

Having high-priced tickets may stroke your ego, but it is no good if no one buys them. There's no shame in pricing a little lower than what the market will bear and selling out quickly if it means that you make your target. When setting ticket prices, we do not have a crystal ball, so the best we can aim for is to reach our targets. Optimising for more than that is the work of dynamic pricing and yield management, which will come later. Right now, we need to concentrate on not butchering the on-sale by getting prices so drastically wrong that we cause people to be actively disinterested in our title. If that happens, we'll need to win them back around later with expensive marketing, so let's try to get it right first time.

Concentrate more on what you expect audiences to pay and the proportion of tickets you actually expect to sell. These prices must get you to your targets, and also be realistic for your product in this marketplace. This is an exercise in cold realism.

A good starting point for determining pricing is to consider the average ticket price (ATP) you expect audiences to pay. It's a handy metric because you can easily compare it with the actual achieved at other productions (both your own and in the marketplace), and it can serve to ground your thinking. Is this show really worth 20% more than what the last smash-hit achieved?

Yield-Occupancy Matrix

The yield-occupancy matrix can help you work through different scenarios for what happens once your show is open. Across the columns on top, list percentage occupancies: 100% full, 90% full etc. Down the vertical rows are increments of possible average ticket prices. It's wise to put in the middle what you achieved last time (or what your nearest competitor did), and then evenly step up and down from there. The top-left cell will show your potential income if you sold 100% of tickets at a very high price, and the bottom-right will show income if you sold many fewer tickets at a much lower ATP.

You can now highlight the cells which are greater than your target, and you'll be presented with a smorgasbord of scenarios to reach your goal. For example, you could sell 90% of tickets at £50, or 60% of tickets at £80. This is a useful matrix to share with stakeholders from production to the venue, as it lays out exactly what is required to reach your goals. Very quickly the highlighted numbers provoke comments like "we could never charge more than £50" or "we'd never be able to sell out 90% of the seats" and so promptly aligns everybody with what a realistic target looks like, and what sales are required to get there. Now that you've filtered down your options, pick one target scenario to aim for.

Two words of caution. Firstly, give yourself some fat. If your target requires you to sell 100% of tickets at the highest possible price, then you've given yourself no room for flexibility when you later suffer the slings and arrows of outrageous fortune from miserly and apathetic consumers. Hence, lower your targets, for it is preferable to over-perform than to suffer the crushing disappointment of not having enough seats left to turn a profit.

Secondly, your ATP on the plan should be higher than your target by 10% to 15%, as a rule of thumb. This is because you want to *finish* on your target ATP, and you will most likely end up losing some yield to discounts or concessions. Pricing for your target ATP from the start leaves you nowhere to go but down.

Ticket capacity: 1000

Target: £50,000

Average ticket price	Ticket occupancy 100%	90%	80%	70%	60%	50%
£80	£80,000	£72,000	£64,000	£56,000	£48,000	£40,000
£70	£70,000	£63,000	£56,000	£49,000	£42,000	£35,000
£60	£60,000	£54,000	£48,000	£42,000	£36,000	£30,000
£50	£50,000	£45,000	£40,000	£35,000	£30,000	£25,000
£40	£40,000	£36,000	£32,000	£28,000	£24,000	£20,000

Value

"The value is what someone is prepared to pay for it… people pay for what they want… they can decide if it's worth it." - Howard Panter[10]

Now that we've established the average ticket price and occupancy level our show needs to play to, let's consider our value proposition.Value-based pricing comes from the perceived value of a product to the customer, rather than from the cost of the product or your competitors' pricing. This approach considers the quality of the experience delivered to the audience, rather than how much it costs to actually deliver it.

Value-based pricing considers factors like the reputation of the on-stage talent, the exclusivity of the performance, the location of the seats, or other added benefits like VIP treatment. Value-based pricing can potentially result in higher profits than either of these approaches, assuming the customer believes your product has a high value. However, it also requires a deep understanding of the customer, their needs, and their perceptions of value.

Consider the "consumer surplus," a term coined by Robert Cross to describe the difference between what consumers are willing to pay and what they actually pay. In his book, Cross explains that businesses often fail to capture this difference and as a result take a significant loss in potential revenue. He gives an example of Super Bowl tickets priced at $250 by the NFL but selling for $1,450 on the secondary market, thereby creating a consumer surplus of $1,200 to the people who bagged themselves a bargain from the NFL[11]. Your goal in setting pricing should be to minimise this consumer surplus.

The alternatives to value-based pricing are cost-based and competition-based pricing. Cost-based pricing involves calculating production costs (set design, actor salaries, venue hire) and then adding a markup to determine the ticket price at which you can make a profit. The reason for not exclusively following cost-based pricing is that it is entirely driven by the

---

10 Howard Panter: High ticket prices are an easy target (27th November 2023) The Stage. Available at: https://www.thestage.co.uk/news/howard-panter-high-ticket-prices-are-an-easy-target (Accessed: 13 January 2024).

11 Cross, R.G. (1998) Revenue management: Hard-core tactics for market domination. New York: Broadway Books.

supply-side and is not qualified by customers, so it can lead to prices which are logical on a spreadsheet but which audiences won't pay. (Or which they will very happily pay because you've priced much lower than the perceived value!)

Competition-based pricing is setting prices based on what competitors charge for similar shows. This involves benchmarking ticket prices against similar performances in comparable venues The competitor exercise will be helpful for challenging and justifying your proposed pricing, but in fact, entertainment products are rarely easy to compare due to specificities in each staging.

I suggest a good approach is to understand your cost base and define broad scenarios with the occupancy-yield matrix. Then set about defining ticket prices using the value-based model, which has a better chance of customers actually being prepared to pay your prices. In the Pricing Experiments section we shall discuss the Van Westendorp approach to scientifically understanding the cash value which customers place on your tickets. Finally, refine and optimise your plan by evaluating what competitors are charging and the sell-through rate of your tickets.

Price differentiation

Price differentiation is the strategy of charging different prices to customers of the same show. Prices can be differentiated by seat location, time of purchase, or audience segment (students, seniors, or groups). Different customers will have varying willingness to pay, and with a large theatre, we want to cater to as many customers as possible. Charging higher prices for preferable seats or peak performances can help capture more revenue from those willing to pay more for a specific experience.

On the other side of the coin, by offering discounted tickets to specific groups (like students or seniors), or lower prices for less popular days of the week, we can attract a broader audience and fill seats that might otherwise remain empty.A range of prices means audiences can choose what they're willing to pay for. Those who value a better view or a peak performance time can opt for higher-priced tickets, while others might prefer more affordable options even if it means compromising certain aspects. It also imparts an element of fairness, because the person who pays the most can justifiably expect to have an enhanced experience over another who pays less.

Opportunity cost

There is a spectrum of how consumers could be spending their time, with sitting at home playing Scrabble at one end (nil cost), going for a few drinks in the pub (some cost) all the way up to booking the presidential suite at The Ritz (crazy money). Think about the dozens more options for spending leisure time which exist for customers in your location, and where your show sits on that value spectrum.

We need to ensure that we don't underprice our product, because if the cost is the same as sitting at home playing Scrabble, then audiences will rightly infer that the value of it is the same. By similar logic, tickets should not be observably much more expensive than more valuable experiences (like the Ritz) because an open market means consumers will choose that instead. We need to price tickets in terms of the value which consumers perceive.

This price of the opportunity cost for a comparable experience is a good starting point for setting your mid-range price, and by extension your target ATP. In the West End, this would typically be your Band C price, but the important thing is that your target ATP is in the middle of your range of prices. You will, after all, need to sell many tickets cheaper than this price, because you likely have much more inventory than the comparable experience, and some of your inventory will be inferior due to poor sight lines and you'll need to use price as a lever to fill those. Likewise, you'll also end up selling many tickets higher than this mid-range price, to people willing to pay more for a specific seat or date.

With your mid-range price set, make a reduction in price to the minimum at which you want to sell tickets. This should be the lowest price you think the performance is worth, based on the quality of the script, music, and performances, as well as the intangible experience of "being in the room" of a desirable show. In the West End, this would be your Band D price; in other contexts it will simply be your lowest or entry-level price.

With your mid-range and lowest prices defined, we can now set your highest prices. In the West End, this would be Bands A and B, but in other contexts you may only feasibly be able to have one high price. Where the auditorium allows, you want this high price to cover the most seats, as it will produce your highest per-seat yield (unless you also sell premium tickets, of which more in a moment). This, then, should be a price that most of your audience will desire to pay without hesitation for a good seat at the show. If you're in the West End and this is your Band A price, set Band B equidistant between A and C.

If you're in a smaller venue, or producing a show where the convention is to have only one price for all tickets — such as comedy shows or some family shows — I would still advise that you experiment with adding more price levels where you can. For example, you can offer restricted view tickets at a lower price or front-row tickets at a higher one. Even when these are tied to specific aspects of the product in this way, price differentiation will always open your show up to a wider range of audiences.

Finally, it's worth noting that even if your show doesn't have reserved seating — i.e. it's sold as general admission or first come, first served — this doesn't preclude you from offering multiple price levels. In many cases, when you are purchasing plane tickets you are not able to pick a specific seat at the time of purchase either, and yet airlines still sell seats at different prices. As above, you should experiment with ways to differentiate your pricing based on the qualities of your product. Perhaps some tickets could be sold with an add-on like a bundled drink or programme, or a meet-and-greet with the performers after the show. Others, like standing room seats or stools near the bar, could be sold for less.

Premium Tickets

In the early 2010s, Broadway and West End theatres experienced a problem where touts were buying Band A tickets and then, once the show had sold out, reselling them at wildly inflated prices to tourists and people desperate to see the show. This is the "consumer surplus" we discussed earlier, and just as with the NFL, theatres were leaving money on the table because of it.

The industry responded by taking some of their best Band A seats, pricing them up significantly, and labelling them as "Premium Tickets." The business of touts soon dried up, because these high-priced tickets meant there were usually still seats available at the last minute from the official channels, and the price was comparable.

In the intervening years, the industry has learned that there is significant appetite for premium tickets, and it is now commonplace for 20% of a West End theatre to be priced as premium. Customers are quite happy to buy premium tickets months in advance and, importantly, are comfortable doing so from on-sale — the performance does not need to be sold-out for customers to choose premiums.

The audience for these seats is more diverse than expected, too. More than just tourists, a range of customers decide to buy premiums as a way of ensuring they have the very best experience, and to treat their guests on special occasions — though in fact, no West End theatre currently offers any added value on these tickets, and it is precisely the same experience as the adjacent seats.

Curiously, sales and marketing professionals struggle the most to reconcile premium tickets, perhaps because we understand the system better than the general public and can't rationalise why someone would pay so far over the odds. This is a "Homo economicus" viewpoint which mistakenly presupposes that customers make rational decisions which maximise their own profit, when in fact, homo sapiens are far from rational whilst holding a credit card.[12]

---

12 Kahneman, D., Knetsch, J.L. and Thaler, R.H. (1990) 'Experimental tests of the endowment effect and the Coase Theorem', Journal of Political Economy

My experience is that for every performance, there will be a superfan or two who are prepared to pay well over the odds. It may be the parents of the leading child at the school play, or someone who has flown over from Australia especially to see their favourite Hollywood star live on stage — but every show will have someone like this. In some ways, we owe it to them to ensure that a premium ticket is available, so that they can enjoy what will be a very special performance in their eyes.

Crucially, this is true whether we are talking about a West End or Broadway theatre that literally has a type of seat called "premiums," or whether we're talking about a black box studio theatre in the suburbs: someone will always have a reason to pay over the odds, and we should make sure they are able to.

In a standard West End auditorium, premiums are generally a ring of very-good seats in the front-centre stalls. Depending on your market's price sensitivity, you may also choose to have an inner doughnut of 'super premium' tickets. Either way, the rationale is that this the area where you will have the best experience of the show: the best sightlines, the closest proximity to the orchestra, the quickest route to the interval ice cream, and so forth.

If you're not in a West End theatre, think about where people will have the best experience of your show, and place your premium-priced seats there. If your theatre doesn't have reserved seating, think about what else might make the best experience for your audience: early entry to the auditorium, perhaps, or a dedicated bar or queueing area beforehand.

The pushback against these kinds of initiative is less often from the ticket-paying public, as they appreciate that there is a value attached to a desirable ticket to a hit show. In fact, the pushback most often comes from public relations teams who fear negative coverage, or from cautious producers who don't want to 'rip off' their audience. In those conversations, I would remind the producer that the value of their show is whatever someone is prepared to pay. If we receive complaints after the show that it isn't worth the ticket price, then that should absolutely be addressed. But criticism that a price is too high from someone who will not buy it anyway is an irrelevance, so long as someone else will.

If you are publicly funded, receive donations or are a mission-driven organisation, some additional nuance may be required. But in purely commercial terms, the price of premium tickets should be dictated by what the market will pay for them (including through secondary channels), and anyone's opinion on whether it is ethical is irrelevant if you can demonstrably sell them and achieve your objectives.

Finally, there is the question of premium tickets going unsold. The first school of thought is that if all of the other seats are sold except the premiums, and they are not selling, then they should be reduced in price until they are at the same level as Band A, or your next highest price, which has already all been sold. The rationale here is that there is evidently enough demand for all seats to be sold at a lower price, and that it is better to sell the ticket now than risk it going empty in the hope of being sold as a premium.

The second school of thought is that if a few last seats are empty, they should be left as premium, and that the potential of earning substantial incremental per-seat income outweighs the benefit of one more Band A sale. Plenty of shows worldwide have premium seats going empty every night because it helps reinforce their prestige position, and they've made a budgetary rationale that they can achieve their target without selling every seat.

As with everything to do with pricing, the art balances having just enough premiums on sale without leaving money on the table. On a long-running show, it may be to your benefit to regularly have a couple of premium seats going open rather than for word to get out that it is possible to buy discounted tickets on the day, as that will surely damage your advance sales.

Model pricing

Here is an example which shows the relationship between each price band, as well as the distance between them. Obviously this shows the pricing model for a standard West End show; if you're working in a smaller venue or with a narrower range of prices, you can omit the bands that aren't relevant to you, still starting with Band C as described above.

I will later discuss the left-digit effect and how you might want to turn £50 to £49.50, but have kept to whole numbers here for ease of converting to your own circumstance.

Super premium: £180
Premium: £150
Band A: £100
Band B: £85
Band C: £70
Band D: £50
Standing/restricted view: £20

You can use this framework to model your own prices. To do that, determine your own price for a Band C (for example, £50) and divide it by the amount in the model above, £70. This gives you 0.714. Then multiply each of the model prices above by this value to ascertain prices for your own event (super premium would be £129, premium would be £107 and so forth). That will give you a starting point for your own work.

With your basic pricing decided, it's good practice to build additional price tables for different performances. At the most basic, a peak and off-peak plan can give you the benefit of more yield around high season whilst encouraging sales at quieter times of year with lower prices. For example, you might add £5 to every price during the school holidays. This framework is common with ticketing businesses that need easily communicated pricing, such as theme parks, museums, and attractions which cater to very high volumes (10,000 tickets or more per day).

More sophisticated versions of this idea are to have different pricing plans by day of the week (e.g. Saturday evenings are more expensive than Wednesday afternoons), or even to use dozens of plans which are activated on specific performances dependent on the time of year, anticipated demand, tourism trends, etc. I worked on one long-running West End musical that had five agreed seating plans and price tables, and we would assign them very specifically to performances years in advance, using all of the historical data and forecasting we had available.

The lesson is to use price differentiation, but only where it is needed. On one show I worked on, a significant Hollywood title was being transformed into a stage production, I observed that it was sure to sell out months' worth of performances within hours of on sale. Curiously, the production nevertheless wanted to make reduced-price tickets available for the preview period (i.e. first few weeks of performance) as is the general custom in London.

In a standard sales pattern, we would expect performances to "front-fill", i.e. the more immediate performances to sell first and taper off towards the future, perhaps only for a few bumps around seasonal periods. This is natural given that prices are presented in chronological order on websites, with customers tending to click on dates which are presented to them earlier, as well as a human desire to do things sooner rather than later. Preview pricing makes sense if you need to build a critical mass audience to see the show and then spread positive word-of-mouth — but for this production, performances were bound to sell out on the strength of the IP alone, and, if anything, audiences would have been more keen to see it in previews than later on, as they wanted to be the first to witness this exciting event. It was certainly a mistake for this particular production to use preview prices because it caused an unnecessary 10% reduction to grosses for the first fortnight, and created a steeper cliff in attendances between previews and main-run than would have occurred otherwise, and therefore a starker challenge.

If you expect to sell plenty of tickets before opening night anyway, then there's really no reason to hand a discount onto every audience member as well as the privilege of seeing it first. Pricing isn't an incentive for these customers, so save your levers.

Example seating plans

If all seats in the auditorium were priced the same ("a one-price-house"), then the heatmap of how quickly each seat sells would look something like the page opposite.

Obviously this map represents a standard proscenium arch theatre with multiple levels, but most auditoriums will fill the same way if customers are given the chance: they will intentionally gravitate towards the best seats in the house, which are generally towards the front and centre, with the rear and sides left until last. If you do have multiple levels, the circle will generally fill in the same way, with higher levels filling last. Perhaps they'll avoid the front row if this has sightline problems from a high stage. Perhaps there will be dark patches behind any structural pillars. Americans tend to favour being downstairs more than Brits, who'll sooner take the front row of the circle. But on the whole, this is the general pattern of consumer preference.

As you can see from the heatmap, you should avoid having a centre aisle at all costs. The seats which you would remove to install a centre aisle are the most desirable for audiences, and therefore the most lucrative, so resist all efforts to install one if it comes up in discussion.

When we price up a seating map, we should use this latent demand for each seat as a way to determine how much to charge. So the most desirable seats demand a higher price, and we will use the less-desirable seats as inventory for lower-priced tickets, to attract consumers who are more price sensitive. The next page is a model of how that could look.

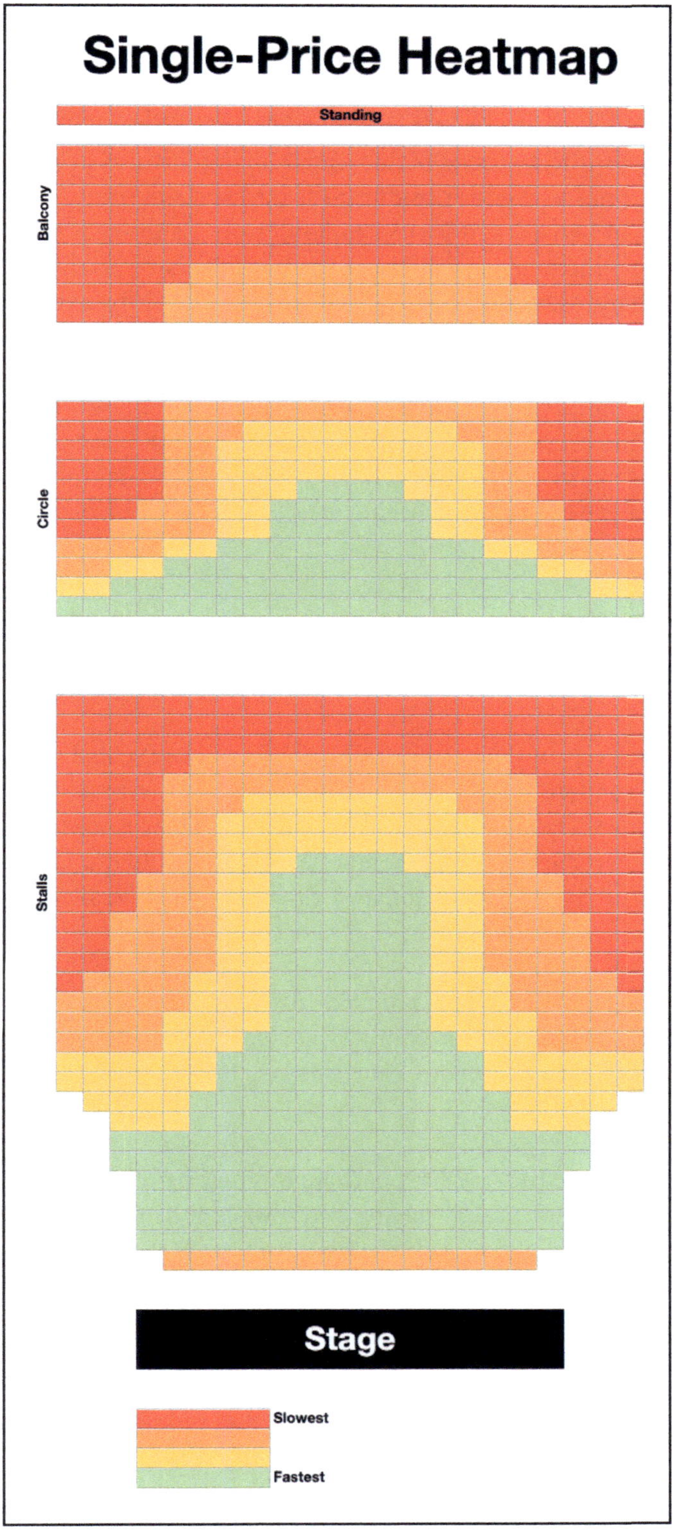
Single-Price Heatmap
Standing
Balcony
Circle
Stalls
Stage
Slowest
Fastest

Working from front-to-back on this plan, the stalls (orchestra) front row are utilised for an accessible-pricing initiative (eg. £10 on the day for TikTok followers). Then there is a donut of premium tickets around the super premium section, in precisely the area which is most desirable for customers and has the highest level of demand. Moving further back, Band A dominates most seats as they are amongst the best seats in the auditorium, and then Band B and Band C taper in towards the rear stalls. Depending on the auditorium, aisle seats can sometimes have poor views, or otherwise be in large demand from people who appreciate the extra legroom, so you may price these up or down as appropriate.

The front row of the circle usually offers a great view for shows which have large sets, so the centre here is priced at Premium, with Band A either side, and then tapering into Band B and Band C further back. Towards the edges at the back of the circle are restricted view, so these are placed at the very lowest price.

The balcony replicates this model and is home to most of the cheapest tickets, as well as standing tickets which will only be released if all seats have sold out.

Typically the back row of the balcony will be the cheapest seats in the auditorium, however there is a counter viewpoint that these should in fact be the most expensive. The logic goes that if someone is actively seeking to buy the back row, then the performance must be virtually sold out, and hence there is a higher market value to pay for the final ticket available to a performance.

You can of course have the best of both worlds by ensuring there are always a few premium and super premium tickets left in good stalls seats, so that you aren't left trying to convince a customer that the back row is worth the highest price.

We have deviated from the original heatmap by creating the premium and super premium section, and by having two rows in the balcony at Band A. The reason for this is that the super premium section is the single most desirable part of the house, and we can almost guarantee to sell it at Band A price at any time in the sales cycle. Therefore we are wise to mark it up and bring in extra revenue from customers looking to get excellent tickets closer to the time of performance.

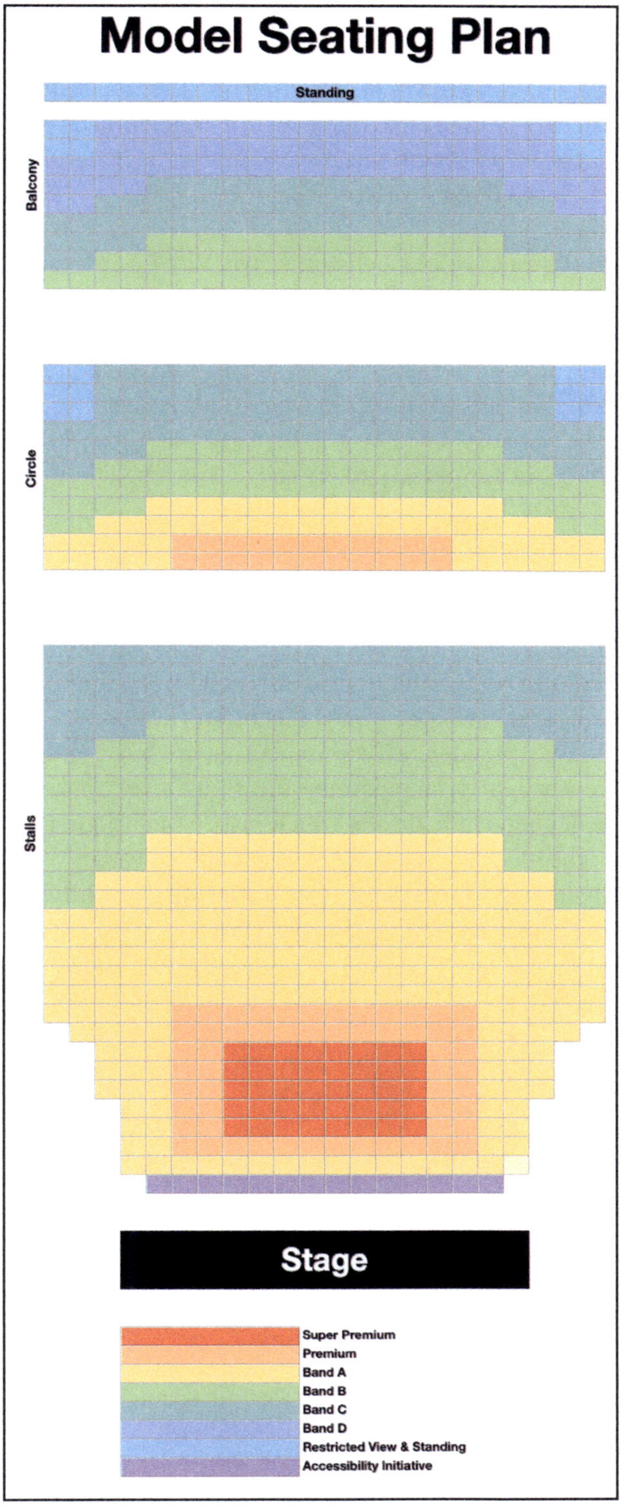

Model Seating Plan
Standing
Balcony
Circle
Stalls
Stage
Super Premium
Premium
Band A
Band B
Band C
Band D
Restricted View & Standing
Accessibility Initiative

Having Band A tickets in the balcony may be a diversion from what this venue has tried before, and the rationale is that these seats are worth Band A if all other Band A seats have sold. We aren't expecting them to sell as quickly as the Band A tickets in the stalls, but a customer will objectively choose these seats over the remaining Band B seats, and so at that point in time, they would be worth the Band A price.

Crucially, the question is not "would a customer pay Band A prices in the balcony if they could sit in the stalls?" but rather "would a customer pay Band A prices in front of the balcony rather than Band B in the rear of the balcony?". As long as the answer to that question is affirmative, then it is justified to place some higher-priced tickets in every seating tier.

Using these prices, the auditorium will likely sell out per the diagram opposite.

Demand is now much more evenly spread across the auditorium, leading to higher occupancy and higher revenues. Consumers will naturally gravitate towards the front rows of each price band, which is particularly visible in the stalls. Premium seats will intentionally sell last so that touts don't try to make a profit, and each seat across the auditorium is maximised for its potential. It's a desirable plan because we have sold most of our unattractive inventory early, so medium- and short-term bookers are presented with a range of good stalls tickets which justify their higher prices. In each section, the emptiest seats are towards the rear, so customers are generally looking out on sold seats, rather than swathes of empty seats - promoting a positive audience experience.

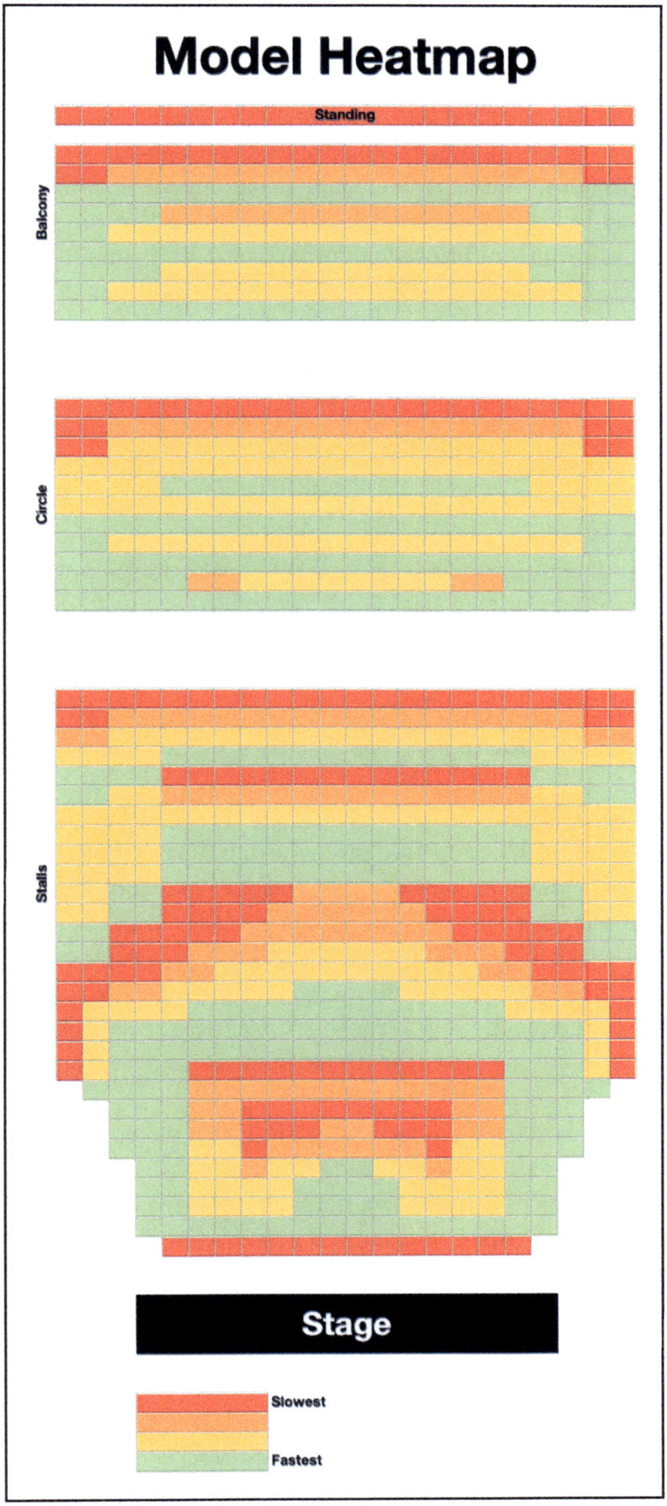
Model Heatmap
Standing
Balcony
Circle
Stalls
Stage
Slowest
Fastest

Round numbers

There is a temptation to settle on round numbers (£50, £70 etc.) as these are cognitively simpler for staff and customers to deal with. In the later section on consumer psychology, we will learn about the left-digit effect and how £49.99 is more appealing to customers than £50.00. In selling tickets, there are some additional factors which aren't considered in conventional research, and you will want to put thought into them.

Firstly, do you plan on charging any booking or transaction fees? There is no point in pricing yourself just under the £20 threshold at £19.99 if a £1 booking fee will make the price to the consumer £20.99. It completely undoes all of your hard work, and if you're going to go above £20 anyway then perhaps you'd have been better charging £23.99 all along.

The same applies to restoration levies which the theatre might apply. I've seen prices where the producer has clearly budgeted for tickets at £10, £20 etc., and then when they've been informed that a levy of £1.50 is required on each ticket, they've hastily added this on top — so that prices are published as £11.50, £21.50 etc. It makes for ugly pricing, which has had the opposite effect of its intention.

To generalise, customers who attend entertainment events tend to go in pairs. So £54.99 may seem like a sensible price for one ticket, but a pair will cost £109.98, which takes the basket value over the psychological threshold of £100. If you expect to sell most of your tickets in pairs, then would it be better to sell them at £49.99, so that the big total number facing your customer before they enter their credit card is two digits rather than three? Try different pricing on different performances to see whether there is an uptick in transactions to make up for the loss in per-ticket-yield.

If you're working in a large, mature market, with many ticket agents or other secondary sellers, it's also worth considering how these will impact the presentation of your prices. In London, it's commonplace for ticket agents to add 20% of fees on top of the face value. In my model pricing earlier, Band B was set at £85, but a 20% commission takes this to £102 and thus over the £100 threshold. It may be in everyone's interest for you to have a conversation with your ticket agent to reduce this by £3 to £99 so that consumers have a more attractive price.

Packages

I first encountered packages whilst working at a regional theatre which had its own restaurant. Management noticed that the theatre was a magnet for visitors to the town, but audiences chose to eat in nearby pizzerias rather than at the in-house restaurant. To tackle this, the theatre decided to offer show tickets with an upsell of a restaurant meal. Benefits were manifold; customers had one less reservation to make and knew that chef would have them done in time for the show; the restaurant would surely fill up more tables from being positioned in front of every booker; and paying for the package meal in advance was a significant change to the scourge of people who never show up for their restaurant reservations.

If restaurant-as-upsell is version one, then restaurant packages are version two. Here, particular seats are selected to be 'packaged with' a restaurant meal. A £100 ticket might become £150 for dinner-and-the-show. These could be the best seats (as a mechanic to make guaranteed restaurant income from seats which are sure to sell) or lower-end tickets, which can effectively be discounted under the radar into an attractive package price.

Though packages can be an effective ticketing strategy in theory, they are often contentious with both audiences (who begrudge having to buy a restaurant meal to access the best seats) and producers (who earn no financial upside from restaurant sales). I'll also admit to having passionately fought against packages when I felt that ticket sales were being inhibited, and we could have sold more tickets if we didn't insist that they were sold at a much higher package price.

There are ways to avoid consumer pushback around packages. Most importantly, you should clearly communicate the value proposition. ("£100. Includes show plus three-course meal and glass of wine" is more appealing than "£100. Package seat.") You should also be very sensitive about how many are ever displayed on the plans. If you have lots of seats left to sell, then it's bad optics to have all of the best seats set as packages; limit these to just a few pairs. If you're nearly sold out, then consumers will be more forgiving that most of the remaining seats are at the higher rate.

Holds

Common reasons for holding tickets off sale are to provide space for patrons who use wheelchairs, to leave room for the sound desk, or to restrict sales of specific seats for fear that sightlines may be impinged upon by a large set.

I am a big advocate for another kind of hold: revenue management holds. These are tickets distributed throughout the auditorium that do not initially go on sale. Instead, you can release them at your discretion throughout the sales cycle, determining when, how many, and at what price, dependent upon the uptake of sales so far. Revenue management holds are a great way to hedge your bets on pricing for a show if you aren't certain how it will land with consumers.

Without revenue management holds, if you expect high demand and are wrong, you could be left with a ton of distressed inventory at a high price. Or, if you expect demand will be low and are wrong, then there's the even worse scenario of selling out too cheap, with no recourse to undo. Revenue management holds allow you to put a proportion of tickets on sale, gauge demand, and then price the held seats according to that demand; typically, either pricing up if demand is higher than expected and down if demand is lower than expected.

Revenue management holds are also a helpful tool for dressing the house, for if sales are meagre you don't ever need to release the seats farthest to the back. The audience experience is improved by having everyone sat towards the front, and neither the actors nor the audience is gazing upon swathes of empty seats.

Tactically, I suggest it is best to position your inventory management holds along the borderlines of each price break, such as the row where Band A meets Band B. This makes for a straightforward process to either price them to Band A if the show is selling well or Band B if it's doing poorly. If you suspect that the show will do very well, then be sure to have enough seats held in your premium section, as this is where you stand to make the most incremental revenue.

A note of caution is that it's easy to get giddy with the opportunity presented by inventory management holds — but imaginary money is no good to us. If the show is flying, you're better off putting the seats on sale at the super premium rate now, rather than concocting some clever scheme to release your holds later. The moment of heat may pass you by, and the endless internal conversations about "how high can we go?" may cost you more in staff wages than the 10% extra it earns.

Revenue management holds are an insurance policy for when you are uncertain about demand, so don't confuse them with a golden ticket a lottery ticket or, indeed, dynamic pricing.

Private Property Seats

Private property ("PP") seats are a peculiar anachronism that are very profitable for their owners. The premise here is that specific seats within an auditorium are not, in fact, part of the regular seating, but instead are the "private property" belonging to the theatre landlord. They may choose to sit there themself, but, more likely, they will be sold to the general public, and 100% of the takings will go direct to the theatre owner — bypassing any splits or deal structures.

In days of yore, these were literal seats which could be numbered, but now they are figurative and tend to exist only within the ticketing system. So a contract for venue hire may specify that whichever ten Band A seats sell first, they will be the PP seats for that performance, thereby guaranteeing the landlord their income regardless of attendance each night. The convention is that PP seats are always Band A, and customers are never aware of where the PP seats are, or if they have purchased one. In a London auditorium of 1,000, there may be as many as 10 PP seats, earning the landlord significant extra income over the course of a single show.

Because this tradition has been written into contracts for hundreds of years, there is no debate to be had with the venue owner about this state of affairs. Instead, you must simply be careful to reconcile the PPs within your own seating plan, budgeting, and settlements, so that you aren't mistakenly planning on earning from those tickets.

Pricing for different customer segments

I choose the words "customer segment" rather than "audience segment" because our interest is with the customer and the nature of their transaction: high or low yield, long- or short-term, one-time booker or member. This differs from audience segmentation which categorises people based on factors like their demographics (age, gender and ethnicity), socioeconomic position (wealth and earnings) or engagement with arts and culture. These two systems may overlap, but for our purposes, we shall concentrate on how patrons behave as transactional customers, because that is what impacts our ability to sell them tickets. Different customer segments have their own preferences, budgets and willingness to pay, so price differentiation strategies like membership priority, single-seat-discount or group rates are a way for us to cater to their specific needs.

Robert G Cross gives an example of two customers purchasing airline tickets who belong to different customer segments[13]. The first is a business traveller who wants a seat available on a specific flight and is prepared to pay for it. The second, a discount passenger, is looking for a last-minute bargain on seats which would otherwise have gone empty. The airline is able to satisfactorily service both segments without upsetting either party, and fulfilling its own goals of maximising occupancy and per-seat yield. Consider who your own customer segments are, how their needs differ and what they each value.Pre-sale and early-bird tickets can effectively build hype around the show before tickets are officially on sale. However, be careful to avoid the pitfall of unnecessarily handing discounts to the customers with the greatest propensity to book. Pre-sales are opportunities to reward fandom through exclusive access to the best seats, but discounting rarely services your objectives.

For those who view pre-sales as an opportunity to build an advance and get some seats sold before the general on sale, I suggest using other tactics to achieve these ends. For example, holds are a good way of making the auditorium look better sold than it is, and advertising dollars may be more effectively spent in promoting the general on sale rather than the two-step of paying to acquire customers for a pre-sale list and then re-activating them again to make their booking. The target figure will be for the number of tickets sold by the end of the general on sale, so the proportion bought during the pre-sale is an irrelevance.

---

[13] Cross, R.G. (1998) Revenue management: Hard-core tactics for market domination. New York: Broadway Books

Stunt pricing

There is a common temptation among arts leaders to propose radical, headline-grabbing schemes to show off their venue as a champion of increasing access to the arts. These include initiatives like free tickets for under-30s, or pricing all tickets for a specific performance at £10, or promising that the first thousand people to book a ticket may do so for £5. I can think of at least three such schemes in London in recent years, each of which has garnered the media attention they were seeking. Yet whilst they have certainly had catchy premises, I've yet to read a positive post-campaign analysis of any of them.

These stunt-pricing initiatives are intrinsically flawed because, in their hope of offering greater access and bringing down the cost barrier to art, they in fact do the opposite. Invariably the people who purchase tickets from these schemes are the customers who are already the most engaged your organisation, who have likely visited your venue many times before, and are very familiar with the dynamics of booking tickets. They know what's hot and what's not, they are savvy enough to spot a deal quickly, and are tuned into the zeitgeist. As a result, these schemes are invariably wholly sold out when the true target customers hear about it.

This kind of programme also rests on the common fallacy that the main barrier to young people attending is price, and that if only tickets were free (or near-free), then youths would put down their Playstation controllers, switch off Netflix and come out of the pub to instead spend a pleasant evening in the company of a string quartet. I suggest that young people are not totally without means and that if they can afford a few drinks in a club or a film at the cinema, then they can already afford a reasonably-priced ticket for your show — if that's how they really want to spend their free time. (Recall our discussion of opportunity cost.)

Producer Yinka Ayinde articulated this neatly at the Theatre 2016 conference when he said "You want a new generation of theatregoers, so let's attract them through their interests and not just put on what we want to and then tell them to come and see it."[14] In fact, making tickets cheap or free only devalues your own show, when in fact, attention would be better directed to the other Ps, besides price: product and promotion. Namely, do

---

14 Yinka Ayinde: 'connect to popular culture' to attract new theatregoers (May 16 2016) The Stage. Available at: https://www.thestage.co.uk/news/yinka-ayinde-connect-to-popular-culture-to-attract-new-theatregoers (Accessed: 13 January 2024).

young people even want to see a string quartet, and is an accessible pricing scheme the best way to inform them of it? I suggest that adjusting your program to accommodate more contemporary products that appeal to young people, and promoting them in their forum (TikTok), will yield better results than blanket ticket discounts.

A case study of how these schemes miss the mark is "A Night Less Ordinary," a two-year UK-wide scheme supported by £2.4m of government funding, which distributed 400,000 tickets for free or at very low cost.[15] According to the Arts Council England's own evaluation, the scheme failed in its objective to "increase the number of young people going to theatre for the first time," and instead got engagement from a minimal number of people (80,000) who each made liberal use of the subsidised initiative and, on average, claimed five tickets each.

More seriously, of those 80,000 people, only 12,800 (16%) had never visited the theatre before. A proportion as low as 16% shows that the scheme was overwhelmingly being taken up by frequent theatre-goers, and it's intended end-users barely got a look-in. Further, this number is lower than would be achieved by simply putting on a high-quality show with broad family appeal (like a pantomime, or a musical based on a popular film). By comparison, 60% of audiences for *Harry Potter and the Cursed Child* in it's first year were first-time theatregoers[16].

Whilst price was a barrier for some young people to attend theatre, the *Night Less Ordinary* scheme demonstrated the deeper problem that young people's leisure interests aren't aligned with the offerings at most theatres. According to the ACE report: "young people do not necessarily value something free; what is important is the attractiveness of what's on offer". Furthermore, the government targets meant that theatres were forced to shift their efforts away from reaching non-attenders, to the lower-hanging-fruit of re-engaging previous visitors. The government curtailed the scheme early, but I suggest that its real legacy should be a lesson for theatres to think more creatively about widening their funnel before jumping to stunt pricing.

---

[15] Sam Culture Ltd for Arts Council England and Department of Culture, Media and Sport (2012) A Night Less Ordinary Evaluation. Available at: https://www.artscouncil.org.uk/sites/default/files/download-file/Night_Less_Ordinary_evaluation.pdf (Accessed: 2023)

[16] https://www.bbc.co.uk/news/entertainment-arts-41302602

Customer-price differentiation

There is a long cultural tradition of offering discounts for seniors, but, as with preview pricing discussed earlier, we should first consider why we are doing it at all. Any reduction in yield should always be in service of your sales strategy, and "because it has always been done that way" is not a valid excuse when you fail to meet the target.

Commercially, it can make good sense to offer reduced-price tickets to particular groups, but only under certain conditions: if it helps to sell more tickets than would have otherwise been sold; if it targets particular inventory which you are having difficulty with; or if the offer has neat criteria (such as seniors) that means you won't be overwhelmed with the whole audience demanding a discount.

Seniors and students are the classic examples of such an initiative, with good reason. These groups represent straightforward categories to use for a ticket offer because an individual can easily prove their eligibility, and there is a convenient network effect where they can spread the word amongst their peers, who tend to fall into the same group. Yet the intrinsic booking behaviour of the two groups can be very different.

As a rule, seniors prefer to plan ahead, making arrangements for their companions to join them and planning around transportation options. There is also a convenient symbiosis with matinee (afternoon) performances because these are difficult to sell to mainstream audiences, who are at work during the day, but convenient for seniors as they can enjoy more accessible travel and get home before dark.

Students, on the other hand, often prefer to be out in the evening. And enjoy the flexibility of making impulsive plans, so last-minute tickets tend to be more desirable for them. Consider each customer segment's characteristics, motivations, and needs to inform your decisions around discounting.

Don't, however, simply offer a senior discount without thinking about it. As an example, consider a Gershwin musical I worked on. It was selling poorly, and someone suggested offering a discount for seniors. Unfortunately, this was a bad idea, because seniors were the main customers who were already booking, and we would simply be handing them a discount for no good reason whilst still facing the challenge of finding broader audiences.

On the other hand, offering a student discount might have helped young people who had been considering the title and needed some convincing to buy a ticket, thereby expanding our customer base. Students are comparatively much easier and cheaper to reach because they live online, so a simple TikTok advert about the discount would have gone a long way to reaching our target group and substantially widened the top of our funnel.

The lesson is not that student discounts are always better than senior ones. Rather, discounts for both seniors and students have their place. Before you implement either, however, you should consider what your objectives are and whether you are cannibalising your own sales rather than widening your funnel.

Tourists can also be a good customer segment to offer a discount, because you have no brand reputation to defend with them, knowing they won't re-visit anyway. Depending on your location, tourists may also have countless other options for spending their time, and a discount might be the only lever you have to open up this customer segment and make them pick you.

If you are offering a tourist discount, as mentioned above, it is important to speak directly to tourists so as not to alienate your core customer base — so when positioning your discount, consider places or channels that tourists are most likely to frequent, such as airports, local travel guides, travel agents, and hotel concierges.

For example, the city of Split, Croatia, offers a free "Split Card" that gives tourists free or discounted access to theatres, museums and attractions. This is a great way of improving visitor numbers to these destinations whilst protecting full-price sales from locals. Similarly, if there are other businesses in your area that target tourists, then talk to them about partnering your efforts so that a tourist who has enjoyed your show gets 20% off at the nearby museum and vice versa.

It is worth being aware of the unchanging truth that there is a correlation between average ticket price and distanced travelled by the customer. Statistically, international customers will generally pay the most per ticket, followed by domestic tourists, followed by locals. The pattern is the same for venues of all types throughout the world, and is presumably a consequence of customers having already paid a great deal to travel, where the cost is comparatively much higher than a premium theatre ticket, and therefore they are more amenable to a luxury experience. For that reason, I would offer tourist discounts only on lower price bands as a means to widen the funnel, and encourage them to 'level up' to a full-priced Band A or Premium ticket during the booking flow.

Corporate audiences are another customer segment worth considering, because while they can be hard to attract, they are lucrative when you succeed. They might use your theatre as part of a hospitality offering for their clients, or as a year-end reward for staff, and so will be keen that tickets are of the highest quality to the best show in town. However, cautious as we always should be at losing any yield from the most-desirable tickets, you could suggest that instead of a discount, they enjoy some champagne on the house or use a VIP lounge.

For example, I once had a premier league football manager ask to book hundreds of our best seats over Christmas to reward the team winning the season. Rather than give up any discount at this lucrative time of year, the manager was delighted when we instead offered the team a meet-and-greet with our leading stars, a money-can't-buy experience. Any added value you can offer will surely be attractive to corporate bookers, and helps you maintain yield on the best seats.

Finally, family pricing, such as "two adults and two children for £100," can be compelling because it's easy for the customer to understand and intuitively feels like a deal, regardless of the base price. Suppose you expect to have open inventory anyway, as children's theatre often does when programmed in mainstream venues. In that case, it matters less how many tickets you give away in the offer than the total basket size for each transaction.

In other words, you're better to sell the four tickets for £100 than only three at £30 each, if you are going to have empty seats anyway. Where this is the case, budget for it from the start and assume that most of your tickets will be at the discounted rate, rather than misleading yourself with a gross potential where all of the seats could be sold at the full-price adult rate.

Loyalty

Selling one ticket to a show is good, but the concept of cost-per-acquisition (CPA) teaches us that it is preferable to sell that same customer two tickets to a show — or, better yet, two tickets to two shows. If your average ticket price is £50 and your cost-per-acquisition is £5, then 10% of your income goes on marketing. However, if we can encourage every customer to make a second booking, then only 5% of income needs to go to marketing. We have halved our marketing expenditure just by selling one more ticket to each customer.

The concept of CPA also reveals the wisdom in pursuing higher-value customers. Rather than having a £5 per-customer budget, we could increase the CPA to £8 per customer, but use that extra budget to find people who will purchase for two shows — if they do, we're still saving £2 per customer.

You can see how, very quickly, these savings begin to mount up, and how lucrative it can be to have an audience who are reliably turning up time after time. Once you have this base of reliable return customers, you can then invest marketing into initiatives like diversifying the audience or pushing more challenging titles.

Imagine a hypothetical thousand-seat theatre where the cost per acquisition is £5. Even if you sell out every performance, if you never get any return customers then it costs you £5,000 to sell each one.

Now suppose that 10% of one audience can be persuaded to come to one future performance (with an additional investment of £2 per ticket to re-engage them). In that case, the cost of selling that single future performance comes down to £4,700. These gains quickly multiply if you can sustain this level of re-attendance over time; if 10% of every performance is someone who has been before, then over a standard eight-performance schedule you could save £2,500 per week in acquisition costs. Now imagine that an even higher 20% of each audience is someone who has attended before: now your weekly savings in acquisition costs are £4,800 — essentially a whole performance for free, in terms of marketing spend.

Churn

In a typical regional UK theatre, approximately 40% of the audience will be returning, and 60% will be new to the venue. This is even better than our hypothetical example above, but it's still relying on a lot of new customers to attend each show. These regional theatres could each save hundreds of thousands of pounds in marketing expenditure per year by reducing the amount spent on customer acquisition and reinvesting it in customer retention. However, even long-running West End shows can stand to benefit from an intelligent approach to customer loyalty.

The benefits of a customer retention strategy compound each time someone returns to your show or venue. I have analysed these statistics for organisations in Wimbledon, Ayrshire, Stockholm and Des Moines, and the pattern always remains the same: if 20% of first-timers make a second booking, then 30% of second-timers will make a third booking, 40% of third-timers will make a fourth booking, and 45% of fourth-timers will make a fifth booking.

That is to say, someone's likelihood of booking again increases based on the number of bookings they have already made. After five bookings, we have near 50:50 odds that someone will make another booking, so we can drastically reduce the amount of direct marketing spend on them because we have such confidence that they will be lifelong attendees. The insight is that we should do all we can to push people up that frequency ladder because, once they have seen a few shows, it becomes a habit and a self-fulfilling cycle. We just need to get through the hurdle of turning one-time customers into two-timers.

Creative thinking in this area came from the renowned dance organisation Sadler's Wells. Their data showed that most customers only booked for one performance, but that the chance of re-attendance greatly increased once a customer had seen two performances. In response, they ran a scheme whereby new customers were offered a discount if they booked upfront for two performances. This side-stepped the problem of customers not coming to a second performance, because they were already committed. It provides an insurance policy of sorts because even if the customer dislikes the first performance, they have already bought the second, and so venue has another chance to win their affection.

If you're a long-running West End show, it would be ambitious to ask someone to buy tickets to two different performances at once, as Sadler's

Wells did, however you're never without opportunities to re-engage customers. When a new cast is announced, for example, you can email past bookers and invite them to see the show again. Seasonal performances also provide a great opportunity for repeat business if you can establish a family tradition of always going to *Matilda* for Christmas. Or perhaps you could offer past bookers a discount if they bring a friend at full price. Each time you can persuade a previous booker to return, you're saving on the acquisition costs versus a new customer.

Some of this flies in the face of traditional arts policy, which has focused on getting newbies to the theatre and prioritised the proportion of an audience who are "first timers" on funding applications. I suggest that the more nuanced approach is to look at how many second-timers an organisation attracts, because that is a better indicator of their sustainability, audience relationship management and potential for growth.

The arts consultancy TRG has long been at the forefront of this work, and it has particular relevance in the North American context, where they suggest a ladder of patron loyalty. This ladder begins with first-timers, who step up first into repeat attendees, then subscribers, and finally donors. Their work shows that one renewing subscriber brings the same revenue as two new subscribers or eight single-ticket buyers (first-timers), and donors are twice as valuable again. Audiences must be nurtured at each stage on their ladder to foster a subscriber base and donor pool.

A good customer retention strategy will encompass pricing, marketing, customer relationship management and more. As a first step, look at understanding the value which returning customers already bring to your organisation, and calculate the marketing cost involved versus your acquisition cost for one-time audiences. Do this by summing the cost of advertising which is targeted to previous bookers — such as email blasts and brochure mailings — as a percentage of the income which you earn from repeat bookers. Then compare this against the cost of advertising to new audiences — such as out-of-home and television — and the respective income from sales to them.

Digital campaigns are broadly either targeted to existing customers (where you've uploaded a list of customer email addresses, for example), or where you're asking the advertising network to find new customers for you. Some media — like outdoor posters — will convert a mix of new and returning audiences, but for the purposes of attribution I would suggest counting it towards new audiences, because there are much more cost-effective ways of activating your returning audiences and so it is only pulling it's weight if it is cost-effectively bringing in new bookers.

Another helpful exercise is to look at the number of customers who booked a ticket from you two years ago and how many of those individuals have gone on to buy tickets to more performances since. Your goal should be to reduce the level of "churn", or customers who don't return each year, because they are costing you money in needing to constantly acquire new customers. A modest estimate would see a thousand-seat venue spending £1.5m annually in new customer acquisition, so each customer who can be convinced to return is contributing to a significant budget saving.

If it costs you £20 to acquire a customer then reducing churn will reduce your need for customer acquisition and increase each customer's lifetime value.

Subscriptions

North America has a flourishing culture of ticket subscriptions at performing arts venues. These offer great perks to audiences, including the peace of mind that a years' worth of performances has been organised upfront; that customers will always be sat in their preferred seats; and, whilst this is often not quoted as the most important factor, that they may enjoy a discount on the advertised ticket price.

In turn, the venue's cash flow is much improved by having a year's worth of sales done at once, while visiting producers can enjoy substantial advances with houses 60% sold-out at launch, leaving only the minority of seats left to be advertised and sold to single-ticket buyers.

There are several reasons why a similar system has never taken off in south England, including the high density of performing arts venues within a commutable distance, audiences' tendency to visit multiple venues, the lack of "seasons" in the same sense of the word, and the different balance of financial risk between visiting producer and venue.

I collaborated with one UK venue where this was the case, which created "The 100 Club," by identifying the hundred customers in the database who visited most frequently. The theatre director hand-wrote each a card, thanking them for their patronage and welcoming them to the club with a pin badge. Before the week was out, ushers reported audience members proudly wearing badges on their lapels and claiming membership in this complimentary program. It served to greatly enhance the customers' feeling of reciprocated loyalty to the venue, and defended our position as the theatre of choice for the highest-value customers amongst the intense regional competition.

Each loyalty package is unique because each venue has its own peculiarities of programming and product, and the dynamics of how your audience relates to your venue in the context of their other leisure-time pursuits will affect what they need from a membership or subscription. So consider what your audience would need from a package, how many shows it would include, what the perks would be, and the ideal purchase path from the customer's perspective — and then set about a small trial to gauge interest. Transitioning from a wholly single-ticket-selling organisation to one which promotes subscriptions is seismic, so don't take on all the challenges of organisational change and massive ticketing system upgrades all at once.

Instead, consider the minimum viable subscription product your audiences would utilise, and take the engagement from that as evidence for how you need to grow your scheme. Think about who on your database you would want to first join as a subscriber. It will likely appeal to someone who already visits several times a year, and they will be keen to give you plenty of helpful feedback about what people like them would need from this sort of scheme. Don't waste efforts trying to get first-timers to become subscribers right away. To quote TRG's Jill Robinson, "Developing patrons is like romance; you don't propose on the first date."

Resale

There is a common practice at some venues of allowing customers to resell their tickets through the box office if performances have sold out. If you work at one of these venues, think about how best to price these returned tickets. If you don't work at one of these venues, but you have events that regularly sell out, consider whether you might be able to start a resale programme.

If a performance has sold out, then there are favourable odds for being able to resell a handful of tickets. Tickets up for resale tend to have been booked furthest in advance – where plans have changed – and so tend to be priced lower than the latest round of dynamic pricing. On a sold-out performance, the most recent tickets which will have been available will have been premiums, and hence there will be a vast delta between the price which was commanded for the last full-price ticket that sold, and the original price of a ticket up for resale.

The options for pricing a resale ticket at sold out performance are therefore: price lower than originally sold; price in line with the original price (possibly with some facility fee); or price higher than originally set.

Pricing lower is an option but isn't commercially favourable to the box office, because the only revenue potential will be in fees, it requires an outlay of technical effort or administration, and it encourages customers to wait for last-minute discounted tickets. Even the original customer doesn't get much satisfaction of recouping their investment, because they are still out of pocket from the experience.

Selling at face value may seem like a "fair" option at first thought, as the new customer will pay the same as the previous customer did – but fair to who exactly? Certainly not the dozens of customers who recently paid a premium price for what they thought was the last inventory on a sold out performance. Not fair either to the customers who paid at the higher rate when dynamic pricing came into force, when this last-minute customer has got themselves a deal. The inaction of not changing the price is in fact a substantial action, where putting a ticket on sale below the most recent market price is markedly unfair.

I propose that on these hit performances, the box office is best advised to price tickets up, entirely on the grounds that the final ticket to sell for any performance is worth a substantial premium to its buyer. For ephemeral entertainment and the audience member who has not endeavoured to purchase as quickly as the first thousand patrons, and who has such high desire that they insist on being in that room — there is a premium to pay. This may be partly impacted by its location in the auditorium, but not much.

When these customers approach you at the counter, begging for a ticket, their eyes light up with gratitude at the mention that you might have one seat available — and they stop listening when you discuss where it's located, as hands dive into their pockets for a credit card before you change your mind.

Hence, be straightforward about the quality of the seat, but more than ever, the value is defined by when it is purchased rather than its relative position, given that there are no other tickets available from which to shop around. For anything other than a ticket originally sold at your lowest available price, I would price any ticket for resale on a sold out show at somewhere between the latest price for Band A and a premium. Be overt about restricted views, of course, with very clear advisory messages.

I use my experience at the counter here as an illustrative example of the customer motivation, but its intended to describe the urgency which customers feel when looking for resale tickets online also.

There may be some who shudder at over-valuing a ticket which had previously been sold at a lower price. To these people, I remind them that value is not defined by an asking price, but by what a customer is willing to pay. There is no hubris to pricing up a ticket when circumstances have changed (the performance has sold out), as long as a customer buys it.

Supply is usually greatly outstripped by demand on these type of events, so you shouldn't need much, or any, price differentiation when advertising a range of resale tickets across the auditorium. Going back to my experience working on the box office counter, we'd have customers queuing up for returns from 5pm and, by the time we offered them anything at 7pm, the first in line would bite our hand off for anything, and we'd work our way down the queue offering progressively less desirable seats. As far as I can remember, no one ever turned down the ticket which was offered to them.

As a discussion point, talk to your team about how you'd feel about the last ticket to sell being the highest-priced, and whether it matters where it is in the auditorium? What principles do you each hold? Which opportunities do you have coming up soon to test this out? What does success and failure look like for ticket resale?

There are a number of reasons why you may be looking at offering tickets for resale. Depending on circumstances, consumers may have a statutory right-to-return, or the venue have signed up to an industry code-of-conduct which allows it. Your organisation may use its discretion to offer it, either in pursuit of excellent customer care or with eyes towards a commercial opportunity. The resale could have limits to when it happens such as returns permitted only within days of the original booking, or sales disallowed until the week of the event. It could be in-person only, as an under-the-radar way to service the most die-hard fans, or online to be more accessible.

If the performance has not yet sold out, then your resale calculations will be very different, and will depend on your potential earnings from the sale of each ticket, either as producer, venue or ticket agent. The commercial calculation is to work out what your expected revenue is for selling a virgin ticket, versus a resold one. For the producer, you might expect to earn £50 on a virgin ticket, but net £0 on a resale ticket (because the original ticket needs to be refunded to the first booker). There's a further cost to factor in, however, as you've effectively paid for advertising twice over to sell the same seat — when that marketing cost could have been offset by the sale of a net new seat. So the cost per acquisition on that exact seat is double. Ouch! Perhaps there's an uplift for repricing and some fees to take into account, but still vastly less than the £50 for selling one of the remaining unsold tickets.

For the ticket agent, their revenue is likely in line with the sale of each ticket, and overall occupancy may not matter. If the ticket agent is bound by rules limiting booking fees, then adding in facility fees for the administration of handling resale tickets could be a handy way to earn more profit from each transaction.

Finally, the venue will have its own incentives for favouring either, depending on whether the show is on a split or guarantee, and whether or not they've hit their break. It may be that the venue is incentivised to sell new tickets until the show is 60% full, but then better off doing resales past that point. Do your own calculations based on your own circumstances.

Pricing experiments

The goal of advertising is to identify people who may be interested in our product, to educate them about the proposition, and to lead them to our shopfront. The goal of a ticketing manager is to make a sale from as many of those approaching customers as possible. The proportion of people who buy a ticket out of all those who approach the shopfront is called the "conversion rate".

Conversion rates are inversely correlated to the number of prospects, so you should expect that as you increase the number of potential customers who you are speaking to, the conversion rate will drop. Hence, focusing your efforts on the most relevant prospects will maintain conversion rate and therefore profitability.

If you have limited inventory and the performance is near-guaranteed to sell-out, then the conversion rate is irrelevant because you can wait for the right customer to come along. However, it is more often the case that shows are programmed into venues which have greater capacity than there is demand for tickets. Hence, marketing needs to focus on finding qualified customers who are in the market for a show, and have the requisite budget for our range of tickets — whilst we need to do what we can to ensure that everyone who enters our proverbial shop leaves with a ticket.

To accomplish this, we need to have a ticket for every wallet. However much the qualified customer can afford, let's have something available for them and ensure that no one leaves the shop by being priced out. This is easier to do behind a counter when you can control the messaging about available seats, and more challenging online where we don't want to cannibalise our top-price sales by over-advertising the cheaper options. Some clever ways to get around this are to ensure there are many more high-priced tickets shown on the plans than lower-priced ones at any time, thereby drawing the customer's eye to the better seats.

Conversion rate is one of the most critical metrics for the success of your sales. All mainstream web analytics software, such as Google Analytics, will allow you to measure the number of people visiting each page on your site — so set up a tracker which records the number of visitors who look at your "production webpage" (the page which describes the content of the show), followed by the number of visitors who visit your "calendar view" (the page which invites the user to choose between upcoming performance dates), then the "ticket selection" (where the user selects their desired ticket, sometimes from a seating map), and finally the order confirmation page (on completion of a booking). Track conversion between each step of this process.

This gives us a very detailed perspective on the final stages of the marketing funnel and is usually relatively accurate because it is all within the realm of one website domain. If your event only has one date, then naturally you won't track a calendar view; if your event is general admission or doesn't have a seating plan, track the webpage where users select how many tickets they want and at what price level, where appropriate.

Take an example where one thousand people visited the production webpage, one hundred visited the calendar view (10% of the previous step in the funnel), fifty visited the ticket selection (50% of the previous step), and ten visited the order confirmation page (20% of the previous step). The overall conversion rate is ten bookers out of one thousand prospects, or 1%. In conjunction with the website team, our goal is to increase this. As sales managers, we can't affect how many people arrive in the funnel (one thousand) because that is the realm of marketing and demand — but we can influence the proportion who come out the bottom of the funnel (1%), and hence the revenue earned.

One word of caution: this sort of detailed conversion tracking relies on user tracking, which — as you will know if you have visited a reputable website recently — it is easier than ever for customers to opt out of. If you've followed my advice about not using dark patterns to influence user behaviour, your website will by default not track users at all unless they have consented to your doing so. In such gold standard implementations, it's not unusual for up to 80% of users to opt out of tracking, so you will never be getting a full picture of the top of your funnel. Tech companies play a game of cat-and-mouse between themselves where some try harder to advertise and track users, whilst the others use increasingly evasive tactics to protect user anonymity.

For most high-traffic websites, this is not a problem, because the numbers of visitors are so huge that you can still draw useful conclusions from the percentage who opt in. However you should be aware that your conversion tracking may be skewed towards the users who visit your website regularly or already have a positive view of your show or organisation.

You should consider whether these customers are truly representative of the audience you're trying to reach — and always compare the results of your conversion tracking against real sales. If your conversion rate goes up but your sales stay flat, it's likely that your funnel is much leakier than your analytics suggest, so don't rest on your laurels.

To improve the conversion rate, begin by identifying the largest area of opportunity: the steps with the greatest drop-off between them. At which stage are you losing the most customers from the funnel? If it is the first stage, then perhaps the production page could benefit from better-written copy or more compelling images; if it's the calendar view, then think about whether you could make the options more straightforward or add more convenient dates; if the seating plan, then look at whether your range of available prices matches with customer preferences, or if there are extra seats you can release to fulfil demand.

There are thousands of potential micro-optimisations which you can make to a purchase flow on a website: adding information, taking it away, making buttons larger or smaller, having more or less prices on view at a time, and so forth. Almost certainly, there will be a few minor tweaks which you can make to your booking flow which will have an observable increase in sales. The challenge is to identify which one.

A/B testing is where we create two versions of a webpage (Version A and Version B, hence the name) and show them to different segments of website visitors simultaneously to see which performs better.

Before you begin the test, formulate a hypothesis about what you believe will improve the website's performance. This could be something like, "Displaying events by popularity will lead to more ticket sales than listing events chronologically."

Then create two different designs for the page: for example, one where performances are listed in chronological order (Version A) and another where performances are listed based on popularity (Version B). Traffic to the website should be split randomly between the two versions to avoid bias, so half of the website visitors would see Version A and half see Version B.

The test should run long enough to collect a significant amount of data. If the test period is too short, the results may not accurately represent user behaviour. Once the test is complete, analyse the results and determine whether they are statistically significant. If one website version has a statistically significantly higher conversion rate, consider implementing that version as an ongoing feature of your main site.

It's important to remember to test one change at a time, to isolate the effect of that specific change on customer behaviour. Multiple changes at once could muddy the results and make understanding what led to observed differences difficult. The process is iterative, so once you've tested one change, you can identify another potential improvement and run a new test. This process allows for continuous optimisation.

The ticket selection page has the most opportunity for ticketing managers to get creative because there are so many parameters available for us to test. Think about having all tickets on the view or having some on revenue management holds — would that perceived scarcity encourage more customers to make a booking? If you add premium tickets to the plan, will the conversion rate go up because it is perceived as a quality product, or down because it's too expensive? A good next step is to set up a spreadsheet tracker which logs the conversion rate at each stage in the funnel, and then begin planning some interventions to increase the rate. Keep what works, disregard what doesn't, and iterate.

Price elasticity and market dynamics

Price elasticity quantifies the sensitivity of consumers to a change in the advertised price. If a small price increase causes fewer people to buy tickets, then demand is "elastic." This is because the demand stretched (increased or decreased) due to the price change. But, if a price increase doesn't affect the number of tickets sold much then demand is "inelastic."

Conversely, if the demand is relatively inelastic, meaning that price changes have minimal impact on attendance, the producer can consider setting higher prices without significant repercussions. This scenario allows for potential revenue maximisation, as the producer can capture higher profits from the audience's willingness to pay.

Pricing is only a lever if your customers know about it. If they can't see that tickets are cheaper on a Monday, then they won't look at Mondays, it won't drive any more sales and you'll just be giving yield away. You need to showcase it at all points in the funnel — on ads and in the calendar view.

You can calculate price elasticity as a ratio of the percentage change in the quantity of tickets demanded, over the percentage change in the price. For example, if an increase in the average ticket price from £50 to £55 causes a reduction in weekly ticket sales from 100 to 80, then there is a 10% price increase (£5 / £50) and a 20% volume reduction (20 / 100), so the price elasticity is 2 (20% / 10%).

If the price elasticity is greater than one, you have elastic demand. This means that the demand for tickets is sensitive to price changes — a small percentage increase in price would cause a more significant percentage decrease in demand, leading to a decrease in total revenue. If the price elasticity is less than one, demand is inelastic, indicating that changes in price have a smaller effect on ticket sales. In such a case, an increase in price would lead to an increase in total revenue.

When demand is elastic we should be careful about raising prices because we can potentially lose a lot of business. But if demand is inelastic then there is is opportunity to increase prices because most people will still buy tickets even though they're more expensive.

Van Westendorp's Price Sensitivity Meter

Before launching a new show, it is helpful to know what price customers are prepared to pay. Our dilemma is that, when asked, people have a bias towards naming a price lower than what they would actually pay. The Van Westendorp model[17] attempts to overcome this by instead asking four questions, and quadrangulating price sensitivity. It quantifies the point at which consumers would dismiss the ticket price is too good to be true ("you get what you pay for"), at which point it unaffordable, and where the sweet spot lies.

Prospective customers are presented with a survey and, after an introduction to what the show is, are asked the following questions:

1. At what price do you start to question the show's quality?
2. At what price do you think the show is starting to be a bargain?
3. At what price does the show begin to seem expensive?
4. At what price is this show too expensive?

Respondents need to answer each question with ascending values, and some survey platforms bake this in as a feature. If your platform doesn't include this, then manually discard any responses which don't meet the criteria.

Responses are then visualised on a line graph with price on the x-axis and proportion of recipients on the y-axis. Each of the questions forms its own line and colour. As price increases, so too do the people who believe it's too expensive, and the number of people who believe it is too expensive diminishes.

The intersection of people from questions one and three is the point of marginal cheapness and should be the floor to any prices, because anything lower and customers will believe it's too good to be true. (£35 in the example chart). On the other side, the intersection of questions two and four is the point of marginal expensiveness and is the ceiling to which most people would pay. I suggest that within the arena of ticketing, we can afford to have a minority of Premium tickets above this point which cater to the most affluent. (£48 in the example chart)

---

17 Van Westendorp, P (1976) "NSS-Price Sensitivity Meter (PSM)- A new approach to study consumer perception of price." Proceedings of the ESOMAR Congress.

The intersection of questions one and four is the optimal price point and the value which most customers would be satisfied in paying. (£40 in the example chart). Van Westendorp suggests that our prices should congregate between the point of marginal cheapness and the point of marginal expensiveness.

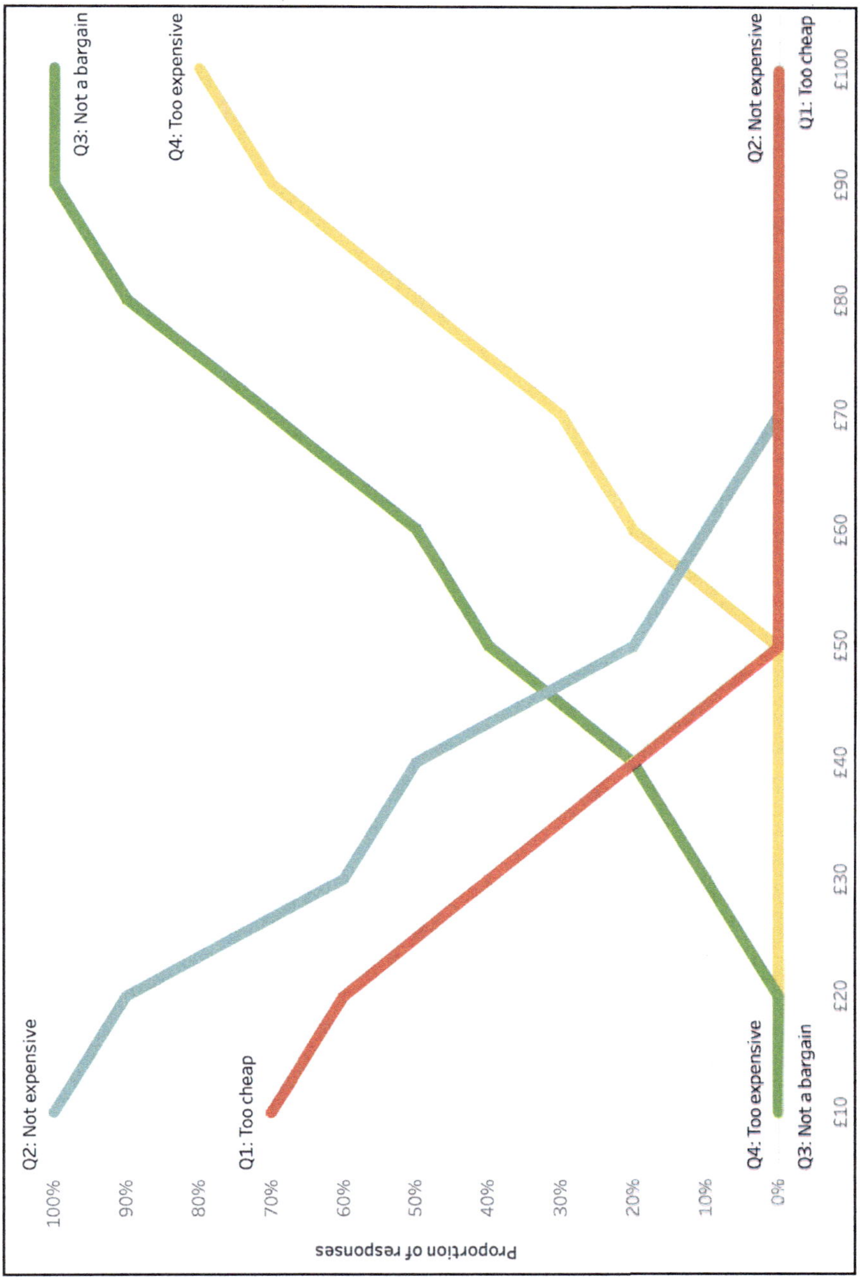

Gabor-Granger

An alternative approach when researching potential pricing is Gabor-Granger, which is better for understanding the optimum point for maximising revenue and is useful in competitive markets to see the maximum cost which the market will bear. Rather than asking respondents to name prices at which they would buy, it presents different potential prices and asks whether or not it is an acceptable cost, thereby reducing the ambiguity from Van Westendorp's survey questions. Typically survey platforms will semi-randomise the initial option which is presented, and then follow up with subsequent options based on the respondent's feedback.

An example survey might look like this;

Would you buy this product for £10? (yes)
Would you buy this product for £15? (yes)
And so on, increasing the price incrementally.

The process continues until the customer indicates that the price is too high for them to consider a purchase. This method allows for the collection of specific data points at different price levels, giving a clear picture of price sensitivity and the optimal pricing point.

The responses are then analysed on a demand curve, plotting price against the proportion of customers willing to purchase at that price. This curve helps in identifying the highest price that the maximum number of customers are willing to pay, as well as the potential income earned at each level.

It's advisable to use a specialist surveying tool for Gabor-Granger to allow for the intricacies of follow-on questions and randomising the initial value.

Gabor-Granger is especially effective when the product differentiation is low and the price is a significant factor in consumer decision-making.

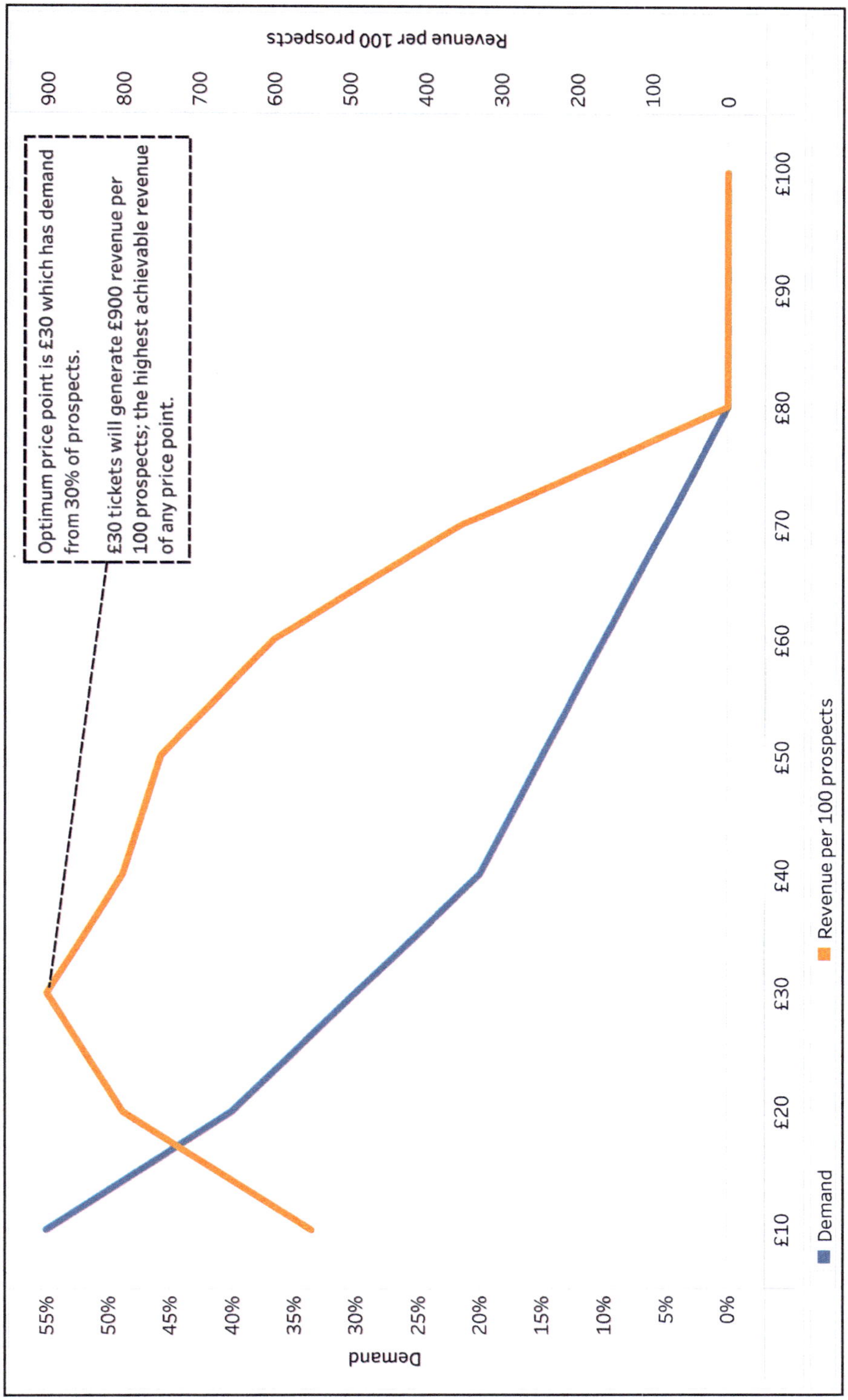
Optimum price point is £30 which has demand from 30% of prospects.
£30 tickets will generate £900 revenue per 100 prospects; the highest achievable revenue of any price point.
Demand
55%
50%
45%
40%
35%
30%
25%
20%
15%
10%
5%
0%
Revenue per 100 prospects
900
800
700
600
500
400
300
200
100
0
£10
£20
£30
£40
£50
£60
£70
£80
£90
£100
Demand
Revenue per 100 prospects

Qualitative approaches

Qualitative market research is a way to understand customers' preferences using interviews, focus groups, and observations. For example, you can conduct in-depth interviews or surveys to understand how much customers are willing to pay for a ticket. By discussing their thought process, we can understand the perceived value of the show, what factors influence someone's willingness to pay, and what price point might deter them from buying.

Focus groups are structured discussions with a small group of customers. They can provide valuable insights into the trade-offs customers make between price and other factors like seat location, added value included with the ticket, or the event's exclusivity.

Social listening involves monitoring social media platforms to understand what customers say about your event and similar events. This could give you insights into how consumers feel about ticket prices and what they consider fair value for their money.

However, I find that qualitative research specific to the subject of ticket price preferences can be unhelpful and is often misaligned with the reality of actual consumer behaviour. A customer may say that they would pay "up to £20" for a ticket, but in fact, when the event comes on sale, and it's the talk of the town, they find themselves spending £40 without hesitation.

The inverse also happens when a focus group is primed to focus on the question of one show, hears a well-rehearsed pitch for the show, and proudly announces that they will be first in line to buy a ticket. Between the focus group and the on-sale, however, life gets in the way, the small advert towards the back of the season brochure doesn't sell it as compellingly, and the sales don't correlate with the enthusiasm of our focus group.

Generally, qualitative research involves a smaller sample size than quantitative research. Thus, the insights gained may not represent the broader population or all customer segments. Conducting in-depth focus groups can be time-consuming and resource-intensive.

Qualitative data isn't numerical, making it difficult to measure or compare results objectively. This can be a drawback when trying to decide on a specific ticket price.

This isn't to say that qualitative studies can't be of great value for understanding who a target audience should be, how a title is perceived, and what an audience needs from its marketing. But the specific question of ticket pricing is best handled by quantitative approaches rooted in actual transactions.

Discounting

When evaluating a discount promotion, consider these questions:

- Will new people either be made aware of the show for the first time, or give fresh consideration to a purchase because of this discount? If not, then you are just cannibalising your own sales.

- If you didn't do the discount, would the seats go empty, or do you think you might sell them closer to performance time but at full-price? Use your Weeks Out report (illustrated in part two) from previous shows to understand how many tickets you can expect to move in-week of performance, and compare it to the number of tickets you currently have open.

- How many additional tickets do you estimate that you will sell from this discount versus not doing it? Look at what uplift the venue saw from similar offers on other performances.

- If the discount is successful, how much do you expect it to effectively cost you versus selling those tickets at full-price? The delta between full-price and discounted rate, multiplied by the number of discounted tickets will give you the theoretical cash which you could have earned without discounting.

- Is the per-ticket discount lower than the cost-per-acquisition on your mainstream marketing campaign? In other words, is your £5 discount cheaper than the £8 which it'd cost you to find a customer with social media advertising? If not, would you be better off investing that money in marketing for tickets that will sell at full-price?

- If you are using a third party to sell the discount tickets, what else are you giving up as a result, and does that matter? For example, access to customer data and opportunities to upsell.

- Does a discount devalue the product and discourage people from booking because they assume the show will be cheap? Use the point of marginal cheapness from Van Westendorp to quantify it.

- Would offering discounts to this show train audiences to wait for discounts on your next show and thereby undermine advance sales?

- Will discounting solve a discrete short-term challenge you are facing, or is there a deeper problem like lack of top-of-funnel demand or supply-and-demand imbalance which needs addressing systemically? Discounting should only be used to solve a short-term challenge and shouldn't be used as a crutch to replace marketing or scaling the house.

Generally, customers will give greater consideration to deeper discounts, which will yield more units sold. However, the more discounts you offer, the more you will train your customer base to wait for a discount to appear, making your wider marketing campaign less efficient. Think about whether you can mitigate the drawbacks of discounting by being more targeted in your approach, for example, by having consistent messaging about when it applies ("10% off for seniors on midweek matinees") or keeping tight reins on where it's advertised (e.g. in a student newspaper).

Discounts are a necessary evil. If you offer discounts, make them targeted to specific audiences and performances, with a clear book-by date, through particular sales channels and with a clear objective in mind. Like a shark who smells blood, consumers can sniff out discounts, and once they've tasted one, they will keep coming back for more. So don't expect that once you've experienced the sales uplift from an above-the-line discount promotion, full-price sales will return to their previous levels when it finishes. Consumers will be baying for increasingly deep and frequent discounts, so know your limits and have a strategy ready in case the discount offers don't work.

If you are approaching a difficult season in the year where tourist numbers decline, then instead of discounting, consider hunkering down by reducing advertising spend and limiting running costs for a few weeks, and then re-emerging when the climate is more favourable. This approach can avoid haemorrhaging money on discounts and reset the team's expectations — so that rather than chasing complex sales, they're focusing efforts on the future, where a more significant prize is to be won. This will be a difficult conversation to have with the producer who'll expect to houses to reach a minimum occupancy, so assure them that its not a case of idleness, but instead a strategic application of resource. Remind them of the overall objectives which you set together - such as to reach an ATP of £x, or a ROAS of £y, and these can't be achieved with prolonged discounting whilst the market is cold. In short, discounts are one of the most powerful ways to put rocket fuel into your sales, but be careful when playing with fire.

Groups

In terms of return on investment, groups are one of the most effective ways you can focus your discounts. You are five times better off if a group booker buys ten tickets from you, rather than an individual booker taking the standard two.

Group organisers are often leaders in their social community, and enjoy bringing their friends together for a theatre trip. The group might be members of some social club, or pupils at a school. Professional group organisers might own a travel company, and create a package where locals can simultaneously book transport and a theatre ticket. Audiences benefit from having the work done for them and coming down together, theatres benefit by filling many seats in one go, and the organiser benefits by earning a commission or a free ticket.

If you're trying to sell tickets to a group booker, however, you need to consider how their needs will differ. Perhaps they need easily-digestible marketing material which they can share with their companions, or the price removed from the printed ticket, or the functionality for you to send out ten separate booking confirmations?

Mystery tickets

This inventive initiative aims to diversify the audience by giving good seats to less affluent customers, filling empty seats, and reducing audience reliance on last-minute deals.

The basic principle is that customers can buy an advance ticket for a price which is a little more than the cheapest available (non-restricted view) seat in the auditorium. Whilst customers are guaranteed to be sat with their companion, they are given no other assurance of where they will be sitting. So it may be in the cheap seats (aligned with what they've paid), or they may get a fortunate upgrade into a Band A or premium ticket.

This is facilitated by the ticketing office on the day of the performance, allocating all of the mystery bookers into the best available seats. The immediate benefit of this process is that the house will be better dressed. But long-term, because the mystery tickets are only available for advance purchase, bargain hunters are incentivised to book ahead for the best deal, instead of waiting for the last minute in hope of a discount. A nuance of the initiative is to guarantee that a certain number of mystery seats will be in the Band A section, thereby upping the chance of payoff for customers.

One high-profile iteration of this scheme was launched by the English National Opera (ENO) after consultation from Baker Richards, and many other venues have adopted the novel model.

Perennial discounts

A sushi restaurant opened opposite my office several years ago, and this poster outside proclaimed a 50% off discount. The poster stayed up for four years, and passing tourists were duped into a deal that wasn't a deal at all.

The strategy worked with tourists because it created a hook which set this sushi shop apart from the three others on the street. However they never got any repeat bookers out of local office workers because we could see that an always-on discount wasn't a discount at all. These perennial discounts are a cheap trick and are easily exposed when the consumer realises that the "now" price is just the market rate.

In some countries, there is a regulation about the duration that a product needs to be sold at "full price" before a percentage-off offer can be promoted. In any case, it's best avoided if you want consumers to return — or recommend you — with any certainty.

Incidentally, since writing the above, the sushi shop has closed its doors. I hope the new tenants take a more honest approach to pricing and are rewarded with better success.

Ethical practicalities

Theatre has long been an art form which tries to be populist but often finds itself in the patronage of the elite. Unlike a can of Coca-Cola, a ticket to the Louvre, or a Netflix subscription, we do not have an infinitely available supply of tickets to our shows. We cannot guarantee entry to everyone who might wish to attend. When this limited inventory coincides with high demand, we have the opportunity to command very high prices for our tickets. However, a question then arises: do theatres have ethical responsibilities when pricing tickets?

On the one hand, theatres need to sustain themselves economically. Revenue from ticket sales contributes significantly to covering the capitalisation of production, actors' salaries, and the upkeep of historic buildings. Thus, a compelling argument exists for pricing tickets at a level that ensures economic viability. However, high ticket prices can also limit access to the theatre to a privileged few, contradicting the notion of theatre as a shared cultural activity. Economically disadvantaged sections of society may be effectively priced out of the cultural conversation.

Another line of thinking is that theatre productions involve significant creative expertise, and value-based pricing should reflect the artistic quality involved. However, critics argue that attaching a high price to art can undermine its intrinsic value. They maintain that creative expression, community engagement, and cultural discourse — all integral components of theatre — should not be reduced to a commodity priced beyond the reach of many.

Dynamic pricing can allow theatres to maximise revenue and sell more tickets by adjusting the cost of tickets dependent on demand. Rather than charging a flat rate for all tickets, pricing some at a higher level can offset others to be sold at a lower price to those in financial hardship. However, opponents argue that dynamic pricing compromises the principle of equal access. Dynamic pricing can perpetuate socio-economic divisions and further theatre's status as an elite art form by making the best seats available only to those who can afford more, or hiking prices for popular shows. Once dynamic pricing takes root, lines can quickly blur between how much extra revenue can be offset against cheap seats versus going straight into the producer's pocket.

Finally, some argue that theatres, as cultural institutions, should prioritise community outreach over profit. Schemes like discounting tickets for underprivileged communities can promote cultural literacy and social cohesion. However, detractors argue that first and foremost theatres exist to educate and entertain, that their future can only be assured through a self-perpetuating cycle of paying audiences, and that other organisations like drama clubs are better placed to service community outreach.

My view is that theatres should be accessible to a diverse socioeconomic spectrum of society, and pricing should be designed to prevent potential barriers for those with limited means, thus promoting equity and social inclusivity. Implementing tiered pricing, discounts for specific demographics, and "pay-what-you-can" schemes are tactics to uphold this principle of broadened access. To those who ask "how can our audience best resemble our constituency?" I answer "don't charge £300."

The solution lies in achieving a balance that respects both the cultural role and the economic needs of selling tickets, whilst transparently educating the ticket-buying public about the purposes behind differential pricing. A robust access program will inspire new audiences to try theatre for the first time and, hopefully, will nurture them over several years into repeat theatre-goers, with content that appeals to them at an affordable price point. Once they mature from the entry-level scheme, a 'graduate' program of accessible tickets ensures that they do not walk out. Identifying who in your catchment area can afford to pay more for tickets, and the extra value which they'll expect in return (preferential seats, early booking etc) can equitably offset these cheaper tickets.

Being transparent about the pricing structure and ensuring that there is a ticket available for all wallets will create some balance between commerce and art-for-all.

Getting on sale

It is tempting to think that the sooner you can go on sale, the better, as it will offer you the maximum amount of time in which you can sell tickets. This is a fallacy: you only have one moment to make your splash, so it makes sense to have a rational plan for when this moment should be. Strategise the optimum time to go on sale and coordinate with a tactical marketing plan which maximises all of your opportunities to sell, leverages organic customer demand and reduced market competition, and hits at a time when there is the highest consumer propensity to spend, such as around payday.

The optimum moment for you will be when there market is quietest and your announcement can cut through, whilst still giving you enough time to have several sales moments and capture valuable advance bookings.

If you have a seasonal show like a Christmas pantomime then put it on sale as soon as possible. These audiences want to plan their busy festive calendar months in advance so, if your event isn't available, they will buy tickets for another Christmas event. If possible, put tickets on sale for next year's Christmas show before you've started performances for this year's. That will empower marketing colleagues to send cross-promotional post-show emails to audiences who enjoy the show each night and make sales whilst memories are fresh. Those early sales act as great comfort when sales hibernate from January to the Autumn.

Performance schedule

The performance schedule is a a key factor in determining whether your show will sell out. There will be hard limits to when you can perform, such as the contractual availability of the venue, working hours of cast and crew, and any local licensing regulations about opening hours. Attending performances is a cultural event, so you will also want your show to align with cultural norms. Start by reviewing when similar events have been programmed, as well as the timings of any neighbouring events so that you are not in direct competition for the same audience.

If you have a social media following made up of a relevant audience, there is no harm to polling them on their preferred timings. Consider the public transportation schedule and the opening hours of nearby restaurants that the audience may visit before or after the show. A varied schedule with some afternoon and some evening performances can give diverse options for audiences who might have caring needs in the evenings or are at work in the daytime.

Human societies tend to work on a weekly rhythm, and you can generally use the same schedule each week, but remember that there are times of the year when this gets disrupted. For example, in Britain, Monday 24th December is not a typical Monday: it is Christmas Eve, and therefore behaves more like a Saturday, as does the whole period between Christmas and New Year's Day, a string of six Saturdays, one day after another. Schedules should therefore not have any performances on the day of Christmas and New Year's, but play as many as possible in the intervening days, except for the evening of New Year's Eve where revellers prefer fireworks to theatre. In the United States, the fourth Thursday of November is not a typical Thursday, and the day after is not a typical Friday: they are Thanksgiving and Black Friday respectively, days on which audiences turn their attention elsewhere. Think about the times of the year at which you must adjust your standard schedule.

If you have many performances per day, such as an promenade performance where audiences enter at regular intervals for several hours, your performance schedule gets more complicated still. In that case, you will need to choose what time your first and last entries will be. There is a curious phenomenon where, faced with 15-minute increments (7.00pm, 7.15pm, 7.30pm etc.), customers invariably choose the half-hourly slots (7.00pm and 7.30pm), while avoiding the quarter-past and quarter-to intervals. The rationale for this is presumably that these times are slightly unusual and might be more challenging for people to remember. The learning is only to advertise half-hourly slots and admit customers on a first-come, first-served basis within these. This benefits audience members, who all have a memorable time slot, and also benefits your operational team, who have some buffer when audiences invariably arrive early or late.

Production notification

All shows can benefit from a production notification: a one or two-page document for internal use only, outlining all the on-sale details in black and white. The production notification is used by producers, ticketing managers, venue staff and anyone advertising the show, to ensure everyone is working from the same, correct information. Once all the details are agreed upon, the production notification can be signed off by the producer, venue, and ticketing manager before being rolled out. Even in an age of digital, cloud and APIs, there is outsized benefit in a two-sided sheet of A4 which spells out all of the core details at setup, and saves many hours of clarification-seeking later on.

It can contain:

- Name of the production
- Performance schedule
- Advertised booking details (e.g. phone number, website)
- On-sale dates including any priorities and their eligibility
- Marketing copy
- Age suitability
- Running time
- Key dates, such as first preview, opening gala night, first midweek matinee, final performance
- Billed creative team, cast and producer
- Specifics of any seating which will be off sale or held (e.g. holds for producer, company, lighting and sound desk, press, audio description/captioned/sign language)
- Pricing matrix of performances and price bands
- Discounts (e.g. disability, young people, seniors, members, schools, groups, concessions)
- Customer booking fees
- Commission arrangements for third parties to sell tickets
- Internal contact details for questions about the production (e.g. marketing, advertising, PR, production, ticketing)
- Allocations (e.g. for VIPs, media partners, friends and family, sponsors, house seats)
- Performance schedule including around national holidays
- Trade nights
- Press night holds
- Revenue management holds
- Day seat / rush / lottery holds

Pricing checklist

These won't all be required on every show, but make sure you've considered them by the time you go on sale so you don't have any difficult questions later on.

- Standard pricing
- Group discounts
- School discounts
- Other education discounts
- Concessions (e.g. seniors, unemployed, veterans, etc.)
- Access/disability discounts
- Preview discounts
- Accelerator discounts (where customers are rewarded with a lower price for booking by a specific date)
- Booking fees and levies, both inside and outside
- Complimentary ticket policy for cast/crew/staff

Doing the basics

I am indebted to a former manager who taught me that there is no use in creating fancy new-fangled initiatives if the basics aren't covered. In a creative industry like theatre, it is easy to be distracted by something fashionable and shiny, and not notice a gaping mistake which has emerged on the show website. So my manager would insist that the marketing and ticketing teams start each day by doing the basics, and checking that the fundamentals were in place for selling the show, before moving onto anything more inspired. He'd be the first to rush into my office if he noticed the lineup of standup comedians on the website was incorrect, and thought nothing of my excuse that I'd been too busy preparing a sophisticated approach to CRM.

What follows are the basics that you should be covering, before getting too clever.

Who should do what

Preparing for on-sale

Marketing:

- Produce a marketing plan to generate hype around the onside (explaining how to do this well is a topic for a different book!)

- Organise a community management squad to monitor social media for signs of difficulty with the system, questions or complaints

Ticket office:

- Build the event, performances and pricing within ticketing system

- Set up any offers and concessions

- Have a second pair of eyes proofread the setup for potential mistakes

- Make test purchases to check it is working (and refund them)

- Rota extra staff for the pre-sales and on-sale days

- Hold a briefing for all ticket office staff about the content of the show, changes to the usual seating plan, content advisories, and any seats being held off sale.

Ticketing manager:

- Liaise with ticket agents

- Distribute a clearly written production notification

- Host a kickoff meeting with all stakeholders to discuss cross-functional work required

- Speak to the ticketing software provider to ensure that the system is upscaled for the volume of traffic

- Plan for live system monitoring

The day of the on-sale itself

- Check all details on the website are correct

- Monitor traffic to the website and performance of customers through the booking flow

- Verify that all planned marketing activity has happened to schedule, and log screenshots

- Circulate hourly updates about website performance and sales to venue team, producers, marketing team, and community management team.

At set up

Marketing

- Put in place a digital abandoned basket campaign, which messages customers who put tickets into their basket but don't complete a purchase and reminds them to make a booking. Add an incentive if relevant.

- Check post-show emails are being sent, which invite patrons to re-attend, see another show, or become a member as appropriate.

- Count the number of mouse-clicks required to book a ticket. Do everything you can to reduce this number, because each additional click represents a swathe of customers who won't reach the checkout.

- Preview your booking flow on a range of mobile devices and check it is intuitive and clear to read. The number of customers shopping for tickets on mobile has increased from less than one percent a decade ago, to now being the majority.

- Make information contextual, rather than putting all your important information into an FAQ page and hoping that people find it. For example, if someone is hovering their mouse over a restricted view seat, this is a contextually appropriate time to give details about how restricted the seats are, what action they will miss, and a view-from-seat photo. Tell people the answer at the time that they have the question —

especially with regard to running times, refund policy, pre-ordering interval drinks etc.

Ticketing manager

- Book a ticket yourself and check that language is clear throughout the purchase path.

- Initiate revenue management holds so that no one feels like they are the first to book. No one likes to be first at a party.

- Audiences are like goldfish: they grow with the size of the bowl. If you have tickets you need to sell, then put them on sale right away. Withholding any seats or keeping a performance off sale will mean it always drags behind and becomes a distraction. More availability equals more sales.

- Remove currency symbols from price labels (so £20 becomes 20 etc). Academic research[18] on restaurant menus found that customers spent 8% more when the currency label was removed, and it has become an effective tactic in the hospitality industry. In culture, think about how often "£££" or "$$$" is used as a synonym for expensive. Removing the symbol is a smart way to avoid connotations of cost.

---

18 $ or Dollars: Effects of Menu-price Formats on Restaurant Checks, Yang, Sybil S, Cornell University. https://hdl.handle.net/1813/71169

Daily tasks once on sale

Marketing

- Check the show can be found at the top of a Google search.

- Check website copy is correct.

- Check that your messaging about sold out performances is clear, and that data is being captured from anyone looking for returns.

- Remove any redundant upsells and replace any which are ineffective. Quantify this by A/B testing the booking flow with, and without upsells. If net revenue is higher with upsells then it's worthwhile, but if the upsells are causing enough consumer confusion that conversion rate and revenue would be higher without the upsells then remove or replace them.

Ticketing manager

- Check the show is on sale through all sales channels, and that performances times are correctly listed.

- Check all seats are released which can be.

- Check seating plans for any orphaned pairs of open tickets which have different prices. Reprice them so orphaned pairs are the same price as one another.

- Check the "shopability" of seating plans. What will the consumer think when they see the selection? Is there an appealing range, and does it help them to intuitively understand where the best tickets are, where to get best value, etc?

- Tactically place people visibly into the auditorium who will add atmosphere, for example members of your Young Persons membership tier in the front row of a comedy show will encourage the whole audience to laugh along.

After you have just opened

Marketing

- Carry out an audit of all the sales channels which are promoting the show and put yourself in the customers' shoes, imagining the questions which they will be asking about the show and how they will perceive it.

- Check that all of the advertised details — performance times, prices, "booking until" date, etc. — are all up-to-date and haven't changed since they were first set up. If you've offered any discounts, check that the details of these are up-to-date and nothing has been left advertised past it's expiry date. Repeat the exercise for every ticket agent or what's on guide which is promoting the show, and follow up with any updates which they need to make.

Ticketing manager

- Chase up any ticket agents who aren't yet on sale that should be. If visiting ticket offices or tourist information centres in person, then take a moment to ask the person behind the counter what questions they are getting from customers about the show, and explain to them why it is the show of the season — or better yet leave them some promotional material — so that they can better sell it to walk-ins.

- If you have a longer running show with a great deal of inventory to sell and many months in which to sell it, you might consider setting up a trade night for influential industry figures to watch the show. Slightly different to an opening night gala, the guest list here will be sales professionals who can help you to sell tickets, such as staff at a tourist information centre or ticket booth, hotel concierges, taxi drivers, and anyone else "on the ground" who's word-of-mouth recommendation will carry weight with the ticket buying public.

- When scheduling a trade night, choose an off-peak performance where you can afford a few complimentary tickets, send out invitations for the trade night well in advance, and chase for RSVPs. It's worth schmoozing these individuals with a small drinks reception at the theatre foyer to build an interpersonal relationship around your show or theatre, and to give them any information about pricing or booking periods which they might need when recommending it to others.

- Unlike a red carpet gala night, this is a long-lead sales endeavour, so we aren't expecting an immediate bump in sales the following morning. If individuals can't make the day of the trade night, then there's no harm in them coming on another off-peak day which is more convenient for them, as the outcome is the same.

Ticket agents

“A man may do an immense deal of good, if he does not care who gets the credit for it.” - Father Strickland[19]

Broadly speaking, there are three avenues for selling your tickets. Most preferably, if you own the venue, is to licence some software to sell directly. This could be either a one-time purchase of something like Patronbase, which will allow you to sell unlimited tickets until the end of time, or a modern SAAS alternative like Spektrix, which is licensed on a per-ticket basis.

Music venues and new venues have a habit of deciding that operating their own ticket office is too much hassle and so outsource ticketing to a third-party ticket agent, which sells on the venue's behalf whilst adding obligatory fees to both seller and customer. This is usually more costly than selling direct and removes an element of control from the purchase flow and messaging, but can be less admin, especially when everyone is rushing to get the production on stage.

The third option is to operate your own ticket office *and* sell through a ticket agent (or several). The theory here is that you can retain all of the benefit of direct ticketing whilst also capitalising on elements which only ticket agents can bring. Specifically, they may be able to target promotion of your event to customers who have recently attended a similar show at a competitor’s venue; to advertise it on marketing lists which reach millions more eyeballs than you have in your own customer database; or perhaps to present an “under the radar” discount which you want to avoid your own members from being aware of.

Ticket agents also open you up to selling tickets through many different brands besides that of your own venue. So rather than attempting to be all things to all people, you can confidently offer premium marked-up tickets on one site which specialises to VIP clientele, and last-minute discount tickets on another site for bargain hunters — all whilst preserving the integrity of your main venue website. This isn’t underhand; it’s simply

---

[19] 1897, [1863 September 21: Date on Diary Entry], Notes from a Diary 1851-1872 Volume I by Sir Mountstuart E. Grant Duff, Page 237, John Murray, London.

market segmentation, and diversifying your product across distribution channels.

An incremental sale is one which would not have ordinarily have taken place and is made because an additional customer has been reached who otherwise was not going to have made a purchase. If most of your bookings come from your own mailing list, then going on sale with a ticket agent would help you to put your product in front of lots of new people and make valuable incremental sales.

Generally a ticket agent will not charge anything to put a show on sale, so their business model is made on a per-ticket fee. That is to say, the more tickets they sell, the more money they stand to make, and inversely that you won't pay them anything if they don't sell any tickets. This is a tempting "no risk" approach because you are only paying on success.

Your cost-per-acquisition to sell a ticket through a ticket agent is near zero, because they are doing all of the advertising, unpaid, on your behalf. That makes it a very attractive proposition when you have no marketing budget of your own and only need to pay the inside commission; effectively only paying for successful sales. If you have don't have a mailing list of your own or are opening a new venue, then it gets you in front of a huge audience with no cost outlay. It's also likely to be more efficient for a ticket agent to advertise a show, than for you to try above-the-line marketing, because the ticket agent already has a large database of customers who are in-market for a product like yours and they can cross-promote. Conversion rates will always be higher when trying to sell live entertainment to someone who has previously made a purchase for other live entertainment, compared to a random stranger. Ticket agents help you put your show front-and-centre to these proven ticket buyers.

However, there are downsides to selling through an agent in this way. The customer effectively belongs to the ticket agent rather than to you. That is to say, the customer's relationship isn't with your venue, and their data is owned by the agent, so selling a ticket to one show via an agent won't do anything to help you acquire customers when your next show comes around. (Unless, of course, you return to that same agent.) In terms of customer lifetime value, it may be more cost-efficient to spend a little more to acquire the customer yourself the first time around, so that you can build a relationship with them and market future similar productions to them, rather than chasing the thrill of a one-night-stand from a ticket agent. The best course of action will depend very much on the particulars of your business model, so do your own maths to calculate how cost-effective ticket agent sales will be for your event.

That said, a ticket agent who brings in truly incremental sales — that is, sales you could never have made on your own — is worth every penny that they charge, because those sales can be pure profit to you. The factors you should consider are whether you could, in fact, reach these customers in a more cost-effective way if you thought of the commission in terms of your own marketing budget;, whether the ticket agent is harming the perception of your own product through brand; and whether your customer lifetime value would be improved if you sold the ticket and captured consumer data for yourself. These are not pure profit if you are making concessions with discounts through the ticket agent or leaking your customer database, so think about the specific objectives of your own ticketing strategy when deciding your approach to ticket agents.

You may question whether the agents are reaching customers who exist on your own database, or whether they already exist in your mailing lists. It's a hard question to work out, because you'd need to speak to everyone who arrived at the show, and the agents will never hand over a list of customer email addresses. If you do need to find out, then the solution is to ask the agent for a list of email addresses with a one-way-hash. The one-way-hash is a cryptographic tool which turns the email addresses into a secret unintelligible code which you couldn't use to email people. However, by comparing the list of hashed addresses from your database and the ticket agent, you can see exactly which customers belong on each list and how big the crossover is. It protects customer privacy and means the ticket agent never gives up the details of a customer who is theirs alone.

The effectiveness of a particular ticket agent typically depends on how much they promote your show, and this in turn depends on how profitable it is for them to do so. Ultimately, they want to extract as much value out of each customer on their database as possible, and that means promoting the most relevant product to the right customers in order to induce a sale. The agent, therefore, is not going to make value judgements about whether or not they *like* your show, or for that matter whether they like you. If your show was the top-seller for them last week, then you can be sure that they'll give it lots of promotion next week.

As such, rankings on ticket agent sites are determined by customer market forces in the most brutal way possible. So what makes your show popular to your customers is the same factor, writ large, which will make it popular with ticket agents. Consumers prefer shows which are playing now over shows that are months away, and they prefer discounts over paying full-price. Those elements, along with the intrinsic attractiveness of the product, will have the biggest influence on consumer demand on agent websites.

The other elements, which you have somewhat more influence over, is the volume of tickets which you have available, and the profit the agent makes on each sale (whether in fees to the customer or commission paid by you, of which more in a moment). If you have a very large auditorium, or can give them access to a lot of tickets across a long run, then it'll be more worthwhile for them to put resources into promoting your title — at least, until a show with an even bigger auditorium or willingness to pay commission comes along. It's a fickle environment, so leave your ego at the door and don't overthink your selling points.

If you've made a deal where an agent earns more commission for your show than your rivals, then surely it'll be bumped up in their rankings. But if the show isn't selling any tickets — even if Laurence Olivier himself has been reincarnated to perform Macbeth — then it won't be worthwhile for the agent to promote it. So you should do everything you can to empower your agents with the best marketing materials you have, send them the latest photos, and give them access to as much inventory as you can make available. Their success will be your success.

Ticket agent commissions

Inside commission is a percentage or fixed fee that is included within the ticket price. With inside commission, the event organiser incorporates the agent's commission into the overall ticket price, and the agent receives their portion when the ticket is sold. This can make the ticket more attractive to customers, because it means the agent doesn't necessarily need to charge a booking fee in addition to the ticket price; from the customer's perspective, the commission is not explicitly stated separately, but is embedded within the ticket cost.

Outside commission, on the other hand, is where the agent's commission is added as an additional fee to the customer when purchasing the ticket. The commission is separate from the ticket price and is usually communicated transparently to the customer.

Whilst outside fees have a negative perception amongst the ticket-buying public, they remain prevalent because the producer is able to earn the same net revenue per ticket, and the agents can charge differing fees depending on their business model and advertising costs. It is common to have both commissions in place on a single ticket.

Inside fees are typically used when the producer has a quality brand which they are trying to protect, and don't want to be seen to be offering discounts. By paying all commission on the inside so that the agent can market a "no booking fee" offer, customers can be offered a soft incentive which appears to be from the ticket agent rather than the producer. Whilst I have seen an uplift from these sorts of offers, they are never as significant as offering a standard "10% off" discount, which has more cut-through to customers.

Tiered commission involves different commission rates based on predefined sales thresholds. For instance, the agent may earn a higher commission rate once a certain sales volume or revenue target is reached. This structure provides incentives for the agent to exceed sales targets. It can be a convenient way to navigate the question of incremental sales, as you may believe that the ticket agent will scoop up a base layer of sales from the strength of your show's brand without having to do any work themselves. So you could pay a low level of commission initially, and then a more lucrative percentage once they have achieved a target and demonstrated that they are bringing in incremental business.

In a sliding scale commission structure, the commission rate increases or decreases based on factors such as ticket price, seating category, or event capacity. Higher-priced tickets or premium seating options may yield a higher commission rate, incentivising the agent to focus on selling those tickets.

In certain cases, ticket agents may receive ongoing commissions or residuals for repeat ticket sales, or for customers who attend multiple events organised by the same producer. This structure rewards agents for building long-term customer relationships and generating recurring revenue.

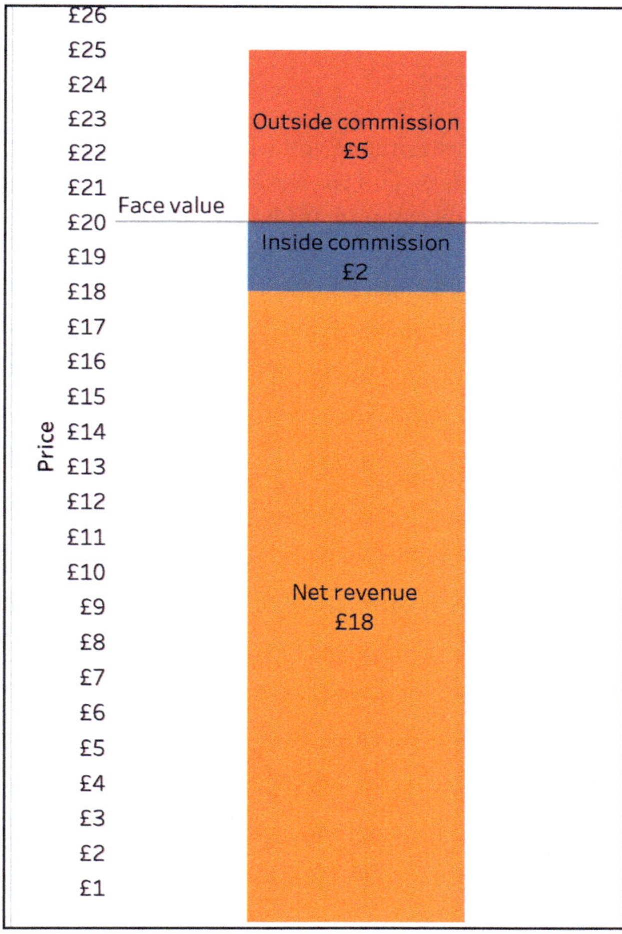

[20]

[20] In this example, the customer is presented with a £20 face value ticket, plus £5 booking fee, and pays £25. Of the £20 face value, the producer earns £18 and pays £2 as inside commission.

Ticket agent promotions

Being on sale with a ticket agent may bring you some incremental sales, and hopefully they'll put some advertising in place that you wouldn't otherwise have had, like inclusion in their newsletter or social media posts to drive business. But if you want to see a big increase in sales, you'll need a ticket agent promotion.

Generally, the two options for ticket agent promotions are a solus, where only your show is being promoted, and a multi-show promotion, where several shows participate in a single campaign. To obtain a solus, you'll need to give the ticket agent some sort of exclusivity. Occasionally this can be in the form of early or sole access to particular performances or seats, but most often it will mean a discount.

The bigger the discount, the more enticing you will be to customers. 10% off, 20% off, 50%... the choice is yours, and the ticket agent will likely give you more exposure the bigger the discount is. If I had limitless inventory, then I'd sell 50% off all day long to guarantee maximum exposure and volume. But auditoriums have a finite size and once a seat is sold at a discount I can't sell it for more if I find a wealthier customer later. So it's a balance between volume (the number of tickets you want to sell) and yield (the per-ticket income you want to earn).

No matter how big a discount you offer for a solus, a ticket agent will probably still spend more budget advertising a multi-show offer above the line, as a range of discounted titles is a more compelling prospect for potential customers than a single show they may not be interested in. The trade-off is that whilst your show will gather more eyeballs, you now face greater competition from being in a line-up with your closest competitors. Much like how car dealerships situate themselves next to one another, I suggest it's generally better to be in a multi-show promotion rather than trying to make it alone.

For long-running shows, you'll need to be tactical about which soluses and multi-shows you participate in, so that you can drive sales for the most difficult times of year without undermining full-price business and training customers to wait for a discount to your production.

Another option are lotteries and rush schemes, which have been popularised by TodayTix[21] and seek to move distressed inventory at last minute to price-conscious consumers. Rather than openly discounting, these schemes have an element of competition — i.e. audience members "win" the chance to buy tickets — and the number of tickets on offer is never revealed. Where Band A tickets are usually £50, customers can get a bargain by winning a £20 rush ticket and sitting in the same seat.

This means that only a pair of tickets needs to be discounted for a Saturday night performance in order to unlock promotional activity from the agent, but that for slower performances producers can subtly dress the house by making more available on the lottery. In theory these tickets are all incremental, as they are made by customers who wouldn't have paid full-price, and can be activated last-minute with an under-the-radar discount.

Some lotteries also offer a "losers rate", which is a novel balance between wanting to sell tickets at full price and getting the influx in demand which a lottery attracts. Whilst you may have a few £20 lottery "winners," you might choose to offer a special discount price to everyone who entered but didn't win. At £30, they feel like they are getting an exclusive deal which isn't available elsewhere, whilst the producer earns £10 more per ticket than the advertised lottery would have done.

---

[21] TodayTix Group is the author's current employer

When to go on sale with ticket agents

The decision of when to go live with each sales channel is a commercial one, and not one you can realistically revert on. You'll never get a second bite at the cherry of going on sale through a given channel, so get the terms right first time.

For a title which is expected to be a difficult seller, or will not be playing many performances, then there's not much benefit in holding back your cards, and you can go on sale with everything as immediately as is operationally possible.

At the other end of the spectrum, for something you expect to sell out very quickly via your direct channels, you may not need to go to ticket agents at all, or can do so later with terms that are very much in your favour.

For venues with a wide season of events each year, your relationship with ticket agents depends on many factors, such as if they will pay to 'buy-out' tickets up-front, versus allocation or API; whether they demand consistent terms on all events or are happy for you to run your own pre-sales; and whether you are bound by visiting artists to make inventory available to their agent of choice.

Where ticket agents can be of most help is for a show of medium popularity which will run for several months or years. Here I will lay out the sequence to pursue in this scenario. You can roll out each step in turn, pausing to exhaust the benefit from each stage before moving onto the next step. The process may take six to eighteen months to compete and the longer and more drawn out it is, the more value each step will bring you. It is generally the case that, the longer you are able to draw out each step, the more profitable the show will be, the more effective its marketing, and the more seats you'll fill.

First, go on sale with your direct-to-consumer channel, which will generally be your venue's own ticket office. You should expect this to form the largest single share of tickets, so a visiting producer will want to do all they can to secure the most favourable commercial terms with the minimum possible inside commission.

If you are a visiting company and have your own ticketing system with a customer database, then next go on sale with this channel. If you can add customer booking fees to the outside, then you may be able to earn greater net revenue here than through the venue channel.

Next go on sale with any other reputable ticket agent who will charge 0% inside commission. The purpose of this is to benefit from their marketing support and wide distribution reach. Because they are 0%, it doesn't actually matter much if they end up selling to some customers who would have bought through the venue box office, because your net income is the same. Do due diligence on their outside customer booking fees to make sure that it is a level which you are comfortable with, and that customers are not being ripped off. Complaints will always find their way to your desk because it's your show, so you need to be able to stand behind any fees being charged.

Negotiate marketing support with the ticket agent at this point — they'll be more likely to offer up something of value when they are trying to secure new product. As a starting point, look for a solus email to recent customers of similar product. This is different to the earlier point about agent discounts, where we were benefiting from the wider impact of a multi-show promotion. A solus is most-effective at on-sale for helping your show to gain cut-through and have a moment to stand out in the marketplace.

Put rules in place about how the agents are allowed to promote your product, and more importantly how they're not allowed to — sales through agents are of no use if they damage your reputation or primary sales channels. For example, you should specify that ticket agents are not permitted to bid on search advertising using the title of the show or the name of the venue ("brand terms").

Next go on sale to groups and schools with 0% commission, so as to open up that customer segment. They will have a discounted rate but the ticket agent won't get anything on the inside at this stage. Start with a straight discount, and then move to an additional accelerator rate in booking period two or three if you want to grow this segment. Again, we'll discuss groups more fully in the section on customer segmentation.

"No booking fee" promotions are next. As I mention above, these often have a limited impact on sales because they're not as attractive to consumers as a discount is. However, they're a good way to reignite lagging enthusiasm from your agents, gain more marketing support, and broaden the top of your funnel. You could offer this as a limited-time promotion to get a quick uptick in sales through a sticky period, before resorting to the world of above-the-line discounts.

Next, utilise inside commission. The agents are double dipping here because they earn both from the producer and the customer, so they're more incentivised to promote your show over your rivals — and the higher percentage commission you are prepared to pay, the higher the incentive still. If you have several agents in your territory, then consider pitting them against one another to secure the most favourable terms.

Next, start offering inside commission on groups sales. This is the biggest bite out of the yield so far, which is why it has waited this long, but should be worth it if it can give you a meaningful uptick in volume. A good group agent — who can sell hundreds of tickets just by making a few calls — is worth their weight in gold, and will see your show through some tough times, so ensure they are incentivised to promote your show over the competition.

Finally, discounts. As the Pringles slogan goes, "once you pop, you just can't stop," and it's equally true of discounts. Think carefully about which customer segments need a discount in order to buy, and which segments you want to protect as full-price sales. Put rules in place about how and where discounts are promoted and their eligibility, so it doesn't become a free for all.

The competition

"We should fear our competitor" was the advice I gave to colleagues at a leadership away day, when they suggested our rivals were inferior or of lower quality. "Never underestimate the competition. Always treat them with incredible sincerity if not absolute fear."

I have enormous respect for competitors simply because they are a competitor and no one is more deserving of respect than a worthy adversary. Even if you are the dominant favourite, they have earned the respect of the audience, who at least view them as a worthy rival. It's a mistake to compare all of the great work your own organisation does behind-the-scenes with the facade of a competitor, who may seem comparatively lacking. Beware the hubris that follows the arrogance of thinking that you are better than the competitor, because they could have all manner of secret plans with which they're about to outflank you. I never, ever, allow myself to think I'm better than my competitors because that moment of blindness is exactly when they'll snatch victory.

Everyone has competitors. You might think that you are better than your rivals but that's only because you know your product inside out and have fallen in love with it. Truly unique shows are one in ten thousand: the original cast of *Hamilton*, the first venue of *ABBA Voyage*, and the thirty-six performances by U2 at the Las Vegas Sphere are the only examples I can think of from the last decade which stand in a league of their own. Everyone else is a part of the milieu of live entertainment. The best people to learn from are our competitors because they are professionally invested in solving precisely the same problems as us, and they are making it work. So study their successes closely.

You should be able to list five to ten genuine competitors to your show, in order to make informed decisions about ticketing strategy. And if you can't, then think harder because you are deluding yourself.

If our job is to understand the audience, then a key component is to understand the marketplace better than the audience do. We should be more informed about the product, pricing and promotion of other shows than our customers, in order to make our offering more attractive. Watch as many shows as you possibly can — especially the ones which you don't think you'll enjoy. I used to watch a hundred shows a year (regretfully less nowadays) and the most powerful lessons about audience appetitive come when you challenge yourself to watch a show which is out of your comfort zone. When I'm watching a show, I'm not thinking about why it's bad — I'm looking at the audience and trying to understand what appealed to them, and what our shows need to do to attract these customers.

The more that you find yourself needing to be specific when justifying your uniqueness is a sign of how unoriginal consumers may find you. For example, you may be "the best educational show for under fives which combines a live stage show with virtual reality". Sure, that sounds perfectly original, but it's not enough unless there are consumers searching for that specific niche (and if there were lots of consumers looking, then it probably wouldn't be a niche). Instead, your target audience will probably be asking themselves whether yours is the best educational show, or whether your event is preferable to using a VR headset at home, or whether their child will enjoy your show as much as anything else playing at the same venue.

When I first became interested in arts marketing, I was advised to read a theatregoers forum, where die-hard fans shared rumours about potential castings, gossiped about early previews, and were ruthless in their critiques. The forum has long-since closed, so today I skulk social media groups where regular theatregoers (often mums) ask for advice about where to sit and how much to pay. I suggest doing some research to find out which online communities exist in your area, as it acts as an excellent grounding in what audiences really care about, and can be a canary to any potential problems.

How long to run for?

"If I was the producer, I'd forget about a West End transfer," advised one critic at the opening night of *Les Misérables* in 1985.[22] Another suggested the show was "instantly disposable trash."[23] *Wicked* didn't fare much better when it arrived on Broadway; *The New Yorker* proclaimed that "not one song is memorable."[24] At the last count, both shows are doing just fine: *Les Misérables* is currently the longest-running musical in London, and *Wicked*'s New York production has earned over one billion dollars.

Neither musical was born a smash hit; they were nurtured into their current form of long-running success thanks to canny management of the performance schedule over a number of different booking periods — a skill we shall explore in this chapter.

Booking periods need not necessarily refer to huge tranches of dates put on sale for a long-running show over a series of years. If you have a one-night comedy show, and later add a second date due to demand, that is a second booking period. A booking period is simply a range of performance dates which are put on sale at the same time. This gives production staff the ability to sign contracts up until a specific date, it gives audiences clear visibility on how long they have to catch the show, and it gives marketing and sales staff a moment of heat, when tens or hundreds of thousands of tickets are made available, around which a successful marketing campaign can be built.

Incidentally, the terminology "booking period" should not be customer-facing and only exists as a means to communicate internally about sets of performances that go on sale simultaneously.

Naturally, different kinds of booking periods require different kinds of sales strategy. Here are a few broad guidelines.

---

22 https://www.telegraph.co.uk/theatre/what-to-see/les-miserables-30-reasons-awful-musical-has-stood-test-time/

23 https://www.latimes.com/archives/la-xpm-1987-03-14-ca-9500-story.html

24 https://www.newyorker.com/goings-on-about-town/theatre/wicked

One nighters

It may be that you have programmed a show for one or two nights and find yourself nearly sold out shortly after on-sale. At this stage, your team may timidly start conversations about perhaps adding another date, seeing whether there is demand, and so on. Don't bother with these conversations: if you are sold out that quickly after on-sale, you should add the extra date immediately and without any hesitation.

At that moment, customers are coming in their droves to book for the show they've just heard has gone on sale, and if they see a single performance that's sold out, they will never return. People's lives are too busy to remember to check back in a few days, and you've already cried wolf to them once by telling them tickets are on sale when they've now discovered you are, in fact, sold out — so when you send another e-shot saying a new date has been added, they'll assume the same has happened again.

Whilst the going is good and customers are coming down the booking funnel, add another date and work out the operational logistics of servicing it later on, when you're a thousand tickets richer.

Tinder: booking period one

For longer running shows, the considerations are a bit more complex, for getting a show to catch fire is like building a campfire: it requires small, careful steps, which start with the tinder.

Being a "tight ticket" initially — where customers are grateful for the chance to be in the room where it happens — sets your production up from the start with a status that forms the foundation for longevity. A limited number of performances means that auditoria are well-sold, and a buzz will develop among early adopters who want to see the show. Booking period one is the initial run of performances and will go on sale weeks or months before anyone sees the show. Crucially, this means your first booking period will be on sale before anyone is able to make any critical judgement — a position you will never be in again.

This isn't to suggest that the first booking period is an opportunity to hoodwink customers into buying a production you expect will be subpar. I only wish to point out that it's a unique moment in the lifecycle of the show that requires a different sales strategy.

During you first booking period, your audience will likely be full of in-the-know people who like seeing things first, are grateful to be there, and are wont to spread good word about it. These ambassadors exist within social groups of all shapes and sizes, and we want to make sure they all see the show early on, when it feels exclusive. A short run of a handful of performances gives your marketing colleagues the ammunition to describe it as a "sell-out hit", which is the social proof needed to get a whole new tranche of customers interested in seeing the show.

For your debut at the ball, be the picky, pretty new thing everyone wants to dance with, rather than the one who is desperate for any dance partner. As with a one nighter, you can then quickly add extra inventory once you've established yourself as the must-have and impossible-to-get ticket of the season.

Kindling: booking period two

Putting booking period two on sale will likely move our sales challenge, from having a few hundred tickets left to sell to possibly 100,000 open tickets — so we need to match the scale of this challenge with an equally sized moment of consumer demand.

Opening night is generally the point of the most heat in any show's sales cycle, so we can capitalise on this by aligning it with the on-sale of a new booking period. If nothing else, this presents journalists with a neat story for their column: "the show is a sell-out success and received rave reviews at its opening night, so today they are adding six months' of new performances due to overwhelming customer demand". It is a tidy narrative which buffs up a middle-of-the-road review piece into a newsworthy article that validates the extension period.

For operational reasons, you may choose to actually have tickets on sale slightly before opening night, so that they are already available when the reviews come out. The key lesson is not to let the most significant organic moment of heat in the show's lifecycle pass you by without making the most of it. As soon as people hear about the show's opening night, they should also learn that it has just extended due to popular demand and that they can buy tickets immediately.

Your number of prospects at this moment is possibly the highest it will ever be in the show's lifetime, so don't waste that potential by putting any barriers in the way like "on sale now for members, general public next week". The people who this news will reach are less engaged customers than those who booked previously, so make the sale whilst you can. If they're only on the website because they read a good review, they won't be around for long and you may never get them back.

Fire: booking period three

By the time we're thinking about booking period three, we have demonstrated to the public that the show is a proven hit and a reliably good time, so we can expand our target customers from early adopters into the late majority who follow the crowd. People in this group are less impulsive and benefit from having more time to make plans, so booking period three should cover a wider range of dates to give customers time to organise themselves. By now we are also reaching a more geographically diverse audience, so a longer booking period helps them plan their accommodation and travel.

If your show is lucky enough to be considering booking period three, it's important to remember that this is when the show transitions from being a one-off into developing a sales rhythm — so it's important to set yourself a cadence you can keep to. Your first two booking periods may have been effectively decided by the availability of the venue, with the show opening at whatever time of year was on offer, but booking period three is the time to think about the seasonality in which you want the show to operate.

Think about which weeks in the year you would organically expect to have higher consumer demand for tickets. In England, this is generally the final two weeks of December around the Christmas holidays, and the six weeks which start from the end of July (when school pupils have their summer break). These timings will vary in each market, particularly in line with tourist trends, but it should be possible to identify them on a calendar.

Booking period three should end immediately before one of these high seasons. For example, in England, the period would run up until mid-December. This is because it gives you the longest possible time to sell the least-desirable dates within the booking period. Then, even though you'll have less time to sell the hot December dates when you add booking period four, this will be balanced out by increased consumer demand.

This creates an equilibrium where consumers naturally fill the less-desirable performances at the end of one booking period before you put the more attractive dates on sale and get the next booking period off to a solid start. Putting this rhythm in place from booking period three will ensure that when new batches of tickets go on sale, they align with organic customer demand and fill the performances which most need attention.

Blaze: booking period twenty three

I worked on one musical up to booking period twenty-three, and we continued to tweak the seating plan, pricing, and performance schedule with each extension, challenging our previous assumptions about consumer preferences with the realities of what the sales data was showing. The work is never done.

The question of how many performances you should have on sale at one time for a long-running show is a hotly debated one, and many intelligent sales managers have vastly different opinions and "evidence".

"The *Book of Mormon* model" is to keep the ticket very tight. For its first few years, the show would only ever have three months' worth of performances on sale, which forced all customers into immediate performances. This created a virtuous supply-and-demand cycle where prices could be forced up because there was so much pressure on short-term performances, and it could proudly announce that they'd never had an empty seat since it opened.

Artificially whipping consumers into a frenzy like this was successful for a musical with so much hype and great reviews behind it, and served to maintain its reputation as a sold-out hot ticket. I hasten to add that I've had no professional involvement, nor inside knowledge, of this show, and this is purely gleaned from looking at their seating plans and online consumer sentiment.

The drawback to this model is that it requires changes, as the production is always three months away from an empty auditorium. The producer has no certainty that the short-term business will come, and so lives on a knife edge, always risking that tonight's performance will be the first with an empty seat. Any disruption to consumer behaviour, such as a pandemic, industrial action on the transport network, or disruption caused by unseasonal weather, can mean that the anticipated short-term sales do not emerge and the house is left half-empty.

Many producers sleep better at night knowing that they have a multi-million-pound advance in the bank from consumers who have booked months or years into the future, which helps their cash flow to pay actors and guarantees their future rent to the theatre landlord. The *Book of Mormon* strategy provides no such comfort, trading a lack of long-term certainty with the high-risk-high-reward possibility of last-minute bumper sales. I suggest that if using this strategy, you need a very reliable consumer base that you can confidently and regularly activate in the short term.

Anything which is less of a no-brainer purchase for customers, or requires them to make plans or consult with others, can benefit from the alternative strategy of a longer range of dates on sale. This might include shows that attract large groups, family shows, shows with higher ticket prices, or anything that else that will require extra consideration and planning from consumers.

These shows will typically always have eleven months of performance on sale at a time, meaning that customers can make plans to book at a significant date for them; birthdays, anniversaries, vacations etc. Anything more than one year into the future can cause confusion (consumers misreading this July as next July), but anything up to this will give consumers all the choices they need and allow for your advance to be as plump as possible.

In this scenario, you will likely have two or three booking periods on sale concurrently. So tonight's performance may be in booking period three, but customers may already be able to book a year ahead for booking period five. There is no rule about how many performances you should have in a booking period, other than that the sensible way of limiting your liability is to only add a new booking period once you have confidence that the existing one will meet your targets for it.

Embers: closing a show

Eventually, whether a show has one booking period or one hundred, the time will come when it must close. This is an enviable time in the show's lifecycle for a sales manager: this is when we are at our strongest, because we have more data available than ever before. In this period we can draw on everything which we've learned about how each consumer segment values the show, what prices can be commanded on week-of-performance sales, and if any seats have especially good sightlines which can justify being priced up. Lean on all you've learned about what works and what doesn't.

For a short run, there is opportunity to price up the end of the run, whether this is its own booking period or simply the last few weeks of the most recent one to go on sale. It is usual for there to be increased demand in the final weeks of a show from people who had been meaning to attend and don't want to miss out, or from fans who are keen to return one last time. If you can, try to squeeze some premium income out of this final surge in demand.

If the show has been running for some time, then closure is usually because sales are anticipated to dwindle. If this is the case then leave no stone unturned, and remember that all options are now available to you. There is no longer a brand to protect, so you can offer bargains to returning customers on your database, openly advertise discounts on posters and take on-the-day bookings at any price. We are now in the realm of a circus packing up and leaving town so there's nothing to be precious about. Instead, earn all the revenue you can, because once the show is over you won't be able to sell any more tickets. Have no ego and sell, sell, sell.

Common problems

"We are all best at teaching the material which we are still striving to master, so I write as someone steeped in ongoing discovery." — Derren Brown [25]

In this chapter I will explore some scenarios which commonly emerge, and my ideas for how to deal with them.

Stuck with last minute inventory to shift

Consider whether this is a one-time problem or a larger issue that will be continuing for days or weeks. If it's the start of an ongoing problem, then don't exhaust all your options at the first slow performance; instead, take a step back and create a broader strategy.

Most likely, there are not enough people coming through the funnel, and marketing need to make an effort to reach more potential customers. If the problem is in the bottom of the funnel, then analyse price resistance and see whether your value proposition (the show + the seats available) are aligned to what customers are prepared to pay. If not, try adjusting this for a few performances; it's low risk and can always be reverted, and will soon show you whether or not price is the problem.

If the problem of last minute availability is a discrete one which only affects one or two performances, then consider what is the most "closed" approach you can use to fill the seats. For example, an offer to friends and family of the cast and venue staff, or local businesses. If there are any groups which have booked, offer them additional tickets at a low price as a one-off. If there are swathes of seats which are likely to go empty, then move customers downstairs and closer to the stage, so that the auditorium feels fuller and everyone has a better experience.

---

[25] Notes from a fellow traveler, Derren Brown, Neat Review, 2023

Disappointing dog

Ticketing managers are the first to get blamed for a flop, and the last to get praised on a hit. If the show had lofty aspirations but has turned out not to in fact be very good, start by bringing down any aspirational targets if they are now impossible to achieve, because it does no one any good to either fool themself that it is still possible, or be demoralised by a number which is so out of reach.

These shows are always long slogs and require much more work than a hit. As a matter of due diligence, check that the marketing team are spending an appropriate amount of money on advertising, that they have attempted to diversify the target audience, and that they are testing different creative and messaging. With a tone of comradely curiosity, check that they aren't spending all of the budget on an advert in a distant cave, and it is in fact being seen by your target eyeballs - because this isn't always a certainty.

Within the realm of ticketing, have no ego about pricing and don't be ashamed to radically bring down the prices from what was originally on the plan. If you also earn revenue from the venue, such as bar or merchandise income, then sometimes these shows can still be worthwhile just to get customers in at almost any cost, in the hopes of selling a drink or two at the bar.

My experience with "seat filling" services — who give away free tickets to a discrete list of audiences on quiet performances — is that they are effective at filling inventory but actually bar sales don't materialise. It turns out that the cheapskates who like free tickets also don't like paying over the odds for a drink at the theatre bar. If you can persuade a seat-filling agency to let you sell tickets to their audience at a peppercorn price, say £5 each, then that is still better than nothing, because ancillary sales could be negligible.

Use ticket agents and distributors to spread offers far and wide. Often you can play one against another by running exclusive deals in consecutive weeks, such that each one feels that they have something worthwhile to promote, and you always have some promotion in market which is reaching a new database.

Tap up drama schools, drama clubs, community groups, and anyone else with an interest in theatre who can be persuaded to take a bulk of tickets at a low price.

By the time that you recognise the show is a dog, then nothing really is going to turn things around and it is a case of limping to the finish line. If all of the signs are there that nothing is working, then it's worth a clear-headed conversation about stemming the loses by cutting performances and closing early.

One-night performance which is bound to sell out immediately

If the performance is bound to sell out immediately, why do you only have one? Add extra performances if you can to capture that high demand.

Price ambitiously. Prices are inelastic on performances which sell out immediately. If the ticket is so hot that you could sell out three times over within an hour, then there is no reason why one seat should be priced less than another — because the demand for them is the same. The only exception is for restricted view where the experience will be legitimately impacted. Apart from those, everyone will be happy to pay top-dollar just to be in the room, given that so many others couldn't even get a ticket at all.

Ensure your ticketing system is stable, with a queuing facility set up. Also be sure to communicate clearly to customers in advance how the on-sale will work and their slim chances of success. If you can, be transparent about how many tickets you actually have available to sell, and the number of customers competing for them, because often rumours can start that there were in fact none available to begin with.

Capture data from everyone who wanted a ticket but missed out, so that they can be first in line if you do add extra dates or have a similar show in future.

Limited run with a celebrity lead

There's a shrewd technique for using dynamic pricing around on-sales, specifically for shows with limited runs that have the potential to be very popular. The tactic is to do a 48-hour priority on-sale for super fans, and then to take tickets off sale for a day.

During this day, you recalibrate your expectations about the level of demand for the show and reprice all of the performances. This approach has the effect of giving the sales manager time to flexibly adjust their approach during a window that would otherwise frenetic. Temporarily taking tickets off sale before the general on-sale begins also means that you can communicate the new prices to ticket agents, so that sales through secondary channels don't have to made at a level which is now too low. It avoids a Twitterstorm from superfans claiming that the show is too expensive, because they are all able to buy mid-priced seats during the priority onsale, and you win legitimacy to maximise the demand for the title during the general on-sale.

As much as you might enjoy the heat of that initial period, you should also have a plan ready for how to sell tickets once the celebrity has left. The trouble is often that, in the mind of customers, the show gets conflated with the star lead, and it becomes harder to sell the show after they've left than if they were never in it — because the heart of the show's brand has been ripped away. So don't wait until the star has left before trying to sell these performances — start early, work with your marketing colleagues to promote the show as something other than a star vehicle, and use price as a lever to point potential customers to these cheaper performances.

Meanwhile, price up all performances which the celebrity is playing in. If the celebrity is concerned that consumers are being ripped off, using their name as bait for higher prices, emphasise all accessibility schemes that you have in place, how your pricing compares to other celebrity-led shows which have been in market, and so on.

When you can't afford a ticketing manager

I've met several producers who, faced with tight budgets, had a preference for trying to handle ticketing strategy themselves rather than to employ a specialist. Their logic is that ticketing is relatively common-sense, and that a combination of their instincts, some steer from the venue manager and their accountant would get the results they need without the cost.

The amateur may observe that ticketing is superficially similar to retail or e-commerce, and that they will be able to utilise the same techniques which they've used in wider business. However, countless times I have witnessed the hubris of intelligent individuals who come from other industries and suffer the consequences of blindly projecting mainstream sales principles onto our sector which is curiously idiosyncratic and so full of individual nuance that professional domain expertise is required for a show to sell out. Whilst plenty of Hollywood studios and media organisations have dabbled in mounting a theatrical production, I'm not aware of any which have succeeded without hiring the assistance of professionals who have experience specifically in live entertainment ticket sales.

I reject the 'we know best' approach wholeheartedly and would firmly advise all producers to make use of a ticketing sales manager whenever one is available. New York, London and Australia all have a cadre of professional sales managers, independent of the venues and ticket agents, who have dedicated their professional lives to helping shows to sell out with relatively impartial consultation. These services are likely to deliver amongst the highest return on investment of anyone employed for the production. The value which they deliver from knowing local nuances, maintaining existing relationships with ticket agents and leveraging their experience from previous deals, will all generate profit. It is an inevitable fact that when someone spends 40+ hours a week, every week, looking at seating plans, pricing and agent deals in any territory - they will be magnitudes better at the task than a well-meaning amateur or jack-of-all-trades. With experience comes the ability to know - within a specific market - which promotions, marketing, deals, times of year - are useful and not. A good ticketing manager will realistically deliver a 100x return on investment so, when faced with a tight budget, look to maximise profit by employing an experienced expert to manage your revenue, rather than cutting costs.

Quiet performances

Sometimes you will unavoidably have a performance which hasn't sold well — perhaps there's another major event happening in town that day, or the transport network is closed. Rather than accepting a smattering of audience across the auditorium, it's preferable to consolidate them into one neat section. Moving all customers to the front of the stalls will create a better communal audience experience and warmer atmosphere for performers.

It is true that many customers will enjoy a ticket at a higher value than what they've paid for, however this concern is only academic given that the seat will otherwise go empty and that the transaction has already happened.

Closing the upper circle a few days before the performance is an easy way to create a more intimate environment and encourage all future bookings into the seats downstairs. Just remember to reband the remaining tickets so that the cheap seats which are off sale are replaced by equally-priced inventory in the stalls.

A note on language, from my experience communicating to customers front-of-house that their tickets are changing. Audiences will fill with tension if told that "your seats have changed", and as a result they will fight for the seat they'd carefully selected when purchasing. Instead, audiences hearts unlock at the phrase "we have upgraded your tickets," and they will follow you anywhere. Small change to the verbiage, big change to the ease at which you can reseat patrons.

I watched a show last week and it was only at the interval that I discovered that I had been subject to this exact strategy: all of the customers had been discretely moved forward, and the upper circle was closed, making for a great show rather than a half-empty one. I didn't notice for hours, because as audiences, we never look behind us.

When touts sell on resale platforms

Resale platforms are websites where ticket buyers can sell-on their ticket to another consumer. This can either be at face value or below, or at an inflated price where the seller earns a profit. The site may be operated by your primary channel, where you earn a commission on each sale, or could be a third party.

The problem with some of the third-party sites is that they are ripping off customers, most of whom don't know they've been ripped off. They charge a price far in excess of the face value, imply that tickets are in a much better seating position than they are, and sometimes peddle tickets that turn out to not even be legitimate. For the venue, this is revenue which they could be earning but is being taken from them; for the customer, they are not receiving the service they think they've paid for, and they're going to blame you.

Whilst this might seem intimidating, aggressive resale only affects a minority of live entertainment performances, and those are primarily one-night performances in stadia by world-class acts. Resale platforms shouldn't be a sizeable issue for most shows because the resale business model is reliant upon such extreme scarcity that potential customers are looking beyond the primary sales channel to find an available ticket. The platforms have most success at one-off events where the customers aren't conversant in where to buy tickets - including ad-hoc events like fireworks night or Hogmanay. Don't assume that just because you have plenty of tickets available, that you will be rid of the resellers, because they often prey on the naivety of consumers. In some countries, such as Ireland, legislation has been introduced where a venue can forbid resale for events over a certain size, so research whether anything like this exists in your jurisdiction, as well as educating prospective customers on where to buy with confidence.

There are some options to mitigate against resale platforms. First, as discussed in the pricing chapter, having premium tickets on sale for tonight's performance massively reduces the incentive for a tout, because you are offering the potential customer a better seat at a better price through a trusted sales channel. The tout is going to struggle to justify pre-emptively buying any of your tickets in the hope of resale, if they know the primary channel isn't fully sold out.

Next, having customer-centric policies for genuine customers who are unable to attend will encourage them to simply accept the convenience of an automatic refund, rather than the temptation of trying to resell. If we make it hard for customers to get a refund, or we try to fob them off with an exchange, then they will be more likely to seek a cash sale from the secondary marketplace — so make it simple for them to take a refund, and get the ticket back on sale through the primary channel. You may even be able to reprice the ticket higher this time around if inventory is tight, and if you take booking fees then you will earn again on this too.

Finally, if touts are really causing you headaches, check legislation in your area, as third-party resale may be prohibited or there may be specific regulations about how tickets have to be displayed on these sites. You may be able to force them to take down sales if they aren't following the required standards.

Overpriced titles

These are curious beasts: good shows which garner a positive audience response, but where the revenue targets are seemingly out of line with customer expectations.

Firstly, work with the marketing team to educate customers on the value proposition. Often these shows have some added value element, such as dinner being included, or an immersive element, or a much longer duration than a normal show. It's easy for this messaging to get complicated, so work with your best copywriter to create simple messaging that tells audiences how you are offering an experience which is much greater than just a show.

Secondly, re-evaluate whether your proposition is objectively more valuable than audience expectations. Research pricing for other shows in market, and consider the opportunity cost for what else an audience could be doing with that time.

Work up some financial forecasts that model how many extra tickets you would need to sell in order to justify a reduction in ticket price. Look at whether this level has been achieved for similar shows at the venue. For example, is it realistic to expect that a 20% reduction in price would see a 20% uplift in customers, and do you have this amount of inventory available?

Talk to the producer and see whether some compromises can be made on the core objectives. If they are able to reduce running costs a little, then this might place less of a burden on the need for ticket price to be so high.

Cancelling a performance

"The show must go on"

When I produced my first show, aged seventeen, my grandmother phoned me the night before because she was watching the BBC six o'clock news. There had been a fatal stabbing outside the theatre and police closed the area as a crime scene. That was the first of many circumstances where I've been faced with cancelling performances, including the venue flooding, the ceiling falling into the auditorium, indisposition of the entire cast, many power cuts, the death of the artist whom the show is based on, and of course the coronavirus pandemic. Not to mention smaller temptations to cancel bookings, like the show not being ready, overbooking seats, or lack of sales.

Canceling a ticket should be beyond our last resort. It is better to have never sold a ticket than to cancel one. When we cancel a ticket, we are disappointing our customers, placing them out of pocket for the travel and accommodation which they have organised, frustrating the plans for childcare and restaurant bookings, and diminishing their faith in live entertainment. It destroys the confidence which has been built up for our show, venue, and industry as a whole.

One hit West End show I worked on developed a reputation for cancelling at least one performance a month. Ticket agents grew tired of processing refunds and actively removed advertising because, whilst the sales were good, it wasn't worth the aggravation of upsetting their customers. Every cancelled ticket also encourages audiences to book last-minute, and goes against all the hard work which the sector has made in rebuilding trust coming back from the pandemic.

It's a pity to observe colleagues who have worked so hard to make a sale being forced to refund it. A ticket is intangible and is a promise of something great yet to come, and the only mandate which we have for dolling out these promises is if we consistently deliver on them night after night. I do not believe that we have the authority to cancel someone else's plans.

There will be tensions when a catalogue of events mean that cancelling tickets feels like the only path to harmony. But I implore you, in those frantic moments of anxiety, to see if there is any way that you can honour the promise made to your patrons.

For example, you could present a performance with scripts in-hand, at a neighbouring venue, with someone else taking on the lead role (understudies, stage management, the director, the ushers), with a changed performance time, with a truncated running time, by arranging complimentary tickets for another show at a nearby venue, and so on. The audience have moved their life to attend this performance, so give them something when they arrive.

Sometimes, of course, there are dire, tragic events outside of our control. If there's nothing else you can do, then by all means cancel the performance. Communicate clearly with your patrons, make sure they've received your message, and keep everybody safe. Send your message with deference to the inconvenience you are causing, provide radical compensation (full cash refund plus free drink next time plus priority booking etc.) and, if the cancellation is within six hours of performance, then be personally present in the foyer to speak to patrons who arrive without having seen the message. Seeing those disappointed, frustrated and angry faces was the education I needed to resist ever cancelling another performance.

Press complaints about high ticket prices

When journalists have a slow news day, it doesn't take them long to reheat the tired story of expensive theatre ticket prices. The article usually name-checks a handful of performances with expensive tickets on sale, and draws conclusions about theatre being out of touch with it's community. The story never gains much momentum, so we can prepare a boilerplate response for this hackneyed enquiry in advance.

Prevention is better than cure, so start by ensuring that your pricing isn't out of touch, has accessible entry points, is affordable to your target audience, and that you've properly communicated where people can find the most affordable tickets. There's usually only enough space in the headline to call out one expensive show, so ensuring that your ticket prices are always a hair's breadth lower than the competition might be worth your while to avoid this situation becoming your headache.

Sometimes a senior figure from the board will be surprised to read this sort of article and rightly make their own enquiries about whether the pricing is fair. To these people - who are intelligent and willing to have a civilised debate - it is worth sitting down and looking at some numbers together. I use the bubble chart specifically for this purpose (illustrated in part two's graphs section) as it pronounces exactly how many expensive tickets there are, how many mid-priced and how many low-priced tickets. Often these news articles jump to point out the highest price on sale for premium tickets, but understandably journalists don't appreciate that this in fact represents a tiny minority of the overall sales because the cheapest tickets always sell first. Use the bubble chart to examine exactly how many tickets are being sold at each price point, how this compares to previous shows or those of the competition, and educate your stakeholders about how this handful of premium tickets is a part of your wider ticketing strategy to bring in the widest audience.

My PR colleagues tell me that these stories are quick to blow over, and that it's preferable to ignore them than to add fuel to the fire. However, if your organisation does decide to respond to the press enquiries, then here are a few lines which you can make use of.

1. Premium tickets help to subsidise cheap tickets.

2. The performance is 95% sold out and we are maximising revenue from the few remaining seats.

3. Consumers are already familiar with dynamic pricing from hotels, airlines and ride-hailing apps, and they know that ticket prices go up when demand is high.

4. The organisation is a charity/community organisation/mission-led, and needs to increase commercial income from ticket sales to support it's education/outreach work.

5. The organisation recently lost subsidy from government or donors, and premium tickets are needed to makeup the shortfall, so that it can continue operating.

6. 1,000 tickets have already been sold at £10 each. The only ones remaining are the higher-priced tickets.

7. Commercial ticketing strategies are balanced by outreach initiatives, such as a free performance for local schools and key workers.

8. Lower-priced tickets are available through access schemes, such as memberships for those aged under 25 and on-the-day rush tickets. Use the press article as free publicity to promote these schemes and ticket availability for your next show.

9. Tickets are much more expensive for opera, sports, etc.

10. The value of the show is higher than ever as it is a world premiere/award winning/elaborate set/direct from Broadway/three hours long/etc.

11. We've price-locked the cheapest tickets for the last five years, and are increasing the top price to pay for it.

When marketing starts picking on pricing

As soon as things start to go sour, colleagues are quick to point the finger at pricing, so it's important to have your response ready.

The clearest way to understand whether pricing is the issue is to look at website page views on this production versus others, to see whether it is attracting the same demand as other shows. Then look at conversion rates from the production page to the checkout, to determine whether people are purchasing at the same rate as usual.

If there are fewer people visiting the production page than usual, then a review of the marketing funnel is required, to see why audiences aren't being attracted to this title. If the conversion rate on the website is lower than normal, that is a sign that customer expectations about value are misaligned with the price.

From there, you can dig into exactly which price points are cutting through with consumers, and which are not. Deep-dive into the number of sales by price band, and the number of opens by price band, to see where exactly the level of customer price resistance lies. If they have bought many of the tickets at £20, £30 and £40, but very few of the tickets priced higher than that, then the answer may be that £50 is their ceiling, and so you could test putting more seats on sale at £40 and tracking whether it improves the conversion rate. Model whether you can reach your overall target by selling more tickets than originally planned at £40 rather than £50.

Part two: psychology, segmentation and statistics

Consumer psychology

"Audiences will go wherever you invite them if the invitation is worthwhile"
Nicholas Hytner[26]

Whenever consumers are interested in buying tickets, we give them choices. Choices of which show to see, when to visit, where to sit, how much to pay, how many tickets to buy, and so forth. As with any matter of human decision-making, there is an element of personal, idiosyncratic bias at play whenever a customer faces one of these choices. We need to be cognisant of these biases, for depending on how we address them they can either lift sales or destroy them.

Heuristics

Heuristics are the mental shortcuts or strategies that consumers employ to simplify their decision-making process when making purchases, often unconsciously. By relying on heuristics, consumers can save time and effort using simplified decision rules instead of extensive information processing. We must be aware of heuristics, so as to not lead our customers into mistakenly making decisions which are not in their best interests.

For example, when we set ticket prices or create a booking flow, we become "choice architects,"[27] organising the context in which people apply heuristics and make decisions, and thereby influencing those choices. Everything about the order in which we present options, and the defaults we choose, will inevitably affect our customers' decisions. If you label certain performances as "Most expensive!" this will naturally have a very different effect on consumers than if you label the same performances

---

[26] Hytner, N. (2017). Balancing Acts. Vintage.

[27] Thaler, R.H. and Sunstein, C.R. (2022) Nudge: The final edition. London: Penguin Books

"Premium tickets available", or indeed if you label a different set of performances as "Best value!"

Choice architecture is often discussed alongside "nudge theory." A nudge is "any aspect of the choice architecture that alters people's behaviour in a predictable way without forbidding any options or significantly changing their economic incentives." Think for a moment about your purchase flow: are you nudging patrons to make a decision instinctively? Perhaps by giving a default donation amount, recommending e-tickets rather than printed ones, or having prominent options for seniors to take a discount? Each of these decisions relies on common heuristics to steer people towards making particular choices.

In this chapter, I will explore how we can leverage heuristics, choice architecture, nudge theory, and much more, to increase sales and ensure consumers are making the decisions that we want them to make. Crucially, however, we will look at how to do so ethically, guiding consumers towards the decisions we want only when those decisions are also in the consumer's own interests.

Dark patterns

Dark patterns are design choices or techniques used in user interfaces that manipulate or deceive users, often leading them to make decisions they wouldn't have made otherwise. They are the opposite of what I advocate in this chapter, employing consumer psychology to the sole benefit of the seller and to the detriment of the customer. When developing your own purchase flow, consider the fine line between positive nudges and negative dark patterns.

Examples of dark patterns include:

1. Sneak into basket. When adding items to a shopping cart or making a purchase, additional items are automatically added without the customer's consent or clear notification.

2. Roach motel. Making it easy for customers to sign up for a service but intentionally making it difficult for them to cancel or unsubscribe from it.

3. Confirmshaming. Using manipulative language or guilt-tripping to discourage customers from opting out of an email list, canceling a membership, or declining and upsell. Confirmshaming often employs wording that makes users feel guilty or foolish for considering alternative actions.

4. Hidden Costs. Concealing or downplaying additional fees, charges, or subscription terms until the customer is further into the checkout process, leading to surprise costs.

There is no need to use dark patterns to sell your tickets. As you will see, there are many ways to harness consumer psychology positively, without tricking users into buying something they don't really want.

Social Proof

People tend to look to others for reassurance when making decisions. Social proof leverages this tendency by demonstrating that others have already made a particular choice, thereby increasing the likelihood of conformity. In his book *Brainfluence*, Roger Dooley highlights the power of social proof as a persuasive tool in consumer behaviour.[28]

One of the many reasons the original Broadway production of *Rent* was so successful is that they started selling on-the-day tickets through a queue system known as the "Rent Line." Fans of the show would line up outside the Nederlander Theatre in hopes of purchasing a limited number of front row seats for $20. When people observe others engaging in a particular behaviour, they are more likely to follow suit. Social proof harnesses this tendency, to create a sense of popularity and desirability around a product or service.

The line for *Rent* tickets often extended around the block, with fans camping out overnight or for several days to secure their spots. The line system became a community gathering, with dedicated fans forming friendships while waiting, and sharing their love for the musical. The Rent Line made people to want to see the musical because it seemed so highly in demand.

Modern digital lotteries try to capture this same effect. Though they miss out on the more obvious social proof of a long line outside the theatre, they try to make up for it by encouraging users to share an image on social media, telling their networks that they are entering the lottery for a particular show. When everyone in your timeline is posting the same image from a show's lottery promotion, this is just as striking as a physical queue.

If you don't want or can't have a lottery or rush scheme, positive testimonials and reviews from satisfied customers can also be powerful social proof. They provide evidence that others have had a positive experience with a product or service, making it more attractive and trustworthy to potential customers. Think about the experience of a customer who has never visited your venue before: how can you prominently display positive customer reviews on your website so that they trust they'll have a positive audience experience?

---

[28] Dooley, R. (2012) Brainfluence: 100 ways to persuade and convince consumers with neuromarketing. Hoboken, NJ: John Wiley.

Critics or local influencers can exert influence as social proof too. Their endorsement or association with your show can enhance its perceived value and credibility. If you have a show which is a "hard sell," think about where you can display quotes from esteemed critics to reinforce that customers will enjoy themselves.

Social media platforms and online review sites provide ample opportunities for consumers to share their experiences. User-generated content, such as photos, videos, and reviews, can serve as authentic social proof that will influence others' perceptions and decisions. Unlike audience testimonials or quotes from critics, organic social media also has the benefit of coming from within a potential customer's own network, thereby increasing trustworthiness and reach.

Beware, though, for not all social proof will have a positive effect. Displaying real-time notifications of recent purchases, bookings, or sign-ups can create a sense of urgency and demonstrate that others are actively engaging with the offering. However, while this can stimulate fear of missing out (FOMO) and encourage potential customers to take action, an effective tactic operated by holiday websites to hurry customers into making a purchase, this often leads to people feeling manipulated and rushed. Customers who feel this way after their first experience with your show or venue may not return long-term.

Perceived scarcity

Perceived scarcity is the belief that not many tickets are left, which leads consumers to perceive the remaining ones as more valuable or desirable. Hotel websites which warn of "only one room left at this price," or a ticket seating plan with only six seats left, have the effect of encouraging customers to make their booking now, or to pay more for their tickets. It taps into the psychological phenomenon that people tend to place higher value on things that are scarce or difficult to obtain.

The opposite is also true in theatre — a production which is advertised as being on sale for months or years, or which apparently has lots of seats available, will have the effect of encouraging customers to wait. Seemingly there is no urgency, so they can take their time to make plans, perhaps come back next year, and maybe drop out of your marketing funnel entirely.

It is, therefore, advisable not to advertise that you have a dearth of inventory available. As discussed in previous sections, this could be achieved by limiting booking periods to the next few months and adding new dates once the first has sold out, or by taking some seats off sale initially so that performances don't look entirely open to consumers. Some ticketing systems can dynamically show only a handful of tickets to consumers at any one time, which makes performances look like they have sold more organically.

Limited edition Nike trainers aren't put on sale, they "drop."

When Apple releases a new product, no one can actually get their hands on one because they've apparently all sold out.

Prime energy drink became a precious commodity and commanded prices ten times higher than incumbent energy drinks, due mainly to its scarcity. The internet is rife with viral clips of kids rushing stores to buy the few cans they could find on sale.[29]

Only 70,000 Birkin handbags are produced by Hermès each year[30], and customers patiently sit on waiting lists for many years hoping to acquire one. Notoriously, it is rare that a boutique will sell one to a prospective customer, but instead affords them only to their most long-standing and loyal patrons.

Nike, Apple, Prime, and Hermès all have the resources to produce more stock if they wanted to, but they manufacture scarcity as a means to drive up demand. This is "artificial scarcity".

On a short-run show, perhaps we can leverage a similar feeling of exclusivity when tickets go on sale. The result might be that customers are prepared to pay more, and feel more urgency to book because of the fear of missing out.

---

29 https://www.youtube.com/watch?v=zP35vol498w

30 https://www.economist.com/special-report/2014/12/11/beauty-and-the-beasts

Anchor Pricing

Nobel laureate Daniel Kahneman and his colleague Amos Tversky proposed the concept of anchoring as part of their work on heuristics and biases in the 1970s, research they later popularised in their book *Thinking, Fast and Slow*[31].

The theory states that the first price a customer sees for a ticket (the "anchor") significantly influences their perception of the show. It establishes a reference point influencing their future decisions about what is reasonable to pay. For example, suppose your posters advertise "tickets from £10." In that case, the customer may arrive at the box office counter hopeful to buy a pair at this price, only to be disappointed when they discover that all of the £10 seats are sold out and that they need to pay at least £20 to see the show.

The principle works in the other direction as well. Suppose we leave ticket prices off the poster, and when a customer approaches the counter we inform them that "we have amazing seats for £40, and some further back at £30." When the customer picks the £30 seats, they feel like they've got a deal, because their expectations were anchored at £40.

Perhaps you have experienced anchor pricing yourself in a clothes shop, where a label says "was £30, now £20." I'm sure you felt a small victory at the checkout, as if you had "won" £10. Similarly, some restaurants list a few high-priced items at the top of their menu, making the rest of the prices seem more reasonable in comparison.

The sample seating plans and price structures provided in earlier chapters show how to adopt this same approach in ticketing. If we know that a performance won't entirely sell out, we can place a handful of costly super premium tickets in the very best position, priced up 30% compared to the surrounding Band A seats. This has the effect of making the Band A seats look like great value to the customer, and giving them the feeling of having got a deal. As ticketing managers, it is a win-win, because we either sell more Band A seats, or occasionally even sell one of the super premium seats at an inflated price. I would always encourage having one price level advertised at a higher price point than what you expect to sell, so that most consumers will feel they've got a small win.

---

31 Kahneman, D. (2011) Thinking, fast and slow. Farrar, Straus and Giroux.

Another way to use anchor pricing is to offer season passes at a specific price and then offer individual show tickets at a cost that, while cheaper on a one-off basis, would be more expensive if one attended all the shows in the season. This can lead consumers to perceive the season pass as offering better value.

Beware of anchoring in surveys. I heard from one producer who ran a survey which asked customers to first select which price they had paid in increments from £15 to £35, and then to give a star rating of value-for-money from one to five. All price tiers gave the show a high value-for-money score, except those customers who had paid the highest price of £35.

The following year, the producers kept pricing the same but added a dummy price option of £45 into the survey. Those who paid £35 were still the highest-paying customers but they now rated it more highly for value-for-money, presumably because they no longer felt that they were the top paying customers in the auditorium. Perhaps this insight could be useful when complaints arrive about sightlines — a bit of context and the customer might feel that they got a bargain, rather than feeling that they missed out.

Left-digit effect

The left-digit effect is where consumers tend to focus on the leftmost digit when evaluating prices, and make judgments based on this digit rather than considering the entire price. A study by Thomas and Morwitz[32] revealed that prices with lower leftmost digits (e.g. £4.99) were perceived as significantly lower than prices with higher leftmost digits (e.g. £5.00). This perception led to higher purchase likelihood and a greater willingness to pay for prices with lower leftmost digits, even when the difference was only a penny. They found that consumers engage in a cognitive process called "left-digit anchoring", where they mentally round down prices to the nearest unit of the leftmost digit. Consider the left-digit effect when setting ticket prices, because what may feel like a slight difference to you — for example £50 rather than £49 — could, in fact, be the difference for a customer between buying and not buying.

---

[32] Thomas, M. and Morwitz, V. (2005) 'Penny wise and pound foolish: The Left-digit effect in price cognition', Journal of Consumer Research

Decoy effect

The decoy effect is when customers are influenced into buying one product because of the presence of another. The purpose of the decoy is to push people towards selecting the option the seller wants them to choose, which is usually more expensive.

Researchers in the 1980s[33] did experiments where they'd ask participants to pick between two types of car. Then, a third option was added to sway them towards picking the option the researchers wanted them to choose. In most cases, the decoy successfully increased the chance of the desired option being chosen. They replicated the work with different products, such as beer and restaurants, and almost every time, the decoy successfully pushed consumers into choosing the seller's preference.

One example of the decoy effect you'll have encountered is at the cinema, where a small popcorn costs £3, and a large one costs £6. Faced just with these choices, you might opt for small. However, when the cinema adds a medium option for £5, the large now looks like great value, as it seemingly costs only £1 to go up one whole size. The cinema might not expect to sell any medium popcorn, but its presence helps to justify the large.

When I went to McDonalds at lunchtime today, I could buy boxes of McNuggets for £3.37, £4.35 or £5.32. Whilst the smallest box works out to 56 pence per nugget, the largest box is only 27 pence per nugget — better than half price. The consumer will convince themselves to pay an extra £1.95 over the small box, telling themself that they've found a bargain. This makes business sense for McDonalds too, because the cost of an extra nugget is negligible, and their main expense is in acquiring the customer to begin with — so they are chasing total basket value rather than per-nugget-yield. (As part of my research for this book, I taste-tested all three boxes and found no difference in the quality of McNugget.)

We can apply this same principle when we have a show that will certainly have many empty seats. Rather than fixating on the per-seat price, it can be worth our while to give away additional seats at negligible additional cost to the consumer in exchange for higher basket value.

---

33 Huber, Joel, et al. "Adding Asymmetrically Dominated Alternatives: Violations of Regularity and the Similarity Hypothesis." Journal of Consumer Research, vol. 9, no. 1, 1982

Let's say that our business model assumes an average of two £50 tickets per transaction, and a marketing cost of £10 per transaction. If a customer wants to buy two seats at £50 each, we could offer them a chance to buy a third for only £10. This is because we have already covered our marginal per-transaction costs and there is no expense to us servicing another ticket with zero cost to acquire. If we're confident the seat would otherwise have gone empty, this offer makes good business sense. We've brought a new person to our venue who will spread the word about the show, buy a drink at the interval, and add an extra 10% to the transaction's total value. I am surprised that this practice isn't more commonplace — especially with genres like children's theatre where there is often substantial extra capacity. The third, fourth and fifth tickets could be sold at half price and still increase the net profit per performance. Imagine how radical it would be to allow customers to buy their tenth ticket to a performance for £1. They'd be delighted and word would soon get around. It relies on the fact that there will generally be open capacity available and that there is zero marginal costs in servicing incremental tickets once the customer has already paid the budgeted basket size. This requires a change in thinking from chasing per-ticket yield to per-performance revenue.

Decision fatigue and a million SKUs

SKUs (pronounced 'skews') are how the retail industry counts their stock, with each SKU describing a product line. Every variation on a product; large, small, diet, strawberry flavour, Christmas edition - are all different SKUs. As consumers, we navigate supermarkets by traversing aisles which have similar SKUs and find a section of half a dozen similar SKUs to choose from. Ticketing makes this infinitely more difficult for the consumer because, whilst a large supermarket might have 20,000 SKUs, a large theatre can have 300,000 and a ticket agent might stock a million SKUs. Every ticket for every performance for every event is effectively its own SKU with a distinct merchandising proposition and we need to help consumers to navigate ten times as many aisles as they would in a supermarket.

When confronted with numerous options, the mental effort required to evaluate and select the best choice can become draining, leading to decision fatigue. The ticketing business is more guilty than anyone of inducing decision fatigue because of the huge number of choices we offer our customers: date, price, seat location, added extras, and so forth. Every extra choice we force the consumer to make costs us in sales.

Imagine walking into a supermarket and wanting to buy a bar of milk chocolate. There are a thousand chocolate bars just for today: bigger, smaller, luxury, bargain, all different flavours. And then there are another thousand chocolate bars for people who want to eat it tomorrow. And another for the day after that. And two thousand if you want to eat it on Saturday. And that's just the milk chocolate! If you want dark chocolate, there's a whole other thousand. It's too much choice for anyone to comprehend or rationalise.

Yet that's the reality we put in front of consumers: a thousand options for tonight, a thousand for tomorrow, and plenty more productions for them to choose from besides that. We have a million SKUs (stock keeping units), and somehow expect customers to navigate our virtual aisles to find the one which is exactly right for them.

With numerous choices available, customers may worry about making the wrong decision. This fear of regret further intensifies decision-making stress and can contribute to decision avoidance or delays. As individuals experience decision fatigue, they may opt for no decision at all and leave the funnel without making any purchase.

We can help our customers with decision fatigue by establishing criteria or preferences that can help reduce the cognitive burden of evaluating a vast array of possibilities. The website for The Bridge Theatre[34] is optimised for humans because it focuses on the most impactful decisions, by asking what show the customer wants to see, whether they want to come on a matinee, how much they'd like to spend, etc. Only after customers have answered these easy questions does the website reveal a set of limited, relevant options. In other words, it tailors its offer to the customer rather than showcasing a deluge of every available option. Much has been written about the audience-first UX at The Bridge[35], so it is surprising that it's not been more widely replicated, seven years later.

I likewise question why we so often show customers full seating plans of a thousand seats when it comes to selecting their tickets. I suspect in many cases we just do it because it is the software default, and not because it's the right thing to do. At best, there are probably only half a dozen potential seats in which they might want to sit in. And if we have 200 seats available in Band B, then we don't need to display them all — we can reduce decision fatigue by just showing the best handful in each price band.

If the customer's budget is for Band B, then they are only going to be evaluating seats in Bands A, B and C at most. It's simple enough to determine the most attractive seats within those bands based on how central and close to the stage they are. Perhaps some customers will prefer aisle seats, extra legroom, or to be close to the exit, so we can reveal those as well. Still, at most that's half a dozen options per customer. We would see much higher conversion rates if we did this thinking on behalf of customers and only showed them the best seats in their budget, rather than overwhelming them with redundant choices.

---

[34] https://bridgetheatre.co.uk

[35] https://substrakt.com/journal/the-bridge-pushing-the-boundaries/

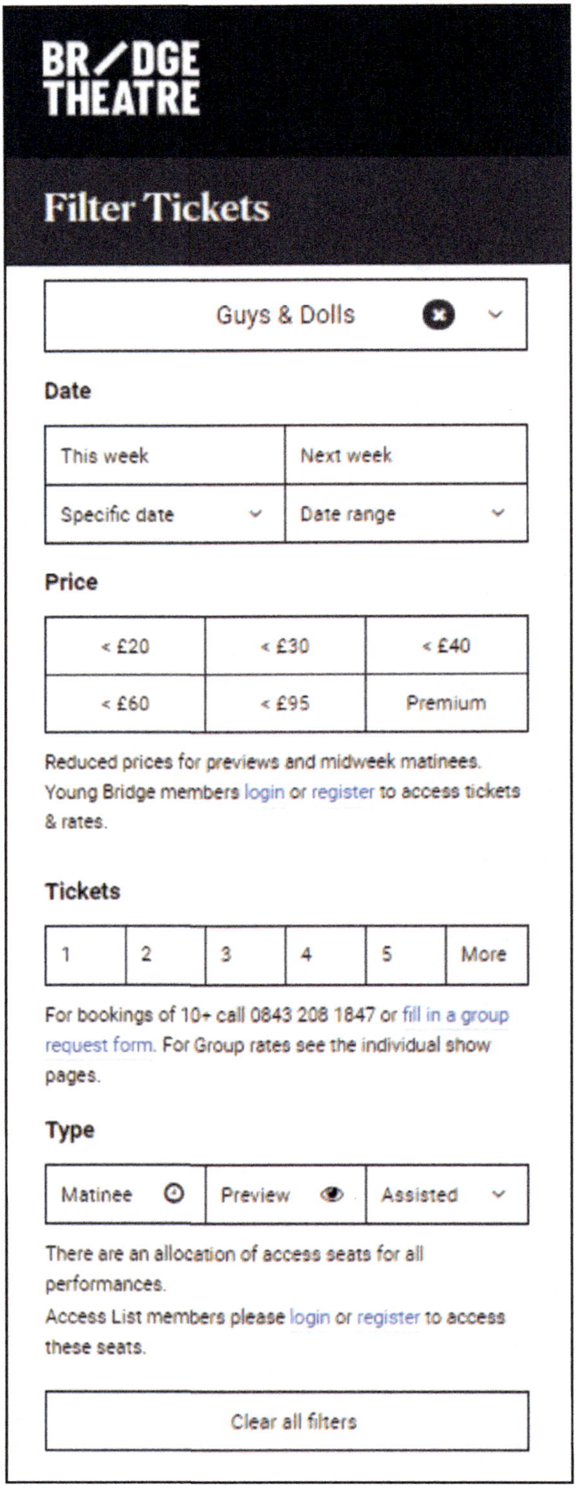
BR/DGE THEATRE
Filter Tickets
Guys & Dolls
Date
This week
Next week
Specific date
Date range
Price
< £20
< £30
< £40
< £60
< £95
Premium
Reduced prices for previews and midweek matinees.
Young Bridge members login or register to access tickets & rates.
Tickets
1
2
3
4
5
More
For bookings of 10+ call 0843 208 1847 or fill in a group request form. For Group rates see the individual show pages.
Type
Matinee
Preview
Assisted
There are an allocation of access seats for all performances.
Access List members please login or register to access these seats.
Clear all filters

Opportunity cost

Opportunity cost is the potential value that is sacrificed when choosing one option over another. It is the cost of the next best alternative that is not chosen.

Often when promoting tickets, we neglect the opportunity cost for our audiences, forgetting that they could just as easily go to a restaurant with friends, get ahead by working an hour later in the office, or spend the evening with their families. I suggest that reducing the price of tickets down to £5, or making them free, doesn't change the opportunity cost to audiences. Their time on this earth is limited, and a free ticket doesn't make spending an evening with their children any less desirable. What it does do, perhaps, is devalue our own show and suggest it's worthless. So consider what the opportunity cost is for your audiences — what are they giving up to attend your show? Make sure your pricing is at least in line with their next-best option to spend an evening — and that your value proposition is at least as good as well.

Information asymmetry

Information asymmetry exists when the customer has less information about a purchase than the seller.

Nobel prize-winning economist George Akerlof introduced this concept in a landmark 1970 paper[36]. Used cars are a classic example where sellers possess more information about the condition and history of their vehicles than potential buyers. (Consider Mr Wormwood in *Matilda: The Musical.*) This disparity in information creates uncertainty and leads to adverse selection, where buyers may be hesitant to pay a fair price due to the risk of purchasing a subpar car — just as Miss Trunchbull does, to her chagrin.

In our sector, ticket sellers may withhold information about additional fees or charges until the later stages of the purchase process. Very commonly, they withhold other information as well, such as poor reviews, sightline problems, underwhelming production values, and so forth. This lack of upfront transparency can lead to unpleasant surprises for consumers, and make them more hesitant to convert next time.

---

[36] Akerlof, G.A. (1970) 'The market for "Lemons": Quality Uncertainty and the market mechanism', The Quarterly Journal of Economics, 84(3), p. 488

I am not suggesting that you should start posting poor reviews for all your customers to see, but in some cases greater transparency is worth pursuing. Ticket sellers should provide clear and upfront information about all fees and charges. In the UK, the law requires that any per-ticket fees are included in the advertised price, and in the United States President Biden has recently called for an end to "junk fees". Similarly, view-from-seat photos provide helpful context about the potential purchase and means consumers have been fairly presented with all the pertinent information they need to decide.

Conspicuous consumption

Thorstein Veblen identified a social phenomenon whereby individuals make purchases not solely for their functional value, but as a means to flaunt wealth and affirm social status. We can observe this when customers purchase the most prestigious seats as a means to display their affluence and position in the social hierarchy.

When formulating ticketing strategies for high-demand events, it's useful to incorporate elements that appeal to this tendency towards conspicuous consumption, because there is a win-win for status-seeking customers and your bottom line.

These premium tickets are not just for those seeking entertainment; they cater to the segment of your audience looking to make a statement about their social status. This clientele isn't just paying for the performance; they're indulging in an opportunity to conspicuously consume, which in itself can be more valuable to them than the actual entertainment.

If the expected demand for these high-status tickets doesn't materialise, they can be re-offered as Band A seats, ensuring no revenue is lost. This strategy not only caters to consumers' psychology, but also maximises revenue potential by capitalising on Veblen's principle of conspicuous consumption.

Customer segmentation

"Each product we buy says something about us, and scoring it in this way can build a picture of what attitudes and beliefs drive our behaviour"

Clive Humby[37]

It can be tempting to think that all audiences are alike, or perhaps that they all behave like you. But in fact, audiences are disparate, chaotic, and behave in vastly different ways to one another. Treating them all in the same way would be bad for business, and so we need to consider customer segmentation.

Attitudinal segmentation is often used in marketing when evaluating which genre to promote to which audience, and demographic segmentation such as Experian's Mosaic can be helpful in understanding a customer's level of disposable income. For our purposes, however, we need only concern ourselves with segmenting customers by their relationship to our show's performance schedule and pricing.

I propose a three-by-three matrix to divide your customers into nine segments. They are by ticket price (high, medium, low) and advance booking time (long-term, medium-term and short-term). To calculate these, sort your customers in terms of how far out they booked, with the first tercile being the short-term bookers, the second being medium-term bookers, and the third containing the long-term bookers. The NTILE function achieves this for databases in Microsoft SQL server and equivalents exist in most database and CRM programs. This will give you three equally-sized groups specific to your show or organisation. Then repeat the exercise for ticket price, dividing each tercile into three evenly sized groups according to how much the customer paid.

Labelling your table with the actual bounds of your data will bring into stark relief what 'long term sales' and 'low ticket price' actually means. It will show you is the range into which your customers fall. It is based not on how you would like them to behave or your preconceptions, but in fact on your actual booker data.

---

[37] Humby, C., Hunt, T. and Phillips, T. (2007) Scoring points: How Tesco is Winning Customer Loyalty, page 140. London: Kogan Page.

Customer segmentation matrix (with example values in italics.)

	High ticket price *(> £28)*	**Medium ticket price** *(£16 - £28)*	**Low ticket price** *(< £15)*
Long term *(> 3 weeks)*	*15,000 customers*	*10,000 customers*	*5,000 customers*
Medium term *(3 days - 3 weeks)*	*10,000 customers*	*10,000 customers*	*10,000 customers*
Short term *(< 3 days)*	*5,000 customers*	*10,000 customers*	*15,000 customers*

If your "long term" bookers are making their purchase a year in advance, then think about how you can help them — perhaps with regular reminders that the date they've booked is coming up, or "one year to go" communications.

In the more likely scenario that "long term" bookers are actually only booking three weeks before the performance, then you've identified an opportunity for the marketing team to stop wasting investment with ineffective season brochures months ahead of the performance, and can instead re-assign the budget to suit consumer behaviour.

This exercise demonstrates that targets are proportionate, and what is long-term to one organisation may be short-term at another. A comedy or festival venue may only confirm shows four-weeks in advance and so the "short term" segment can represent one or two days. Knowing what these values normally are, and tracking against them, is how you can ensure there is a full house come curtain-up.

If you are trying to sell high-priced tickets, then be sure to advertise these early to your long term/high price bookers, and maintain a segment in your email marketing tool of customers who are amenable to buying high-priced short-term tickets, as a way to shift returns of production seats without needing to discount. It's so important not to undermine your own hard-crafted pricing strategy by mistakenly telling too many people about the availability of short-term or low-priced tickets, so this matrix acts a way to give you discipline about which product you are promoting to which people.

If you have a production which isn't selling, then review how many customers you've acquired from each segment. More than likely, there will be one or two segments which have appetite, but it hasn't yet cut through with other valuable sections of audience. Identifying these — and putting actions in place to turn it around — will help to secure a full house by curtain up.

For example, if you observe that medium-term high-price bookers are tracking significantly below average for your current production, then collaborate with marketing colleagues to communicate the quality of this production, upweight advertising to this segment and create urgency around tickets, or if you have enough capacity then consider pivoting your strategy to instead sell many more tickets to medium-term low-price bookers.

You can expand on this approach if your venue has a regular audience base and several shows a year. Our existing matrix shows recency and monetary value. Replace 'advance booking time' with 'weeks since last booking' to measure the recency of your customers' habits. Adding a third dimension for frequency, or the number of shows which a customer has booked in the past year, will present a clear picture of who the most valuable cohorts in the database are. Obviously it's difficult to visualise a three-dimensional cube of customers, but a popular approach is to assign fields in the ticketing database for recency (weeks since last booking), frequency (number of shows in the past year) and monetary (average ticket price). This is useful for segmenting marketing mailings, deciding who to invite to gala nights and fundraisers, and excellent context for your customer service team to look at when answering inbound queries or cancellation requests.

Recency, Frequency, Monetary (RFM)

If you are involved in ticketing at a venue with a varied program, then RFM should be the first set of metrics you look at. It is useful because it helps you clearly define who are your most valuable customers, who has potential to grow into value, and how much you are overspending on costly first-timers.

For each customer in the database, count:

- how recently they made a booking in weeks (i.e. the number of weeks between their most recent transaction and today)
- how frequently they have booked in the last three years (i.e. the count of performances where the transaction date is within last three years)
- their average ticket price (ATP).

With this alone, you've already quantified the value which each customer brings to your venue. Some simple calculations such as the average recency and frequency will reveal the reality of the relationship which your audiences have to the venue. Do they actually book as often as you imagine? If average frequency is low (< 4) then you might have a seasonality issue on your hands, where customers are just returning for perennial events like the pantomime, and you need to work harder to engage them with your wider program.

If recency is high then your program isn't diverse enough for your audience, who are only engaging with periodic programming that appeals to them. Your objective should be to 'ladder up' customers and increase the core venue health metrics of recency, frequency and monetary.

We can do this within a CRM campaign by speaking to customers with language which is most likely to engage them into levelling up. The one-and-done customers are a costly segment so we want to do an initial cleanup operation here. Email them with a one-time discount to book for any show within the next six months, tell them about the next show which you are hosting that is most similar to the one which they attended, and spend some budget reaching them through diverse channels such as digital or direct mail. Our chances of getting a second booking from them are rapidly diminishing with each passing day, so we must try to reach them while we can.

After the cleanup job, set in motion a re-engagement campaign for each of your nightly first-timers. Brainstorm ideas of how you can persuade tonight's first-timers to come back, such as exit flyers, a post-show email, or a special offer if they book within seven days of their first performance? Creating a 1% uplift in first timers to second bookings will have the greatest impact on your entire audience retention, so it is worth the effort to put an ongoing plan in place.

Your warm prospects are a great place to turn if you have a visiting producer who wants to spend some money increasing their marketing activity, because these prospects do legitimately have all the signs of being a good audience member long-term, and are also in need of some nurturing.

The quadrant of high recency and high frequency audiences are your single most valuable group, because they make up your bread-and-butter constituencies who will see you through the tough times. Protect them at all costs, send them a card at Christmas, listen closely to all of their feedback, and set triggers in place if one of these customers stops coming as often — because if they've moved house or don't like the new pricing, then you want to be the first to hear. Keep these audiences happy and your job will be much easier.

Finally, you can apply a decile score (1-10) for each of these metrics as a way to know who are your most important customers, and surface these deciles within the ticketing system. That way, as soon as a customer calls or emails, your counter staff can roll out the VIP treatment and bend over backwards to retain any sevens or above.

You'll observe that I uncharacteristically haven't mentioned money. Partly this is because it's dealt with elsewhere, and partly because I believe it is more important for a venue to foster high frequency amongst their patrons over high ticket prices. If customers attend twice as often, it is better than double the ticket price because, as well as the doubled income, we also save by halving our customer acquisition cost.

I believe that if you can encourage your audience to return regularly then most of the work is already done. They will naturally become ambassadors for the venue, bringing their friends and giving you comfort that the less-desirable shows will still have an audience. Recency and frequency is the name of the game.

Last minute discounts

The worlds of airline pricing and theatre tickets have much in common, but diverge on the subject of last-minute tickets. In theatre, we often sell tickets cheap on the day, thinking of them as distressed inventory which otherwise is going to go empty. This actually perpetuates the problem because consumers learn that they can wait for a discount, and shows become reliant on an increasing percentage of sales happening shortly before curtain-up.

I suggest, therefore, that we should have more confidence that last-minute customers will always come out of the woodwork, and we should charge them appropriately for instant gratification. Instead of seeing our stock like drooping flowers at a market stall, we should maintain inventory at all price levels - perfectly placed for the customer who wants to see a show tonight.

A good way to build your confidence in this respect is to keep a tracker of how many tickets you sell on the day of a performance, and in the week preceding the performance. This will demonstrate for you the minimum and average amount of tickets which you can reliably sell short-term, and at what price. You can even do this retroactively by pulling data on mature performances from your system. Then, when you start the day looking at a half-filled auditorium, you can imagine how inevitably it will fill up as the day goes on.

There is of course some nuance to this, as unexpected transport or weather events may cause your day sales to be lower than forecast, and some days you may have more open seats than you can account for, so relying on your overall sales pattern to fill auditoria is about more than just sitting back and letting the pattern play out. Rather, it requires hands-on-management with an eye to the plan and your environmental context. (One former colleague of mine took delight in predicting how many tickets we might sell on days when train drivers went on strike, or unseasonal snow descended.) There may be discrete “closed lists” of potential customers which can be activated with a short-term discount that doesn’t need to be “above the line”in a way which your core audience can see, such as staff of local businesses.

Still, you must always consider: am I going to make an extra sale by discounting last-minute, or am I just giving a deal to someone who was going to book anyway?

Just as some customers will pay a privilege to see tonight's performance, other time-poor individuals will pay for the certainty of having secured a ticket many months in advance. Think of tourists who are planning their summer holidays months ahead, or a businessperson who will only be in town for a couple of days. Their PA is trying to put together a packed itinerary and doesn't want to risk disappointment by waiting for a deal later on, and the holidaymaker doesn't want to gamble with the show being sold-out once they arrive. Instead, both customers, who we call "planners", will pay over-the-odds for the privilege of having things organised ahead of time.

In these two examples, we have demonstrated that high pricing can be justified at all moments within the sales cycle, and that open inventory doesn't necessitate a rush towards markdowns and discounts. Instead, use your pricing matrix as a guide to balance the price of your tickets so that you are not undercutting your own value proposition.

Groups

Groups are nice work if you can get it.

Groups can be a school trip, friends on an outing together, members of a community group, participants in a theatre club, or individuals on a tour package such as a coach trip or a cruise ship excursion. They will typically have a group organiser who may or may not be getting paid or earning a free ticket for their trouble.

As ticketing managers, we like group sales because they book a swathe of tickets in one go, which makes for very efficient cost-per-acquisition. It also only takes two or three groups for an auditorium to look well-sold. Group organisers can often be persuaded to make repeat visits, either to see each show which you put on, or to bring new customers to the long-running show each time. They act as fantastic ambassadors for the show and reach grassroots theatregoers in a way which would otherwise be challenging.

The common process for a group booking is that the organiser will enquire about availability of tickets. It helps for them to have direct communication with someone knowledgeable in the ticket office, as their requirements will be more complex than an ordinary booking, and the value is much greater than a standard transaction. Phone is useful for their quick questions, and email will be important for going back-and-forth with specific requirements in writing.

You will inform the group organiser whether you have availability at their preferred performance, balancing your need for occupancy with the revenue target of that performance, and how it is already currently selling. If only a few seats remain then it may be desirable to direct the booker to another performance which could benefit from a large sale. A number of tickets then get reserved in the name of the group booker so that they cannot be purchased by other customers, and a peppercorn deposit may be taken, although the convention is that it does not need to be paid until the booker has gauged the level of interest from their companions.

The booker will then share marketing materials with their companions and collect monies, before again contacting the theatre. At this point, it is typical for some seats to be released if there is less demand than anticipated, and the entire booking will be paid for.

It's worth noting that the process described above is the West End convention for group sales. However, it is the rare group booker who does not attend West End shows, and so they are likely to expect a similar process at any venue.

When taking group bookings, it is important to be clear about expectations: how much deposit is required, when seats will need to be paid for, how they will be released if you don't hear back from the booker, how you will keep one another informed about progress whilst they are on reservation, and how you will deal with any requests for extra seats or an extension to the pay-in date. Make sure you have adequate policies about how long tickets can be reserved unpaid, so that you have enough time to sell the seats to normal consumers if the booking is cancelled.

The money related to these unpaid reservations can be tracked and it exists in a sort of purgatory. It is neither earned income as part of the advance, nor potential from an open seat. The expectation is that some of the money will most likely get paid in, but a percentage will never get paid because groups cancel or bookers don't require all of the held tickets. Hence, keep an eye on the figure, seek to get as much of it paid in as possible by proactively staying in contact with the bookers, and don't go spending the money you don't have quite yet.

Given the many benefits which group bookings bring, it can be worth trying to attract them with a discount — but only if this will make the difference between a sale and not. (There is no reason why you can't charge group bookers full price for the current must-see show.) Your cost-per-acquisition should be lower with a group booking, and hence you can still earn more profit on a group sale than individuals, even with a discount.

For school groups, it is commonplace to give a free ticket for the teachers (say at a ratio of 1 teacher per 10 pupils), otherwise the pupils might need to pay a premium to subsidise the necessary staff. When adding a new booking period, a group accelerator rate can be used to incentivise bookers to plan far ahead. Here, you agree that if they have paid for a performance well in advance, they can earn a greater discount than standard. This is a useful way to build your advance for long-term performances.

The arrogance of being sold out

Everyone gets sold out at some point, but for some reason, arts marketers get so giddy when it happens that they start counting their chickens, always forgetting that famine follows the feast. Not every performance will be as in-demand as Christmas, not every cast will have a Hollywood star, and not every season will have a repertoire as popular as the current hit.

So the time to work hard is whilst the going is good. In numbers terms, you have a high volume of people entering the funnel and a high conversion rate going out the end. The problem is that you are then turning away these people who have cash-in-hand. A ticketing manager who takes the long-term view will realise that it would be much more cost-efficient to sell a ticket to these people when you next need a boost, rather than the expensive tactics of new customer acquisition. After all, you've done the hardest work of bringing them down the marketing funnel — so why turn them away?

When you get sold out, release all the holds which you possibly can, add as many extra performances as you can, and then, if you really have sold every ticket which you possibly can, do not let these customers fall through your fingers. Instead, start funnelling them into a sign-up campaign to capture their contact data (email addresses, phone numbers, social media handles, etc). With some certainty, you will produce this same show, or a show like it, at some time again in the future, and it'll be much easier to re-activate these people than to start the expensive task of customer acquisition from scratch. Once you get to sold out, think two steps ahead and build the foundations of data capture.

Measure what matters

Data analysis

In this age of big data, it's easy to assume that you'll need to collect terabytes of data in order to start optimising your sales, but its amazing how much can be achieved with even a small amount.

Take the data points which are printed on a ticket: customer's name and billing postcode, seat number, performance date and time, customer ID, price paid, discount name, performance name. From these eight points, we can triangulate so much information: the most popular events, the average days out that customers tend to book, the top postcodes which the audience comes from, the average number of purchases made per customer, the most effective discount promotions, and so much more. I'd wager that there is almost always more that you could be doing with the data you already have, so focus first on squeezing more juice out of that before pursuing expensive data-capture projects.

Seek feedback whilst putting together a piece of data analysis, before committing to the final version. if you don't get three points of feedback from each person who will be looking at a report or dashboard, then they haven't looked closely enough. Dashboards and reports are so complex and subjective that there will always be three points to raise and most people are too lazy for the task so blindly give their approval. Your report will be meaningfully better for having implemented three pieces of feedback from ten colleagues.

Simplicity

"Simplicity is the ultimate sophistication."
Steve Jobs, after Leonardo da Vinci[38]

I increasingly realise that good ideas need to be simple. Complications are a blocker to the communication of new ideas, and a veil for mistruths. On the other hand, reaching for simplicity forces the speaker to fully understand their core idea before distilling it into its most essential component. When we present our ticketing analyses we should make them as simple as possible.

Earlier in my career I mistakenly thought that the most innovative ideas were likely to have elements of complexity, and that said complexity was a feature of their inventiveness. Whilst this might be true of theoretical physics, I realise now that most ideas relating to ticket sales and audiences can always be presented in a simple form, and that complexity is generally obfuscation. Occasionally a team member has proudly produced a complicated analysis which requires some explanation as to its workings and conclusion. I am so pleased that we did not dwell too long at congratulating our colleague for their innovative new chart, but instead worked to strip it down to its core insight, in a way which had far fewer visual elements but far greater ease of comprehension.

I am guilty as any of presenting overly intricate diagrams, and am grateful to my colleagues who revised them into versions which are simpler to reproduce, analyse and read — and which now form several of the examples in this book. It can't be an accident that the best TED talks don't waste time on the methodology, and instead focus on the insight.

We can be thorough whilst also being simple. The nuance is in only presenting the relevant data points and not unnecessarily detailing your own workings. It's about showing precisely the right amount of context for the situation, no more, no less. Your analysis should have a linear thread from start to finish, with nothing tangential, whilst being entirely truthful and not leaving the observer with unanswered questions. The irony is not lost on me that this section required two illustrative quotations rather than one. I still have work to do.

---

[38] Brochure advertising Apple II, https://www.computerhistory.org/brochures/doc-43729572aadaf/

Helicopter views

When analysing sales, it can feel like there is a daunting amount of data, and it can be challenging to know where to start and which trends are essential to track. I suggest a "helicopter" approach, where you survey your data at the highest level of granularity first, and then "swoop lower" into anomalies to discover where the areas of interest are. This lets you concentrate on the patterns which are deviating from the norm, which can sometimes be the most revealing sources of insight and new strategic initiatives.

Mistaken interpretations of data often arise from starting the analysis at a micro level rather than the macro. It's worth getting your bearings by first working with the largest imaginable numbers, and then zooming in on the problem. I was guilty of this mistake a few years ago whilst researching children's theatre, when I discovered that twice as many bookings are made on a Monday as are made on a Sunday. I mistakenly threw around interpretations about busy parents only getting a chance to make plans once children are back at school on Monday morning. In fact, the trend affects most genres and has nothing to do with children's theatre. If I'd started with coarser data, then I wouldn't have wasted time investigating a phenomenon which wasn't novel.

Another example I encountered recently was when a marketing manager was surprised that 75% of the audience for a stand-up comedy show were female. The statistic shouldn't have been surprising because the same survey had revealed that 75% of the overall membership at the venue are female – so in fact the comedy show statistics were entirely in line with the broader customer base.

Beware looking through a lens too narrow. Start with the broadest possible data and then hone-in on your enquiry like a helicopter. From the general into the specific.

The truth, the whole truth, and nothing but the truth

Lying with statistics is so easy that it's often inadvertent. Therefore it's incumbent on us to be unambiguously explicit in all of our reporting. For example, if sales are up this week versus last week, then it's natural to present a graph showing sales for the past 14 days, and annotate the respective increase. However what we should also do is expand the time period out to the last three months or so, so as to give context about whether the weekly increase is truly remarkable, or simply natural variation.

For the same reason, I would avoid arbitrarily excluding any dates in reports, since it could cause inadvertent misrepresentation. Better to deliver several pages of reports which shows months worth of empty performances, then just to present one sheet showing the next four weeks of performances, that gives a falsely rosy picture. There is a subtle balance to be drawn between simplicity of reporting and inadvertent misrepresentation.

Spurious correlation

A word of caution when using statistics. It is easy — and tempting — to look at two different trends in your dataset and draw a cause-and-effect conclusion between the two, when in fact the observed effect is merely a coincidence, or the influence of other variables. In other words, it's a correlation that doesn't prove causation.

Seemingly there is a correlation between the amount of cheese people eat, and the number of people who die by becoming tangled in their bedsheets. Whilst the two numbers go up together over the course of a decade, are from very reliable government data sources, and have a statistical correlation of 94.71%, there is clearly no common-sense relationship between the two numbers. It's a pure coincidence and no one needs to reduce their cheese intake to avoid death by bedsheet. Tyler Vigen has dedicated his eponymous website[39] and accompanying book to these types of spurious correlations.

In the same way, you might observe that sales are higher when you put posters up on particular lampposts, or that your average group size is correlated to the time of year an event goes on sale. These examples are probably benefiting from chance, and a very small sample size.

Genuine correlations do exist. For example, income from drinks will be higher at comedy or sports events, and lower for children's theatre. Customers will be willing to spend more per ticket to watch a celebrity onstage than an unknown performer. When testing these hypotheses, it's good practice to consider if they make intuitive sense given the other certainties which you have at hand, and compare them with wider data sources (such as sales for other events, or other venues).

On a similar note, beware privileging the hypothesis, which is a cognitive bias where the possibility you believe to be true arises purely from your interpretation of the data. When we privilege a hypothesis, we can easily fall into a cognitive trap where we overlook other more probable explanations or undervalue the importance of obtaining and considering more evidence. Counteract it by considering a range of hypotheses and actively seeking out evidence that might disprove our preferred hypothesis.

---

[39] https://www.tylervigen.com/spurious-correlations

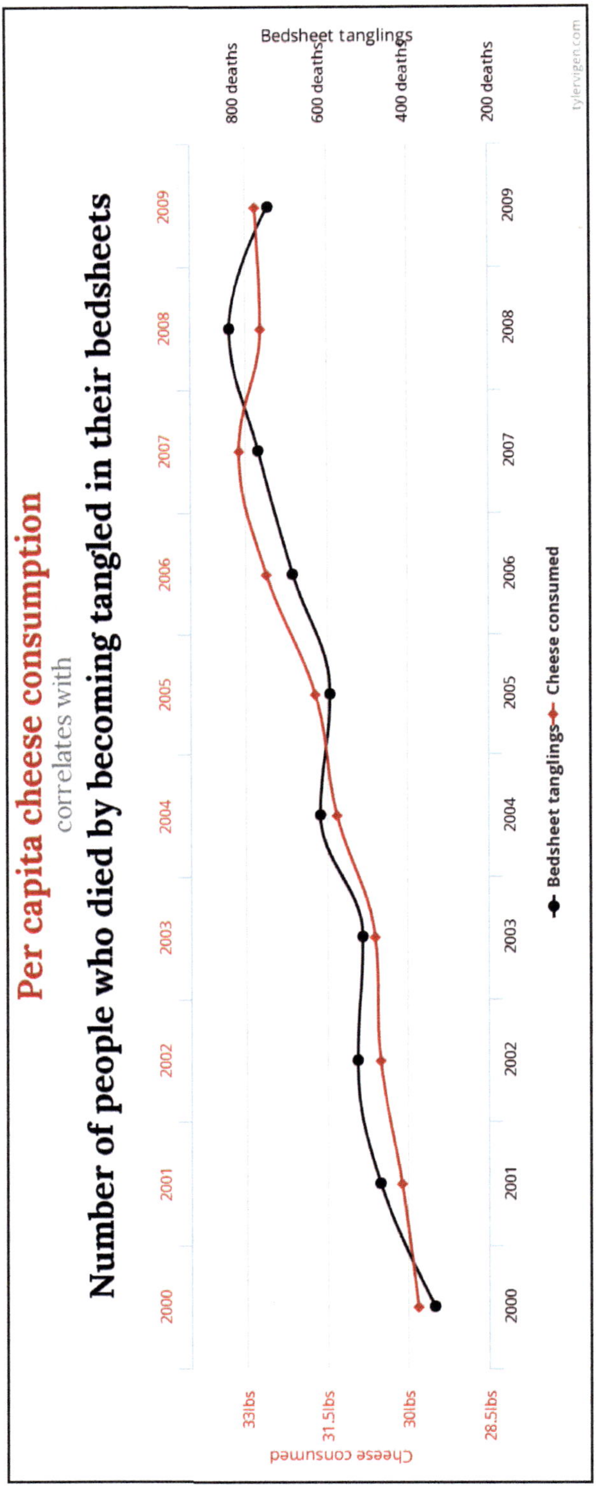
Per capita cheese consumption
correlates with
Number of people who died by becoming tangled in their bedsheets
Bedsheet tanglings
800 deaths
600 deaths
400 deaths
200 deaths
Cheese consumed
33lbs
31.5lbs
30lbs
28.5lbs
2000
2001
2002
2003
2004
2005
2006
2007
2008
2009
Bedsheet tanglings
Cheese consumed
tylervigen.com

False precision

"A museum guide claims that a dinosaur fossil is 100,000,005 years old, since the curator informed him it was 100 million years old when he took the job five years ago."

That joke will have statisticians rolling on the floor in hysterics, so remember it for next time you go to a dinner party with some nerds. Here are some other examples of false precision you might encounter as a sales manager:

"The wrap so far this week is £17,635.25"
"Next year's season is estimated to mature on £200,632.23"
"212 website visitors are women"

In each of these examples, the number is presented in a way that implies much greater precision than is justified. I'd wager that the wrap has increased in the time it took someone to pull that number and recite it, so knowing the number of pence (25) is both irrelevant and inaccurate. Even the best supercomputers would struggle to predict the season gross to the nearest penny (23), but including it in the forecast leads to precision bias, where the reader places undue confidence in it. Unless an a margin of error is provided, the number of significant digits shown in data should only be as many as the data's accuracy justifies. And unless you are looking at truly-live numbers in a database, all figures will be out of date and so extra precision is unhelpful.

The rule of thumb I follow is never to include decimal places in anything (wraps, advance, season totals etc). The only place where seeing pennies (or cents) is acceptable in day-to-day usage is the average ticket price — because it is based on a very large sample, the day-to-day fluctuation is very small, and there are genuine business decisions which can be taken from knowing the ATP to this level of precision, such as whether to increase ticket prices or to start discounting.

The final example above, about 212 website users being women, has a slightly different problem: it uses a data source that is notoriously imprecise, because only a sample of your total website visitors are ever captured. However the solution is still to avoid unnecessary precision. Better to say "approximately 60% of website visitors are women" than to give a false impression of accuracy when the margin of error could be wide.

Analysis paralysis

Analysis paralysis is an easy trap to fall into, where you become ever more intrigued by your statistics, with each set of results prompting more questions. Often this will be genuinely fascinating work which leads to clever insights, but we need to always balance our desire for data with the business purpose — which is to sell tickets.

Analysis should begin with a fact (the ATP is low), then a question like "why is our ATP low?" followed by a hypothesis ("perhaps we are selling too many family tickets"), an investigation (calculating the proportion of family tickets sold), and finally a recommendation based on your findings. ("Yes, most sold tickets are the discount family tickets. Stopping this discount might improve the yield.")

This is what we need in the fast-moving life of a show, where inventory matures every day and can never be sold again: a tight, focused turnaround from analysis to insight to action. This can stem the tide of discounted tickets as soon as the following day and actually supports us in reaching our goals for the show.

When analysis enters paralysis is when we take that first learning but continue to ask deeper or broader questions without taking any action. Such as doing a survey of which customers are families, how many children they have and which other theatres they visit. All interesting questions, but doesn't help with the core issue of raising the ATP.

Analysis paralysis usually comes about either when the original question was poorly formulated, or came from someone who was just interested in trivia rather than pursuing a business goal. Of course, sometimes there is a need for iterative analysis and a couple of rounds of questions, but it should be the exception rather than the norm. Beware analysis paralysis because it eats up time when you could be selling tickets.

WTF is 'insight'?

A job title of 'insight manager' has emerged in recent years, but what even is 'insight'? Aren't we all insightful on occasion, and isn't it grandiose to proclaim oneself as insightful? In my opinion, the discipline of insight is a progression from reporting. Where reporting is rear-view-mirror and reflects on what has happened before, the role of the insight manager is to use data creatively to anticipate what might happen in the future and identify risks and opportunities. Where data and information are factual, insight seeks to draw meaning to the specific business and identify a specific nugget of truth which creates a commercial advantage.

Reporting will summarise data without explanation or rationale, with the purpose of informing stakeholders with a clear overview of the facts which can be used to track performance over time. Insight, on the other hand, will draw conclusions from trends and anomalies, with a goal of understanding the underlying causes and supporting decision making, typically called "actionable insight". There is place for both as management require consistent, factual information on a regular cadence, but marketing need to be on the lookout for creative opportunities or threat to sales. So neither is more important than the other.

Weak insight is the telling of facts or trivia. "20% of audiences vote liberal", "the most popular time to book is 2pm on Wednesdays" and "20% of our audience follow McDonalds on social media" are all fun facts, but don't drive action. A great analyst will have command of the statistics, leave no stone unturned in their analysis, and find new data which tells a meaningful story about the motivation of audiences, and lays the ground for a business decision to be taken. A great example of insight is observing that evening shows aren't selling well with audiences who travel a long distance, and proposing an earlier start time so that these audiences have time to catch the last train. It's about joining the dots, interpreting the data and leading the agenda of what needs to change.

Key Performance Indicators (KPIs)

In one Buddhist parable[40], five blind men encounter an elephant for the first time. Each man touches a different part of the elephant's body; the trunk, the ear, the leg, the side, and the tail.

Afterwards, they discuss their experiences and try to describe what an elephant is like based on the part they explored. The man who touched the trunk thinks an elephant is like a thick snake, the one who felt the ear believes it's like a fan, the person who touched the leg insists it's like a tree trunk, and so on. Each of them insists that his own experience represents the true nature of the elephant.

The moral of the parable is that people can have vastly different perspectives based on their limited experiences and the aspect which they examined. These perspectives can all be valid in their own right, but they may not represent the whole truth. The parable illustrates the importance of seeing things from multiple points of view to gain a more complete understanding of reality.

As ticketing professionals, it is our job to understand the audience for a show, where the barriers to sales lie and what the drivers of sales are - but we can't do all of this in one go - we need to examine the show from many sides.

Look from one direction and sales look positive, through another it appears that Fridays are doing well, and another shows that ATP is up. Only when you piece all of the data points together does it become apparent that weekday performances are empty and the high-priced Friday performances are doing all the heavy lifting. In the coming pages we will learn to analyse sales from many angles, aspiring to build a more complete picture of our elephant.

---

40 Ud 6:4 Sectarians, Tittha Sutta

Average ticket price (ATP)

This is calculated as the sum of revenue divided by the number of tickets sold.

It is useful for understanding the average price which customers are paying, and can be used to easily cross-compare productions which have different capacities or numbers of performances. It is a good indication of the value which customers place on your product. Always look at ATP in the context of number of tickets sold or percentage occupancy, because ATP can be deceptive if you have only sold a handful of tickets. Generally the objective is a high ATP and a high occupancy.

Exclude comps from the calculation, as ATP is intended to show the average price paid by customers, and comps distort this. Showing a 50% drop in ATP because a bunch of comps have been booked in would suggest that there has been a reduction in the value consumers place on the show, or the type of tickets they are buying, when in fact neither is true. A comp patron should only ever be sitting in a seat which would otherwise have been vacant. Comps are only relevant to the question of ATP if their existence is inhibiting ticket sales. Instead, display gross paid average ticket price (ATP) on paid-for tickets, alongside a reference figure of how many comps were issued.

Wrap

This is the value of transactions made in a day for all performances. The wrap is the most real-time guide that we have to how consumers are behaving right now, and gives an immediate indication as to the efficacy of new marketing initiatives. You can use it before a show opens, once it is open, and for venues which have different shows each day.

A high wrap indicates that consumers are interested in the title, whilst a low wrap indicates that marketing may need to be lifted or that there is some macro factor inhibiting sales, such as an economic downturn or decline in tourism.

Bear in mind that wraps will necessarily dip when your success means there is limited inventory left, so always view wraps in the context of open potential and season gross. Past performance isn't a guarantee of future success, but the wrap is the best guide we have as to the current consumer outlook.

Where you've used weekly wrap targets, measure progress against these each week and circulate figures to the entire group immediately. Be consistent in reporting so that there is complete transparency from one week to the next, presenting all targets and actuals so that there is no deception by omission. Control the narrative so everyone judges success by the same set of facts which are prompt, accurate, unbiased and inspire action.

Season gross

Season gross is the revenue earned for all tickets within the production's run, including both matured performances and those in the future. This figure is proportionate to the length of the run and can be more appropriate for comparing historic productions because it shows the total ticket sales rather than just those for future performances.

Average Order Value (AOV)

There is a novice temptation to use AOV because it is made available so easily from digital advertising and web tracking platforms.

However, in our context it is actually an unhelpful metric, because it is a dependent variable rather than an independent one. The elements within your sphere of influence are average ticket price and average group size. There are dozens of strategies to move each of these, which are separate to one another, but average order value doesn't move on it's own.

In a venue which sells many shows, the metrics are much more meaningful when evaluated separately. For example, a production of *Pretty Woman* may expect a low average group size of 2.0 due to it being dominated by couples on date night, but with a high average ticket price. Meanwhile, a puppet show for under fives may anticipate a higher group size of 2.6 from parents, children and siblings, but a lower average ticker price. The AOV could be similar on the two shows, even though the driving factors are different. Hence, AOV is obfuscating the true commercial drivers.

AOV is an e-commerce standard but doesn't hold water in the context of ticket selling, where we have finite inventory and different goals around the anticipated buying behaviour of customers. Blending the two metrics into average order value is a lazy regression to out-of-the-box defaults and, whenever I see it in a theatre's report, I lose confidence in the rest of the figures.

Marketing metrics

Ticketing professionals are often called upon to report on the efficacy of marketing activities as we generally have an aptitude for data analysis and already have the conversion data at hand.

Market share

The Total Addressable Market (TAM) is all of the spend from the entire market in the industry over a year. The TAM for live entertainment in the UK would be the total spend across all venues in the whole country, including theatres, concert halls, comedy clubs, etc. Calculate TAM by reading industry reports, government economic reviews and using market research tools like Kantar's TGI[41].

The Serviceable Addressable Market (SAM) is the revenue which is actually reachable and serviceable by your organisation within the year. For example, if your venue was a theatre in London, then it would only include customers in proximity of London who are booking theatre tickets. All the music and comedy customers would be excluded, as would everyone living outside of the London commuter belt. Calculate SAM by estimating the attendance at your competitors, using their end-of-year reports.

The Share of Market (SOM) is the amount of revenue which your organisation actually earns. Calculate SOM by using the total revenue which your organisation brought in within a year.

Dividing the SAM by the TAM shows the size of your chosen sector proportionate to the entire industry, and can be helpful for deciding whether to move into other or geographies. For example, if your SAM as a violin-only concert hall in Norwich is only 0.1% of the TAM, you obviously have a very tight ceiling on how much of total industry spend you can ever capture; by opening up to other instruments, or touring productions elsewhere in England, you can increase this.

Dividing the SOM by the SAM shows how much market share you are capturing versus your competitors. It can be helpful for understanding the size of the prize if you can increase your customer base or program more shows. Likewise, if you SOM is already 90% of the SAM, you have little headroom to grow even with the best marketing campaign or ticketing strategy.

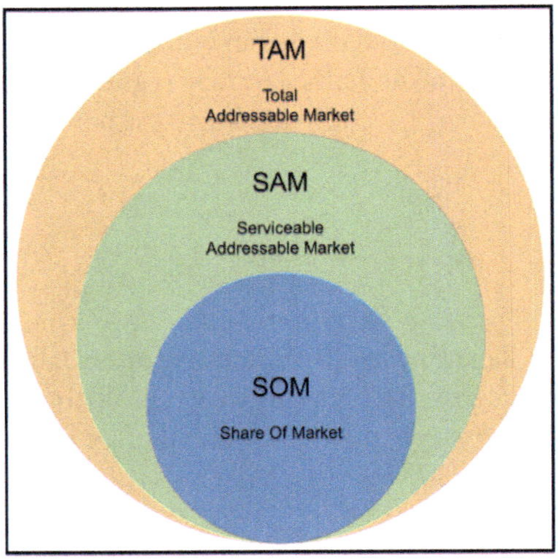

41 https://www.kantar.com/campaigns/tgi

Marketing funnel

Month by month, monitor the approximate number of people in each stage of your marketing funnel: awareness, or the number of people who (when prompted) report that they have heard of your event; consideration, or the number of people who are actively thinking about booking a ticket, and perhaps need to be given some more information or simply a nudge to book; and conversion, or those who have bought a ticket.

Calculate these numbers by looking for the distinct number of customers who have been served an impression through your digital advertising platforms, the number of customers that arrive on your website, and the number who go on to purchase a ticket. If you use multiple advertising platforms, there will be unavoidable double-counting between them, but this should be relatively consistent between months, allowing for meaningful comparison of the conversion rates over time. We are less interested in the actual numbers, but instead in the month-on-month changes to conversion rates.

If you observe a decline in people moving from awareness to consideration, then this may be a signal to change your artwork or copy to something which is more enticing to first-timers. If there is a decrease in people moving from consideration to conversion, then perhaps the show needs to be better unpacked for audiences or made more enticing as a consumer proposal (for example through better pricing strategy).

If you sell a large volume of tickets through a third-party agent, then they may be willing to install a tracking pixel on the confirmation page of their website, which will allow you to measure whether a customer who you have been advertising to has gone on to buy a ticket through the agent channel. When setting this up, take care to ensure that the pixel only fires for your specific event, otherwise you will falsely attribute to your show every single sale for all events on the agent website — a mistake I've seen happen more than once!

Campaign conversion rate (CVR)

This is calculated by dividing the number of purchases attributable to a specific advertising campaign by the number of impressions which that campaign achieved, and is useful for understanding the efficacy of each element of advertising. A higher conversion rate is an indicator of a more cost-efficient advert, whilst a lower conversion rate will need changes to its target audience, placement, copy, or artwork, because the people who are seeing it aren't buying tickets in sufficient numbers.

Conversion rate is highly specific to the product being advertised and the platform being used. For example, one night with Sir Ian McKellen in a hundred-seat venue will intrinsically attract a very high conversion rate because the proposition is so compelling, as will search engine advertising which includes the name of your venue and production — because the people who view it evidently have high intent to book if they are searching for those terms. So set benchmarks specific to your organisation and the channels and genres that you work within. Then aim to increase conversion rates within each stream — just don't expect them all to be equal.

Return on investment (ROI)

Return on investment (ROI) from advertising is calculated as:

ROI = (Revenue - Cost of Advertising) / Cost of Advertising

If you spend £1,000 on an advertising campaign and wrap £5,000 from customers who were served the advert, then the advertising ROI would be 400%. For every £1 spent on advertising, the venue made a profit of £4.

Measuring advertising ROI can be complex for online advertising or multi-channel campaigns, because customers often engage with multiple ads on different platforms before making a purchase, and it can be challenging to accurately attribute their purchase to a specific ad.

Methods such as last-click attribution, multi-touch attribution, or lift studies to estimate the impact of their advertising efforts can be used to put this into context. Generally, the agencies who run your digital advertising will be able to provide these metrics for you.

Ad-sales ratio

This is calculated by dividing the amount spent on advertising in a given time period over the total income earned in the same period. Similar to ROI, it shows how effectively your entire marketing operation is working, based on the number of sales it brings in relative to the budget it spends. It can be used to benchmark against competitors, evaluate advertising efficacy and compare suppliers.

Cost per acquisition (CPA)

Cost per acquisition (CPA) is calculated as:

CPA = Total Advertising Spend / Number of Bookers

For instance, if the venue spends £1,000 on an advertising campaign and consequently sells tickets to 100 bookers, the CPA for that campaign would be £10.

It helps us to understand how much we need to invest in advertising to attract a new customer, and sets a benchmark for what our budget could be to retain previous customers. In this example, spending anything less than £10 to get a previous booker to return would be cost-effective. A higher initial CPA might be acceptable if the customer returns several times (a higher customer frequency and lifetime value), than if they only attend once.

Audience frequency

In the coming pages, we'll move from looking at metrics for performances into metrics around the audience and for a venue which hosts multiple events.

Audience frequency is calculated as the average number of performances which a customer attends within their lifetime. The overall number across all customers may be around 1.1 or lower, so it can be helpful to calculate using only the customers who have made at least two bookings. This is a better indicator of customer lifetime among actual return bookers, separate from all of those who only visit once. If you have individuals in your database who have subscribed to your mailing list but never bought a ticket, then be sure to remove them so as not to sway the statistic.

This is an important number to monitor because high audience frequency is an indicator of overall customer satisfaction and successful retention policies, and forms the foundations for a lucrative membership or subscription programme. On the other hand, low audience frequency will lead to high customer acquisition costs, as the marketing team has to constantly chase new audiences for each production.

It can also be a helpful number to look at through the lens of a show. If the average customer frequency is shorter on one show than usual, consider what about the product or promotion is driving the increased number of first-timers. Conversely, a show with a high average customer frequency has strong appeal to your core database but not at bringing in new visitors.

Customer lifetime value (CLV)

Calculated as the total income over several years divided by the number of distinct customers in the period. This shows on average how much value each customer brought to the organisation and is a factor of both the average ticket price as well as customer frequency.

High customer lifetime value indicates a thriving venue which is successful at commanding high ticket prices and re-engaging customers. If you want to increase the CLV, start by drilling down to see whether the root problem lies in average ticket price, customer frequency, or both.

Net promoter score (NPS)

Net promoter score[42] is an indicator of aggregate customer satisfaction, as well as the likelihood your customers will recommend your venue or show to a friend. As an integer, it is easily cross-comparable between shows or venues, and is very simple to administer in a survey.

NPS is calculated based on responses to a single question: "On a scale of 0-10, how likely are you to recommend the show/venue to a friend?"

Based on their scores, customers are then categorised into three groups:

Promoters (9-10): Loyal enthusiasts who will keep buying and refer others, fuelling growth.

Passives (7-8): Satisfied but unenthusiastic customers who are vulnerable to competitive offerings.

Detractors (0-6): Unhappy customers who can damage your brand and impede growth through negative word-of-mouth.

The NPS is then calculated by subtracting the percentage of customers who are Detractors from the percentage of customers who are Promoters.

NPS = % of Promoters - % of Detractors

The score can range from -100 (if every customer is a Detractor) to 100 (if every customer is a Promoter). In industry at large, a positive NPS is generally considered good, and a score of 50 or above is considered excellent. Theatres generally have scores above 70 because the experience is a comparatively pleasurable one. Most shows are in the range of 75 to 85. The lowest NPS score I've seen for a West End musical was 55 (a critically ridiculed flop), and the highest was 90 for the most incredible production.

NPS is a good high-level longitudinal barometer of how your venue or show is performing when audiences view the holistic experience. However, it takes many years to meaningfully change NPS scores because they are so

---

[42] The One number you need to grow (2015) Harvard Business Review. Available at: https://hbr.org/2003/12/the-one-number-you-need-to-grow (Accessed: July 2023).

affected by the type of work which is programmed, venue transport, restroom and parking facilities, etc.

When implementing NPS, take care to ensure that your scale starts at zero. I have seen organisations find themselves in a muddle trying to analyse results by inadvertently using a default survey question which began at one. The scale should be zero to ten.

Social media engagement rate

Social media engagement rate is calculated as:

Engagement Rate = (Total Engagements / Total Followers) * 100

Generally this is calculated per individual post or piece of content, so that you can discern what types of content resonate most with audiences. For instance, posts about upcoming shows might generate more engagement than posts about behind-the-scenes content, or vice versa, which can inform future content strategies.

Comments and shares can provide valuable feedback and insights about audience preferences and perceptions. This can be particularly valuable when launching new shows or initiatives.

Surveys

Surveying your audience can be a great way to get data about how they respond to every element of the booking flow, their visiting experience, and the work on stage. Popular questions to ask are how much they enjoyed the show, appreciated the customer service, felt it was good value for money, etc. Long form text boxes garner surprisingly in-depth comments, so you should always either respond to these promptly, or make clear that audiences should not expect a reply.

The Audience Agency publishes a standardised audience survey which organisations can benchmark against.[43]

There is some value in the surface-level data, but it doubles in value when you can link it to transactions. For example, being able to see how audience satisfaction changes between productions, or how perceived value for money is affected by the price that customers actually pay, or whether tourists have a better customer service experience than locals.

In each of these examples, the results do vary widely, and looking at an average number across all audiences only tells half the story. I prefer the approach of linking surveys to actual booking data over asking customers how much they spent or where they sat, because question fatigue will set in if we ask for too many difficult-to-remember details, and we have no guarantee that their recall will be wholly accurate.

To unlock the value of the transactional data, embed the customer's transaction ID or booking number within a unique survey link which you send them. (Most reputable survey platforms will have the ability to do this; ask yours for detailed instructions on how.) Then, depending on your survey platform, you can either upload the transactional data into it, or, if that's not possible to do within your survey platform, then export the transactional data from your ticketing system and the survey data from the survey tool, and join both of them together in Excel using the transaction ID. This will then allow you to drill down through any number of metrics and uncover your own insights. If you are uploading transactional data to an online survey platform, then remove any personally identifiable information (such as customer names, postcodes and email address) to stay within the terms of privacy legislation like GDPR.

---

[43] https://www.theaudienceagency.org/audience-finder-core-questionnaire-for-npos

As with any measurement exercise, the transactional data you include depends to some extent on the hypothesis you're trying to test, but could include the ticket price paid by the customer, the number of tickets purchased, the postcode or ZIP code, the customer segment, the seat location, the number of weeks out booked, or the customer's membership status.

Hone your questions so that there is no redundancy of information or room for misinterpretation. Shorter surveys will yield both higher response rates and greater satisfaction from your customers (and therefore more likelihood they'll take a survey from you in future). Whilst I generally err towards shorter post-purchase and post-visit surveys (less than 15 questions), my colleagues who specialise in longer surveys tell me that there is very little variation in response rates between a seven-minute survey and an eight-minute survey, so they are very thorough in asking every conceivable question which could make a difference to the marketing campaign.

Vanity metrics

Advance

Advance is the value of tickets sold for performances in the future. Once a show has begun performances, the advance can become, at best, a vanity metric which makes everyone feel jolly about how things are going. At worst, it can mislead colleagues about a show's fortunes and misdirect the team's attention. It should be the last metric which a marketing team optimises for when a show is in performances, not the first.

A preoccupation on the advance incentivises these types of unhealthy behaviour from a sales and marketing team:

- Turning off short-term sales and not releasing holds, because they mature quickly and don't help the advance.

- Focusing only on costly-to-acquire long-term bookers, like tourists, because they book far into the future.

- Reducing ticket prices so that the show sells out years into the future and has a high advance with a very low yield.

On the other hand, focusing on mature performances and wraps will:

- Maintain a steady inflow of sales.

- Ensure short- and medium-term performances are well sold.

- Discourage harmful short-term promotions because wraps need to remain at a consistent level.

- Make it easier to compare month-to-month sales with specific marketing activity.

Therefore I suggest that, post-opening, the team should focus instead on wraps and mature performances, which will secure recoupment for investors and pay everybody's salaries, rather than the advance which looks good in a report but can prompt damaging strategies.

Gross potential

Gross potential (GP) is the total monetary value of tickets on the plan at setup if they were all sold at full price. The operative word in gross potential is "potential". It is not a forecast or an estimate; it is a potential, which exists only on a spreadsheet. I have potential — to be an Olympic athlete or to win the lottery — but I don't dine out on these aspirations because they are unlikely to come true, and it's money which I will probably never have.

So it is with gross potential: it's an imaginary possibility that will never come true. GP is a vanity metric of selling 100% of tickets at 100% of the price you aimed for, and unless you are *Hamilton*, it seldom happens. As this book's title suggests, selling every seat is a challenging craft, and inevitably you'll find yourself giving up some yield either to discounting, concessions, or company comps. Take a glance over this week's stats from The Broadway League, and you'll see that most shows are achieving an average ticket price below their rate card and are certainly not selling every seat — both factors contributing to deviating from the gross potential.

Impressions

An impression represents one person seeing one of your adverts. Impressions are a vanity metric because they are not born equal: showing a glossy video to one of your subscribers will be much more likely to initiate a sale than showing a static 320x480px advert to a teenager who lives miles away and is browsing a gaming website. There's a big difference in the format, audience, relevance and placement, so attributing both as "one impression" is meaningless. I'd hope that the cost to buy these two formats is very different, and so it's not even a useful illustration to the size of the campaign.

Further, most online adverts are never shown to humans at all but instead to bots, and there is enormous diversity in the price which you can pay an advertiser for an impression based on the quality of their placement. Hence, conversion rates, attributed revenue, and clickthroughs are all better indicators of advert performance than impressions.

Graphs, charts and tables

The coming chapter is a ticketing analyst's cookbook - but without the mouth-watering photography which you might expect adjunct to recipes. That is to say that it will make for arid and academic reading, and it will be better brought to life when you try cooking these spreadsheets up in your own box office. If you selected *How to sell out* to read on your summer holiday, and currently find yourself on the beach with a margarita in hand, then perhaps skip the graphs for now and move to the next chapter: dynamic pricing and inventory management.

For readers who are ready to use statistics to grow their attendance, then the value which these approaches deliver will become much more apparent when you try them out using your own data, so as you read on, I'll encourage you to place book in one hand and laptop in the other - see if you can build a few of the frameworks and look at what trends they expose for your organisation.

Roger Tomlinson pioneered this area, and the inspired reader is encouraged to seek out his publications which lay out various additional standard reports for box offices.[44]

Ready? Then off we go... into the spreadsheets...

---

44 Tomlinson, R., Roberts, T. and Tomlinson, R. (2006) Full House: Turning data into audiences: A Manual for ticketing and Marketing Professionals. Surry Hills, N.S.W.: Australian Council for the Arts.

Tomlinson, R. (1993) Boxing clever: Getting the most out of the box office: A Manual on how to develop the box office beyond ticketing and use box office data for marketing. London: Arts Council of England.

Tomlinson, R. and Baker, T. (2005) Report on the Standard Box Office System Reports Feasibility Study. rep. Audience Data UK, Act Consultant Services.
Archived at: https://web.archive.org/web/20061011083910/http://www.aduk.org/documents/Standard_Box_office_systems.pdf

Performance by performance

Use case: Understanding how well each performance is selling, where the problems are, where more marketing is required, and which performances audiences are currently choosing to book into.

Audience: Marketing and sales teams, producers.

Construction: Most ticketing systems have a version of this as standard within their reporting suite. It can be helpful to export it into Excel so that you can improve the formatting and enhance it with additional metrics, such as movement and benchmarking.

Comprehension: The performance-by-performance gives just enough granularity to be actionable, whilst remaining high-level enough that lots of people in the organisation should find it worthwhile to read on a daily basis. It should become the key document from which you make decisions or set about creating further analysis. The natural expectation is that imminent performances should be well sold, followed by those in the medium term, and then those in the long term. Any deviation from this — such as advance Saturdays selling quicker than short-term Fridays — is an opportunity for further analysis and potential dynamic pricing.

Each column reveals something meaningful about the performance. Look to spot trends in which performances are most popular, how marketing is driving audiences into particular performances, and how the average ticket price varies between performances.

Some columns show the total advance, whilst others show the movement, say in the past week. This is helpful when you've run a marketing initiative and want to see what it has done for sales.

Nuance: Instead of by performance, try aggregating the data by week, month, or year to give a higher-level view of how the whole season is stacking up.

Add a column which shows the cumulative total of the advance as a percentage of the total advance. This is helpful to see how front-loaded your performances are and is a good way of illustrating, for example, that 60% of the advance is held in the next month. Ticket capacity is usually constant. Comps can be deduced by subtracting sold tickets from total tickets.

	Total Tickets	Ticket Movement	Sold Tickets	Reserve Tickets	Hold Tickets	Open Tickets	% of Ticket Capacity	Sold Gross	Gross Movement	Reserve Gross	Gross ATP	Sold Net	Capacity	Cumulative % of Advance
Tue 8 Jan '19 7:30 pm	386	53	386		12	2	100%	£12,586	2071		£33	£9,817	400	5%
Wed 9 Jan '19 7:30 pm	318	34	317		26	56	86%	£10,306	1182		£32	£8,039	400	8%
Thu 10 Jan '19 2:00 pm	375	30	371		8	17	96%	£14,593	1311		£39	£11,383	400	14%
Thu 10 Jan '19 7:30 pm	359	21	359		14	27	93%	£12,622	913		£35	£9,845	400	18%
Fri 11 Jan '19 7:30 pm	324	26	322		26	50	88%	£10,585	1208		£33	£8,256	400	22%
Sat 12 Jan '19 2:00 pm	320	55	320		36	44	89%	£10,104	2503		£32	£7,881	400	26%
Sat 12 Jan '19 7:30 pm	283	21	281		21	96	76%	£10,940	1093		£39	£8,533	400	30%
Sub Total	2365	240	2356		143	292	90%	£81,736	10281		£35	£63,754	2800	
Tue 15 Jan '19 7:30 pm	260	23	256		23	117	71%	£9,904	817		£38	£7,725	400	33%
Wed 16 Jan '19 7:30 pm	258	21	256		26	116	71%	£10,990	383		£43	£8,572	400	37%
Thu 17 Jan '19 2:00 pm	147	8	147	10	25	218	46%	£5,027	0	£370	£34	£3,921	400	39%
Thu 17 Jan '19 7:30 pm	289	0	285		29	82	80%	£13,484	596		£47	£10,518	400	44%
Fri 18 Jan '19 7:30 pm	270	17	270		27	103	74%	£13,122	629		£49	£10,235	400	49%
Sat 19 Jan '19 2:00 pm	192	12	192		27	181	55%	£8,202	580		£43	£6,398	400	52%
Sat 19 Jan '19 7:30 pm	273	18	271		26	101	75%	£10,221	715		£37	£7,972	400	56%
Sub Total	1689	99	1677	10	183	918	67%	£70,950	3720	£370	£42	£55,341	2800	
Tue 22 Jan '19 7:30 pm	291	17	287		22	87	78%	£11,247	328		£39	£8,773	400	60%
Wed 23 Jan '19 7:30 pm	167	6	167		25	208	48%	£5,499	43		£33	£4,289	400	62%
Thu 24 Jan '19 2:00 pm	334	1	334	10	23	33	92%	£14,315	535	£370	£43	£11,166	400	67%
Thu 24 Jan '19 7:30 pm	76	10	76		87	237	41%	£2,008	231		£26	£1,566	400	68%
Fri 25 Jan '19 7:30 pm	298	7	294		32	70	83%	£12,091	222		£41	£9,431	400	72%
Sat 26 Jan '19 2:00 pm	294	6	292		26	80	80%	£13,844	648		£47	£10,798	400	77%
Sat 26 Jan '19 7:30 pm	144	14	144		27	229	43%	£5,938	272		£41	£4,632	400	79%
Sub Total	1604	61	1594	10	242	944	66%	£64,942	2279	£370	£40	£50,655	2800	
Tue 29 Jan '19 7:30 pm	316	8	310		25	59	85%	£15,180	1309		£48	£11,840	400	85%
Wed 30 Jan '19 7:30 pm	246	24	246		25	129	68%	£11,258	608		£46	£8,781	400	89%
Thu 31 Jan '19 2:00 pm	128	20	128	10	27	235	41%	£5,252	585	£370	£41	£4,097	400	91%
Thu 31 Jan '19 7:30 pm	120	17	227		26	254	37%	£10,279	256		£86	£8,018	400	94%
Fri 1 Feb '19 7:30 pm	84	7	84		27	289	28%	£3,002	96		£36	£2,342	400	96%
Sat 2 Feb '19 2:00 pm	248	4	248		24	128	68%	£11,727	388		£47	£9,147	400	100%
Sat 2 Feb '19 7:30 pm	16	10	16		26	358	11%	£520	92		£33	£406	400	100%
Sub Total	1158	90	1259	10	180	1452	48%	£57,218	3334	£370	£49	£44,630	2800	
Grand Total	6616	490	6686	30	748	3606	68%	£274,846	19614	£1,110	£40	£214,380	11200	

Daily wraps and spikes

Use case: Understanding the effect of major marketing and PR moments on sales.

Audience: Marketing and PR teams, producers.

Construction: X axis is the date and Y axis is the value of wraps in your local currency. Bars show daily wraps, whilst a line is overlayed with the number of daily website visits. Key marketing and PR moments are annotated.

Comprehension: Look to see whether top-of-the-funnel interest in the show increased following a major PR moment, demonstrated by higher website visits, and whether this then resulted in higher wraps. Look to see how long the "halo" period lasted after a major campaign, and whether it affected only website visits, only sales, or both.

Nuance: If sales volumes are lower, the chart may be more meaningful to look at aggregated by week rather than day. Spikes only present themselves when marketing/PR is significantly heightened, so only include genuinely major moments and don't try to use this for attributing each element of a campaign (e.g. a single newspaper ad). Do include all major moments, as it is just as useful to learn about what didn't work, as what did.

Graph adjacent show the number of visitors to the website and sales increased around key moments such as the launch party and TV advertising, but some activity like the radio interviews only drove awareness and consideration, without impacting conversions through a respective spike in sales.

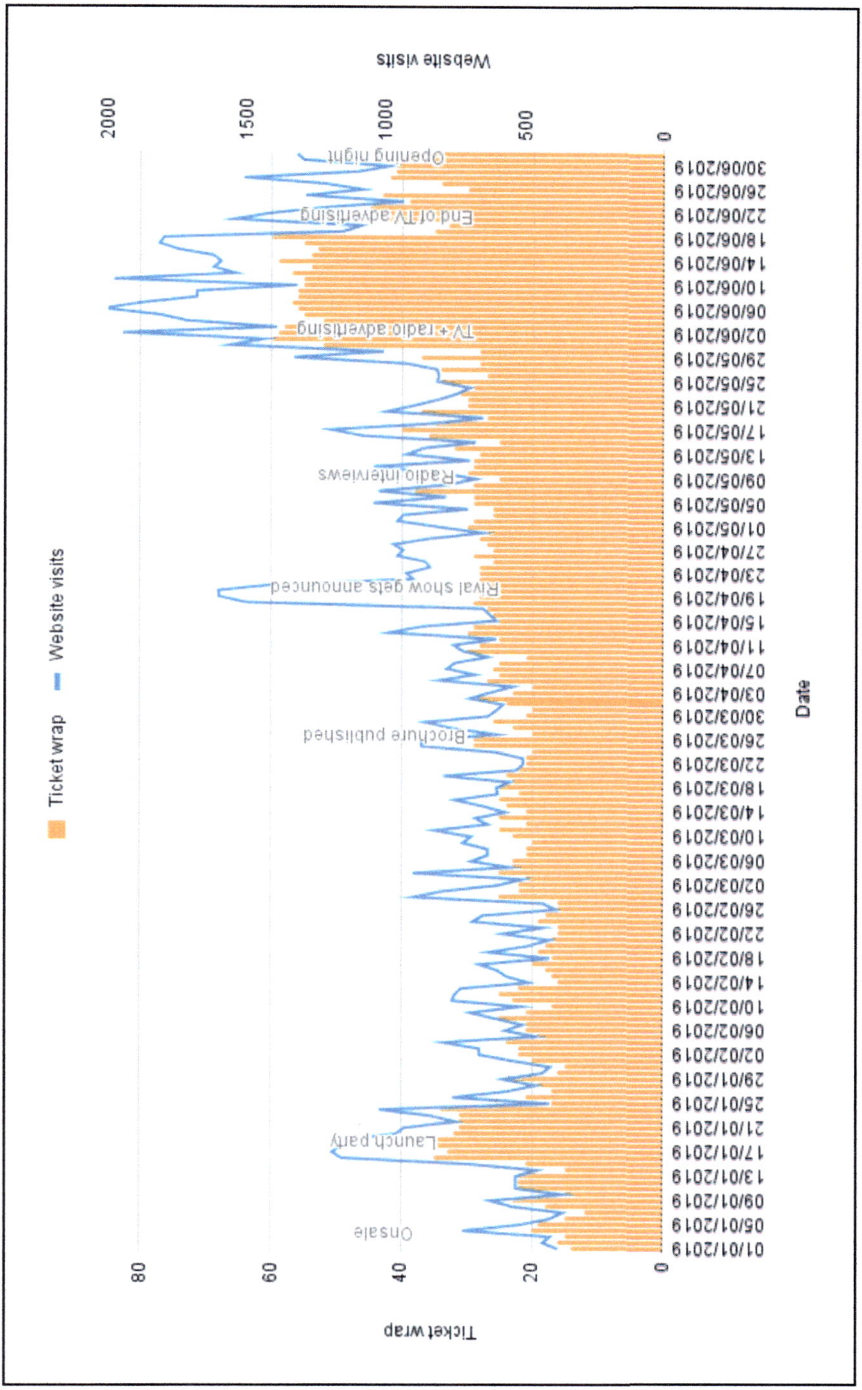
Ticket wrap
Website visits
Date
Onsale
Launch party
Brochure published
Rival show gets announced
Radio interviews
TV + radio advertising
End of TV advertising
Opening night
0
20
40
60
80
500
1000
1500
2000
01/01/2019
30/06/2019

Marketing spend versus income

Use case: To understand the impact of the advertising campaign on sales, and attribute uplift in ticket sales to major campaign moments.

Audience: Marketing teams. (They love showing this to producers to demonstrate how hard their campaign is working!)

Construction: With the date on X axis and marketing spend on the Y axis, plot the weekly spend, using colour to split the bars by channel (outdoor, digital, brochure, radio, TV, etc). Then on a second Y axis, add weekly wraps as a line.

Comprehension: The graph should simply demonstrate how uplifts in marketing investment create an upswing in ticket sales. You should be able to annotate when major campaign moments ran, such as a brochure drop or TV advertising, because of their large spike in investment and accompanying rise in ticket wraps. It is also useful for demonstrating the "halo" of such activity, where the sales continue at the inflated level for some weeks after the initial spend.

Nuance: Be sure to use wrap data rather than mature sales, as the former will be more directly impacted by marketing activity.

This isn't an exercise in econometric marketing mix modelling and so doesn't give you granular detail about the ROI on each element of the campaign, so do keep the data fairly high level. I never go smaller than by week, because meaningful marketing activity doesn't really run any shorter than this, and because it may take a few days for a customer to buy a ticket after seeing the advert. If the show is a few months away and numbers are small, then aggregating by month might be more appropriate.

Top-of-funnel activity will usually have a longer lead time to sale, versus direct-response bottom-of-funnel activity. For example, an email to previous bookers will create a sugar rush of sales in the following 24 - 48 hours, versus a television campaign which will cast a gentler halo over the coming two or three weeks. Therefore, when looking at these charts, you shouldn't always expect to see concurrent thorns because awareness and consideration activity isn't expected to create same-day results.

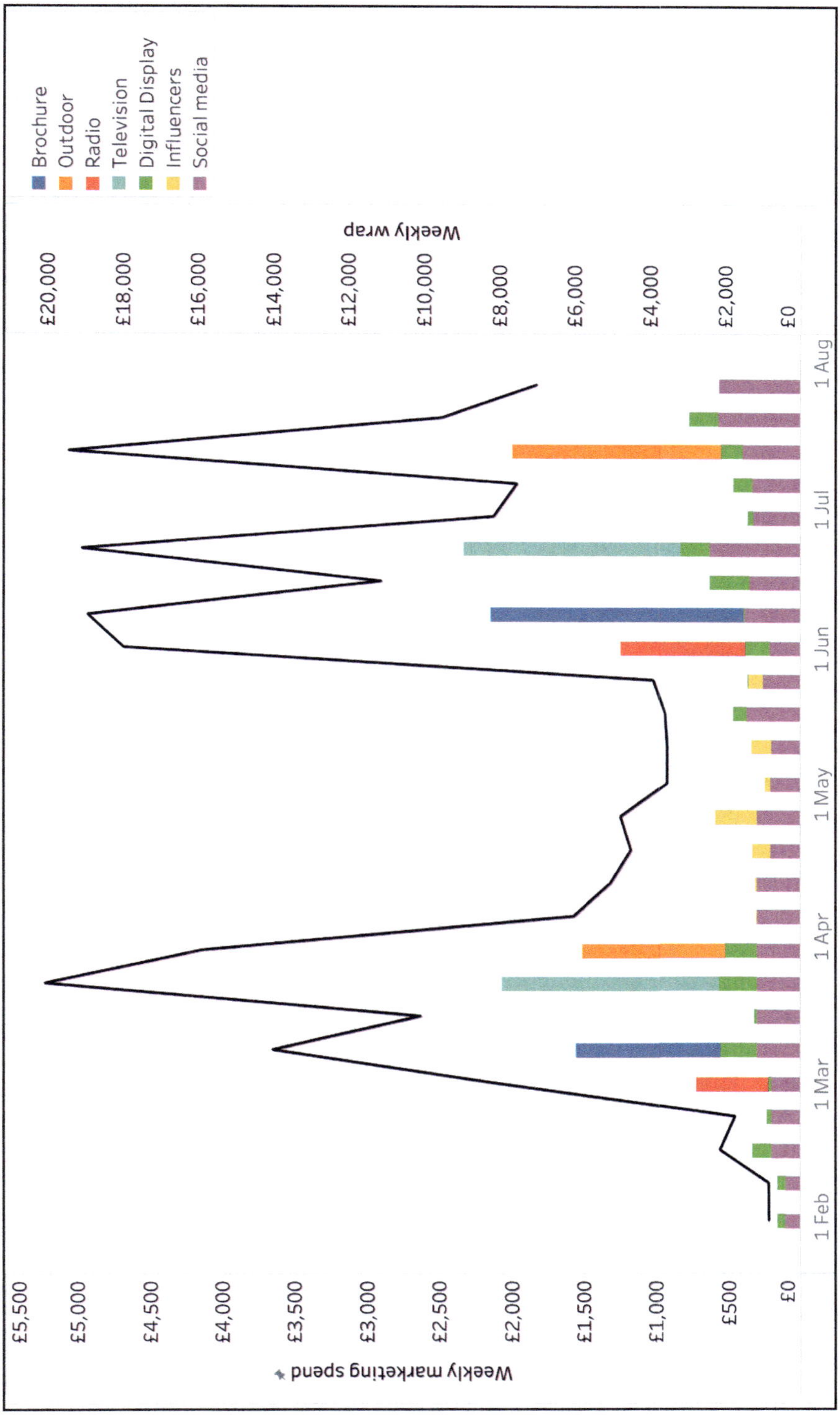
Brochure
Outdoor
Radio
Television
Digital Display
Influencers
Social media
Weekly marketing spend
Weekly wrap
£5,500
£5,000
£4,500
£4,000
£3,500
£3,000
£2,500
£2,000
£1,500
£1,000
£500
£0
£20,000
£18,000
£16,000
£14,000
£12,000
£10,000
£8,000
£6,000
£4,000
£2,000
£0
1 Feb
1 Mar
1 Apr
1 May
1 Jun
1 Jul
1 Aug

Daily emails

Hamlet

Email sent Wednesday 24th January 2024

Wraps

Tuesday's Wrap (23/01/24): £22,062 (245 tickets, ATP: £90.04)
Of which £18,471 (193 tickets, 83% of gross wrap) is Venue Box Office, and £3,591 (52 tickets, 17% of gross wrap) is via Ticket Agents
Down -£3,628 (-62 tickets) on previous week

This Week's Wrap To Date (w/c 22 January): £44,806 (506 tickets, ATP: £88.55)
Down -£6,628 (-122 tickets) on same time last week
This Week's Wrap Gross Target is £172,000

Performances

Tuesday Evening (23/01/24 7:30pm)
Gross: £23,808 (down £250 on last week)
Sold attendance: 299
ATP: £79.62
Comps: 25
Total attendance: 324
Occupancy: 93%

This Week's Performance Gross To Date (w/c 22 January): £43,808
Down -£450 on previous week

Advances

Gross Advance: £2,400,147 (27,660 sold tickets plus 114 Comp tickets)
Gross Advance vs. Last Week: -£38,240 (-474 tickets)
Gross Reserve: £248,040 (4,015 tickets)
Advance, Comp Tickets and Reserve Combined: £2,648,187 (31,789 tickets)

Legend has it that the fastidious founder of one advertising agency would ambush junior executives in the elevator - testing them on today's advance or last week's wrap. Staff in every department soon learned that their promotion relied on them being able to recite these figures like times-tables, such was the import placed on the connection between a marketer's work and the day's takings.

I cannot impress enough how essential it is for everyone connected in the show's sales success to live and breathe these sales each day. To read and understand them, even if not to intone. The daily sales email should be sent to anyone working in ticketing, sales, pricing, press, venue operations, general management and producers so that everyone understands in real time how sales are pacing, how their own efforts are impacting the most important KPI (sales) and to set the agenda for their coming day. Some insecure producers rarify knowledge by limiting the individuals with access to figures. Just as you can't grow flowers in the dark, neither can you expect a marketing team to reach a sales goal without them seeing how they are pacing, so best to put a problem out in the open and use it to focus everyone's energies, than pretending it doesn't exist.

To facilitate this, each morning the ticketing manager should gather together all of the data about the previous day's sales and compile it to the internal sales tracker, before sending out a summary email for all stakeholders.

The email needs to be coherent, concise and consistent. I spent several years honing the format which I will share here, by sending out this email to the teams of over a hundred shows and thousands of individual recipients, and their collective feedback has refined it into a format which works for any show. It should be simple enough to extract from any ticketing system and removes any potential obfuscation created from the peculiarities of any software or show. Ticketing systems can have nuances and slight definitional variations on how the numbers are pulled, so this daily sales email puts everyone from producer to box office clerk on the same page with a single source of truth, and is the grounding from which all conversation about potential marketing activities can sprout.

The email has three independent sections; wraps, performances and advance. Wraps and advance will be present from the first report (the day after onsale), whilst the performances report only gets added once performances begin.

The top line of the wraps section has the most important information; the takings from the previous day's sales, followed by a breakout by primary seller and ticket agents. A comparison to the previous week gives a steer as to whether sales are improving or not. A 'week to date' total helps smooth out some of the day-to-day noise, showing a broader view of how this week is tracking.

If refunds have been processed, the day's total wrap will be lower than the number of tickets sold. Normally, wraps are measured instead of sales, with the exception of calculating return on marketing spend. This is because marketing's objective is to attract customers to the checkout. Marketing shouldn't be accountable for post-sale events. On the other hand, producers are concerned with the net daily effect on the box office. Therefore, I recommend to continue reporting the wrap on the top line.

This should be followed by a note, 'of which refunds -£x', to display the impact.

The performances section lists every performance in the previous day separately, or else a note that no performance was played. ATP should be calculated from sold tickets, and a note made of the number of comps given, which is included in the % occupancy figure, being the occupied tickets divided by the available capacity.

The advance section is focused on sold (paid-for) tickets, before detailing the reserved (held but unpaid) and comp tickets. The combined total is intentionally inconspicuous as it is not entirely a consequence of sales, but also of unpaid tickets and reservations which may not materialise.

It is best to send this email daily but if work patterns don't permit, then list consecutive days within each section. For example, if sending a report on a Monday which covers the whole weekend then specify Friday's wrap followed by Saturday's then Sundays. On a Monday, the running totals for this week will become last week's. I attach to this email a performance-by-performance report each day, and a weeks out report each Monday. Many of my colleagues proudly type this email up by hand each day, and evangelise the benefits for helping them internalise the numbers. For what it's worth, I prefer automated systems which are both quicker and avoid the inevitable typos of data entry, but both approaches have their merit.

Some style guides which I advocate are to only use decimal places on ATP, to only use a - dash to represent a negative number and never in place of a colon, to use full dates in brackets alongside weekdays, to only list percentages out of revenue not tickets, and to begin with totals and then follow it with 'of which' breakouts if needed. When dealing with money, be precise about whether it is gross or net, and wraps, mature or advance. It's not always possible to insist exactly what time the data is pulled, due to other reports competing for server resources, but you should make sure that the source reports include sales made as-of midnight and the preceding 24 hours. The most common cause of discrepancy are when one report is not set to be as-of midnight. Beware daylight savings which can confuse this further. Consistency is paramount, and great value comes from colleagues being able to rely on timely, accurate figures for all shows being delivered each morning. Using the same format across every show will habitualise teams into reading these numbers each morning and framing their work accordingly.

Lollipop chart

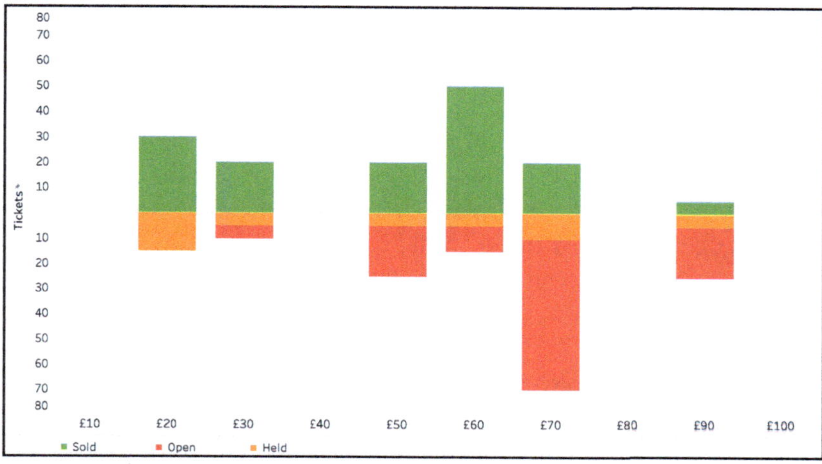

[45]

Use case: To understand which price bands are selling, which are not, and which are held for one or several performances. The purpose of the chart is to bring into sharp relief the contrast between what your plan currently thinks the value of the show is, and the reality of what consumers are actually paying.

Audience: Sales managers.

---

45 All of the cheapest £20 tickets have been sold and most of the £30 seats also. Consider releasing the £20 tickets which are held and pricing them up to £30.

£60 seems to be the sweet spot for customers as this has had the highest sell-through rate, however £70 seems to be sticking. Consider moving some of the unsold £70 tickets down to £60.

Most of the premium tickets at £90 are unsold and will likely remain this way until more of the £60 and £70 seats are sold.

Note that there are no tickets at £80. Consider whether adding some at this price could offer more choice to consumers, and perhaps make £70 appear more attractive.

Construction: Take ticketing data as your data source, with a row for each ticket in a performance, and columns for price and for seat status (open, sold, or held). The chart has price along the X axis, number of tickets on the Y axis, status as colour, and is sorted such that sold is above the zero line, whilst open and held are below the zero line.

Comprehension: The layout of the lollipop shows us where our inventory is sitting: sold or unsold, high price or low. Ideally, we would want the bars to be sitting in the top-right quadrant, which represents sold tickets at a high price. A disaster would be for everything to sit in the bottom left quadrant, which shows most tickets are unsold and currently at a low price.

Most likely, you will have inventory sitting around the middle price bands, probably with more sold than unsold at the lower prices, and some of the most expensive tickets sticking unsold. What you are looking to identify from this chart is where your customers are "biting" — what the sweet spot is for your pricing.

For example, if you see that you've successfully sold a lot of tickets at £50 but don't have many left, and there are lots sticking at £60, then it would be reasonable to reprice some of the £60s down to £50. Often this can be the case when too many premiums have been added to a plan — this example chart clearly demonstrates that the customers would gladly buy those same seats at Band A prices. It also brings the role of Band E seats into clear view, because it often shows that all of these have been sold immediately, and perhaps were priced too low to begin with.

Ideally, we'd like to see a broad bell curve showing in the lollipop chart, but if it looks like a cityscape of skyscrapers then repricing is probably due, because too many tickets are bunched at the same price band. Imagine a large group of prospective customers: they won't all have £50 as their target price; some will be looking for £40 and some for £60, so just ensure that you have a sensible range available.

Nuance: If you have more than ten price bands or are doing a lot of dynamic pricing where they move by a pound or two, it may help to group them together for the purposes of this chart. In my work, I bucket together all prices within a £10 increment, so £10 to £19.99 go together, £20 to £29.99 go together, and so forth. It makes for easier comprehension of the chart and avoids the clutter of lots of small values.

For any discounted tickets, I take the price which it was sold at rather than the rate card. For example, a ticket which was advertised at £50 but which was sold in promotion at £40 would go in the £40 bucket because this represents the actual income which we've earned and at which the customer values the ticket. This is another benefit over looking at seat maps, where perfectly good seats may have appear to have been sold, but deceptively at a discount. It is one of the more challenging charts to read, which is why I suggest it is only for the eyes of the ticketing team. Generally I will then mark up a seating plan with proposed changes when presenting to a producer.

Three lines

Use case: Visualising the trend of advance in context with mature sales and cumulative income. Useful for understanding the interplay between the three metrics.

Audience: Board reporting and senior management.

Construction: X axis is the report date and Y axis is revenue, with a line plotted for each of gross advance (sales for performances that have not yet happened), gross matured (sales for performances that have happened), and cumulative gross wrap (sales made since on-sale, for any performance).

Comprehension: Look to see how gross wrap always increases, and the curve shows any acceleration/deceleration in sales. Advance will increase when wraps increase faster than matured, and advance will diminish when sales mature quicker than new tickets are wrapped. Useful for demonstrating that the advance is not the most critical number, so long as matured and wraps are at healthy levels. Producers often have a preoccupation with advances, or wraps, and I like to talk them through this chart to educate them in what the interplay is between the three metrics, and how an increase in one can pull down another.

Nuance: Project the graph by adding target figures for future dates, to see how the lines are required to extend.

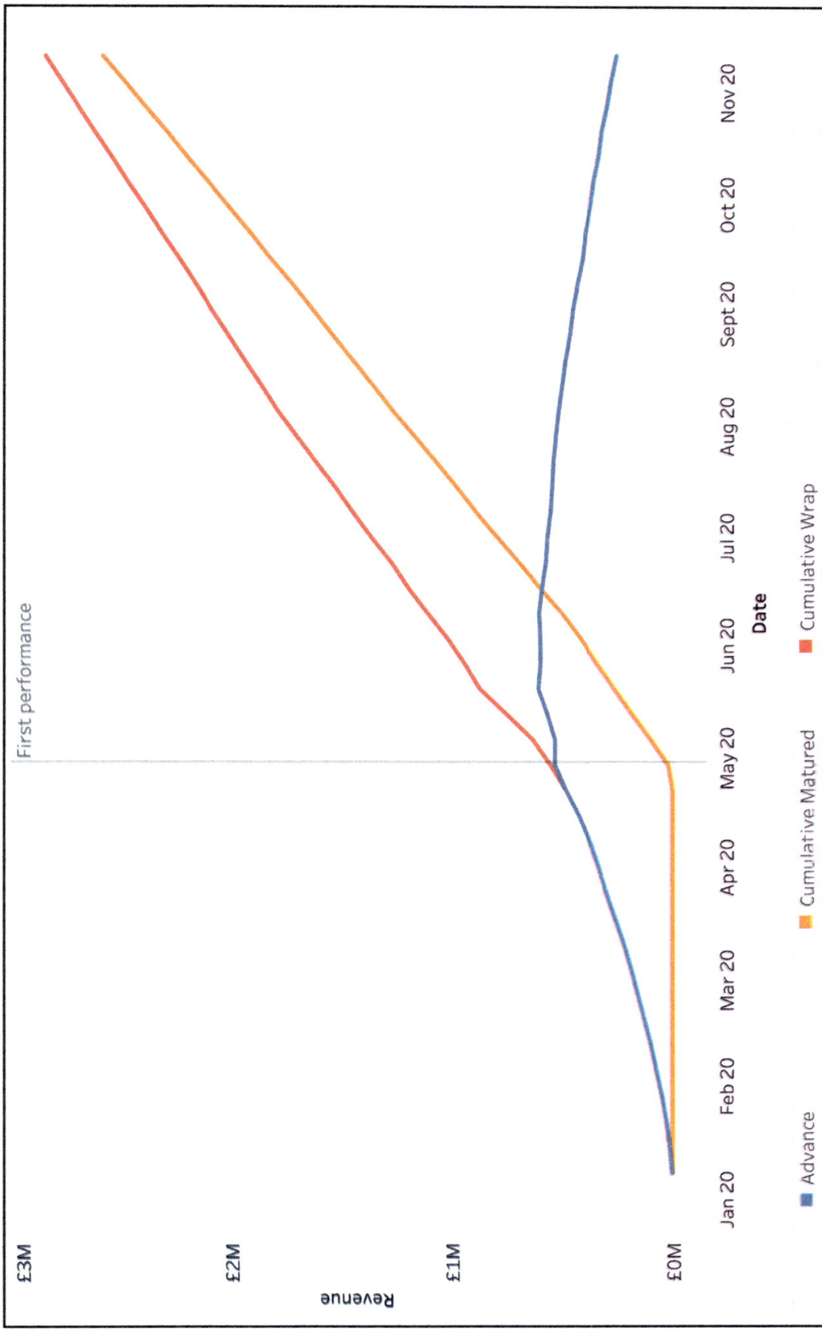

[46]

46 Observe how the advance peaks at post-opening. After this, the show matures off more than it is wrapping each week so the advance declines.

Crossover shows

Use case: Understanding which shows should be cross-promoted, and understanding which audiences have an affinity with a future title.

Audience: Marketing team, producers.

Construction: In your database, take a list of customers who have booked for a target show. Then compile a list of all other shows which these bookers have attended. Rank this list of affinity shows in descending order, by how many customers have attended each one.

Comprehension: Shows with higher crossover are good targets for cross-promotion — for example "if you enjoyed X then you'll love Y" advertisements — and are likely to have a higher affinity with the target title.

Nuance: Crossover lists are generally dominated by the most recent shows and those with the highest capacity, which is unhelpful because it says nothing about the tastes of the audience, and is simply a result of anyone in the database having had a higher likelihood to have attended the shows with the most inventory. To navigate this, you can use the Jaccard index, which adjusts for the relative size of each show. This results in much more meaningful lists, where smaller titles are just as likely to appear in the top crossover lists.

The Jaccard index is the intersection divided by the union in the two lists of customers. So if there are two customers who intersect between show x and show y, and a total of 6 distinct customers total who saw either show, then the Jaccard is 2 divided by 6, or 0.333. You can then rank each show pair by their Jaccard index to determine which has the highest crossover relative to it's size.

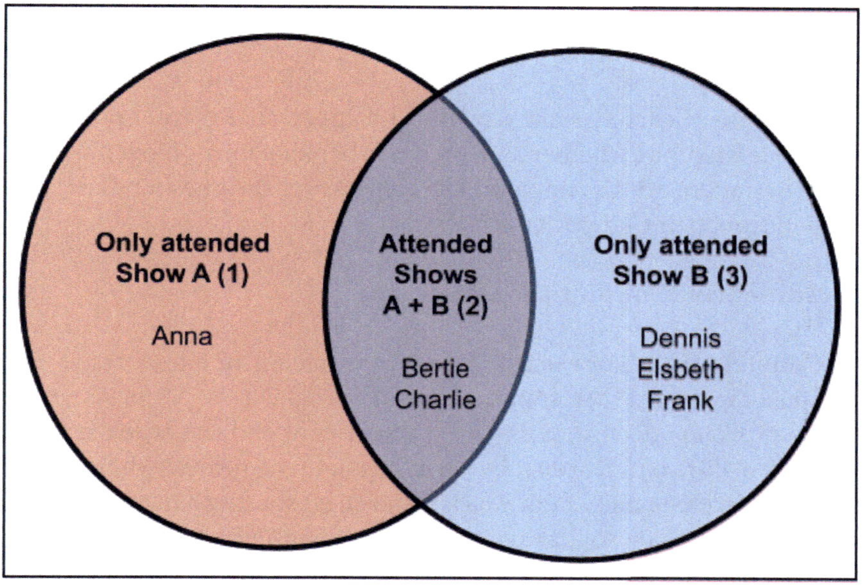

47

		Intersection	Union	Jaccard Similarity
Show A	Show B	2	6	0.333
Show A	Show C	2	7	0.286
Show A	Show D	4	30	0.133
Show A	Show E	1	20	0.050
Show A	Show F	1	5	0.200

48

---

47 In this example, there are six distinct customers, of which two have attended both shows. The Jaccard is 2 divided by 6 = 0.333.

48 If we compare the customers who attended Show A to the customers who attended every other show, then we can determine that Show B has the highest crossover, as the Jaccard value is the greatest for this pair.

Note that Show D has the highest intersection (4), and so it would be tempting so say that it has the highest crossover, but we can see that this is because Show D had many more customers in total (30), so the intersection isn't comparable. The Jaccard shows that the level of similarity between Shows A and D is actually only 0.133, much lower than the combination of A and B.

Average weeks out

Use case: Benchmarking demand and appeal for different productions, and understanding whether audiences are booking long-, medium-, or short-term. Provides a simple KPI to help answer the question "are audiences booking later than usual?"

Audience: Marketing and sales teams.

Construction: For each customer, calculate the number of days between the date of their transaction and the date of the performance. Average this for all customers who attend a show and you have the average number of days out. Divide it by 7 and round to the nearest whole number to see the average number of weeks out. I suggest using a median average rather than a mean, so that an outlying very long-term booking doesn't drive up the overall average.

There are two potential ways to analyse the average weeks out. The first is to plot it as a bar chart, with weeks out on the Y axis and production name on the X axis, comparing the average weeks out across many different productions.

The second is to plot it as a line chart, with weeks out still on the Y axis and now "weeks since first performance" on the X axis. You can now compare how the time between booking and attendance varies over the lifecycle of each production, and see for example whether your audiences are trending towards last-minute bookings, advance bookings, or staying consistent.

Comprehension: Metrics like advance and season gross are often used as an indicator of customer demand in a title, but they are inherently affected by capacity, ticket price and marketing investment. Average weeks out side-steps some of this and is in some ways a stronger measure of how keenly the audience want to see this show. It can be used to compare between different genres, venues, countries, and decades, without needing to make any adjustments for inflation or marketing investment — so it stands up as a remarkably independent metric of customer demand where shows in high demand achieve long weeks-out, and lower-demand titles see shorter weeks-out. This is because consumers who have greater motivation and intent-to-buy will book further in advance, demonstrating the show's pulling-power with higher advance sales.

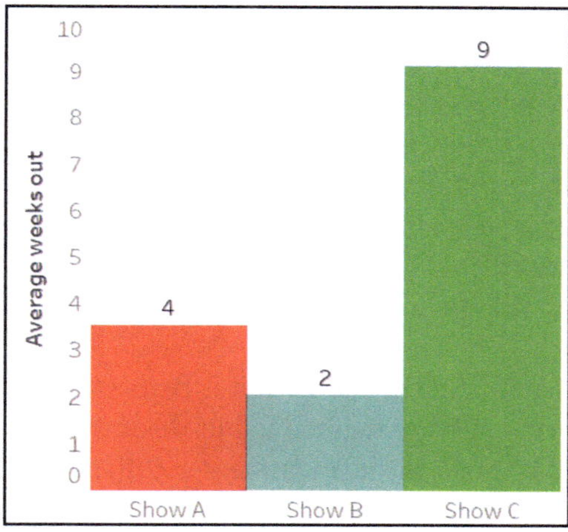

[49]

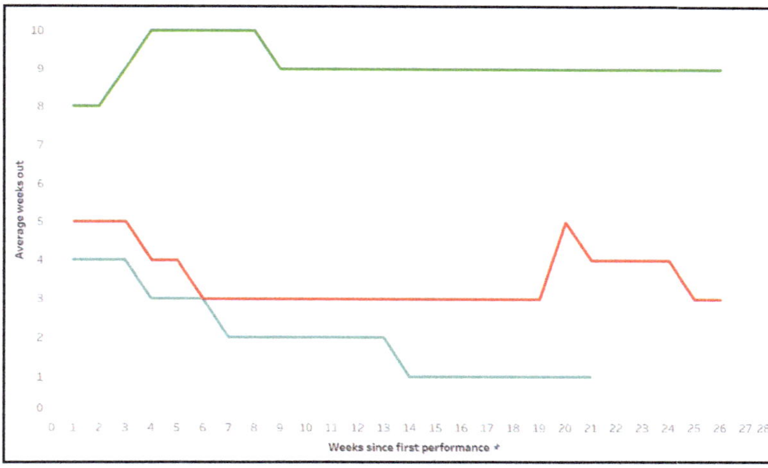

[50]

49 Customers for Show A book the furthest in advance (9 weeks out), whilst Show A has an average of 4 weeks, and Show B has the most last-minute bookings with an average of 2 weeks out.

50 Show A initially has a surge of advance bookings and then settles into a pattern of customers booking 3 weeks out. There is a booking period extension at 20 weeks after first performance which causes an uplift in the average weeks out.

Show B enters into a vicious cycle of short-term availability and so average weeks out continues to decline, before the show closes. To me, the trend of Show B suggests that there is a fundamental imbalance between supply and demand; most likely the show is maturing more tickets each day than it is wrapping, and so the cycle worsens as it has to fill a deepening hole in sales.

Show C has a longer consideration period and so customers consistently book much further in advance.

For example, a performance in a small studio auditorium with a comparatively high average number of days out tells you that audiences are especially keen to watch this production and have made a behavioural change to book early. Conversely, a production in a large auditorium with a low average days out tells us that customers don't feel motivated or excited to book ahead, and there is a risk of sales drying up because the show is overly dependent upon short-term sales. The low weeks out exposes a mismatch between demand and available inventory.

In this example, the advance could still be healthy if it is regularly being topped up as frequently as performances are maturing, but the low number of days out highlights the risk to the business if consumers are disrupted by transport or another show catches their attention.

Two good ways to use this metric are by comparing the average days out for several of your matured productions, as a means to see which attracted the most long-term customers. On a long-running show, it can be helpful to create a graph of the average days out for customers who made transactions in each week. This is a useful way to see how advance booking trends are changing over time. The number will most likely fluctuate up with marketing activity and down in seasons when short-term inventory is available, and it's important to be aware of these fluctuations as they're happening.

Beware that, for as long as there have been shows, there have been ticketing managers claiming that "audiences are booking more last minute". There may a grain of truth to this, but the statement is also influenced by a great deal of perception bias, so use the maths outlined here to quantify it specifically within your organisation and avoid getting swept away with hyperbole.

Nuance: You should only use this metric once the production has begun performances. Until it does so, the number will be high and gradually reduce proportional to the number of days until first performance. So only look at the data once performances have begun.

Seat heatmap

Use case: Understanding which areas of the auditorium are most sought after by audiences, which seats should be repriced in line with customer demand, and how pricing affects where people choose to sit.

Audience: Sales team, producers.

Construction: From your database, pull a list of every instance that a seat has been sold. Aggregate the data by seat (A1, A2, etc), so that for each seat you have the number of times it was sold. Construct a map of your seating plan where each cell is colour-coded based on the frequency of sale to the respective seat. Green for seats which are sold at least two thirds of the time, red for seats sold less than a third of the time, and amber for anything in the middle.

Comprehension: We are looking to identify patches of the auditorium which are in high demand at a low price, or in low demand at a high price, so that we can adjust these and create an equilibrium.

There are some patterns you can expect to see:

In an auditorium where all seats are priced the same, we would expect the centre stalls to be in highest demand – the "greenest" on the chart – as it offers the best view, with demand radiating out from that point. If people have to lift their heads, then the front row of the stalls may be slightly less popular, and the front row of the circle may more popular if it offers a great view. The least popular seats are generally the back rows on the sides in the stalls and circle.

In an auditorium which has conventional variable pricing, we would expect the centre stalls to again be the most popular seats, radiating outwards. Then the front row of each price band to also be very popular, as people hurry to get the best seats at each price band. It is common for the front row of Band E to be amongst the most popular seats because this is comparatively the best seat at the lowest price.

Sometimes a "W" shape can appear in the stalls, where customers desire the centre stalls and aisles, but leave gaps in the less desirable gaps.

One thing which these charts always demonstrate is how desirable the centre is, and hence removing seats to give space for a centre aisle would be disastrous for sales, as it is the most attractive position for audiences. Push back heavily if there is ever a request for a centre aisle.

Nuance: Look to identify seats which are more or less popular than the seats around them. Try to form a hypothesis for why that could be, and adjust pricing to balance out these peaks so that each seat sells as often as its neighbours.

Make sure you are always looking at a good range of performances (at least 10) when creating heatmaps. Anything less than that will have indistinguishable noise and not enough sales per seat to draw meaningful conclusions.

As well as using absolute popularity — i.e. the number of times a seat was sold — consider colouring by relative popularity. This is good for when all seats sell 80% to 100% of the time and are roughly the same shade of green. To implement relative popularity, change your colour scale so that seats which sold 80% of the time are red, those which sell 90% of the time are amber, and those which sell 100% of the time are green. In data visualisation and spreadsheet software, there is usually an option to set the minimum and maximum values. For absolute popularity, you'd use a range of 0% to 100%, whilst a tighter range (for example, 80% to 100%) can be used for relative popularity.

Price can be helpful to visualise where the income is coming from for your producers, so you can also produce a seat map showing the average price per seat. Again, use green for the seats commanding the highest price, and red for the lowest.

Speed is also a useful metric to see how desirable seats are. To implement this, colour seats by the average number of days out from performance that they were sold, where green is a high number of days out and red is low. Sometimes this will expose seats which customers have identified as being great value, such as those in the back row, so super fans log on as soon as performances go on sale to scoop up a bargain. If this is the case, consider pricing up or making them available only to members.

Heat maps are great for optimising revenue to demand, but if you are averaging less than 50% capacity, then there is probably a bigger problem with demand and pricing, rather than with individual seats. I'd therefore neglect heat maps until you have more sales, and first pursue investigation into the marketing funnel and check the entry price is reasonable.

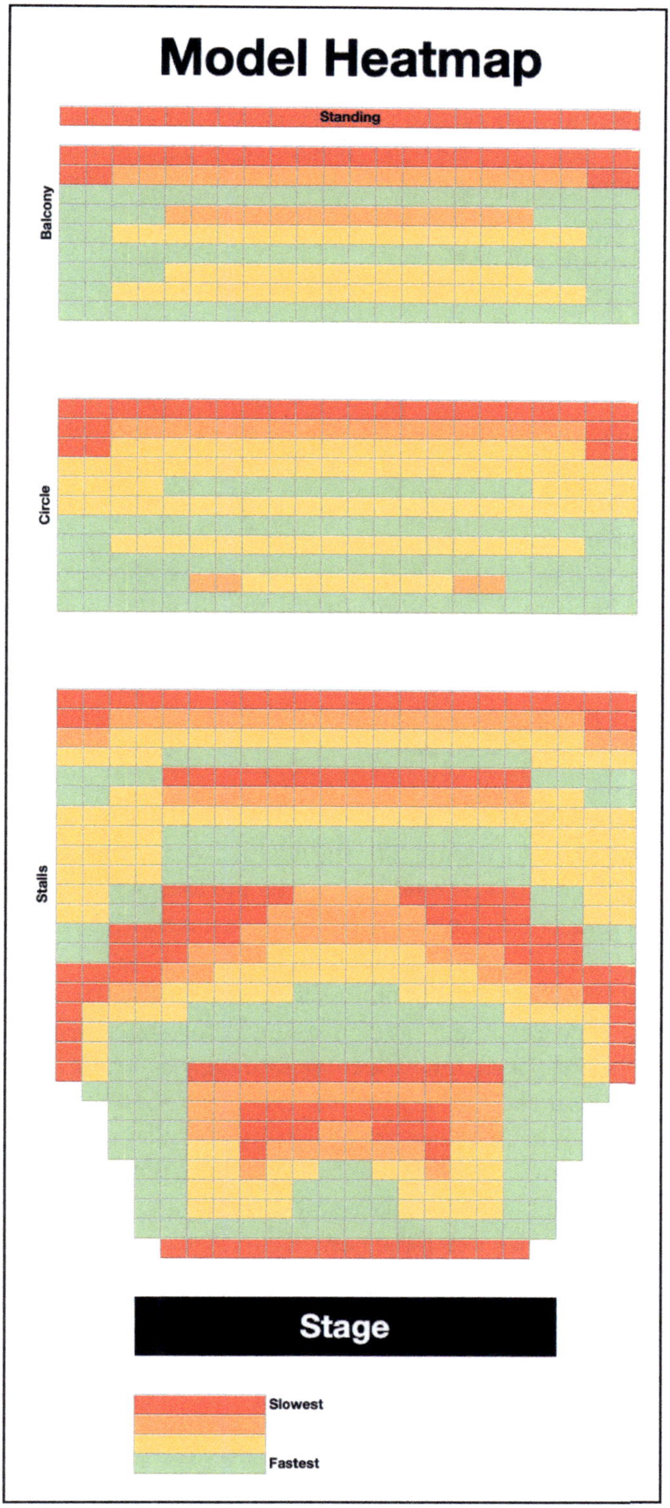

Model Heatmap
Standing
Balcony
Circle
Stalls
Stage
Slowest
Fastest

Bubble chart

Use case: Understanding how your pricing compares to comparable productions in the marketplace, and what the spread of ticket prices is (optionally by volume of seats available).

Audience: Sales team and producers.

Construction: For each show, research the price bands which are currently on sale and, if desired, count the number of seats at each price band. For your own show this will be easy, as you have access to the full seating plan. For other shows, this will require looking at their seating plans online. Evidently some seats will be sold already, so it helps to choose a consistent performance (say, a Saturday in six weeks' time) where there is good availability, and use your judgement to estimate what price you expect the sold seats to have been sold at. For quicker construction and a basic bubble chart, simply take data points for the top (Band A), bottom, and premium prices of each show, and don't count the numbers of tickets. The basic bubble chart is quicker to producer and slightly easier to read, although some detail is lost so I prefer the full version for my own use, even if I give the basic version to stakeholders.

Plot the chart with the show name on the X axis, ticket price on the Y axis, and a bubble for each price band. For the detailed version of the chart, if you have the data, the bubbles should be sized by the number of tickets available. Sort the shows left-to-right by their average ticket price.

Comprehension: Consider which other shows in the marketplace might be valued the same as yours by audiences, and rank your show within that cohort. On the spectrum of all competitor shows, would consumers expect for your show to be the most expensive, least expensive, or somewhere in the middle? Think about your entry price; how does it compare to what other shows have as their starting price? When it comes to your price ceiling, do you want to make a statement by going higher than anyone else, or coast just underneath the norm?

Nuance: Adding all price bands and sizing the bubbles is useful because it reveals that, whilst the bottom price may be £10, only a handful of tickets are available at this price and in fact the £40 to £60 price bands dominate. It is helpful when the shape or size of your auditorium is very different, because it reveals which price bands are carrying the majority of tickets. Ideally, we would aim for a broad bell curve, where seats are split fairly evenly across the middle price bands. However, the specifics of different auditoria sometimes force a ticketing manager's hand to have one price band dominate. The bubble chart will expose this, raise questions about how viable it is for the majority of an audience to be booking at a specific price, and perhaps prompt further investigation about splitting the section into two bands.

Basic bubble chart[51]

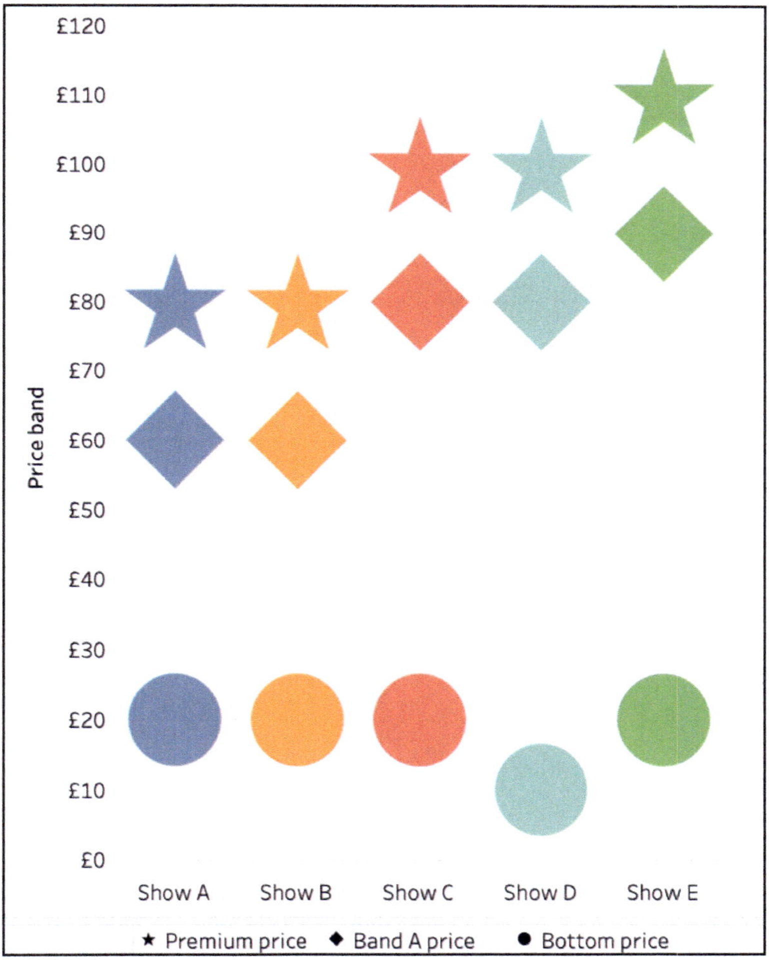

---

[51] Shows A and B are the cheapest whilst Shows E is the most expensive. It is useful for knowing what the market expects for an entry price (£20), and the ceiling on premium tickets (£100 to £110). However, it doesn't give insight about the prices in between.

Detailed bubble chart:

The basic chart doesn't tell the full story because it suggests that Show D is the cheapest show, when in fact it has just made a very small number of cheap tickets available so that they can use it in PR. The chart also suggests that shows C and D have the same premium tickets, when in fact Show C has far fewer premiums on sale than Show D.

Looking at the detailed bubble chart, we can see that:

Show A is a cheap show with lots of low-priced tickets.

Show B has too many tickets at £40 and should spread them more broadly.

Show C is an expensive show which has a handful of cheaper tickets to be accessible.

Show D is an expensive show which is trying to mitigate bad PR by having a very small number of tickets priced lower than any other show, when in reality most tickets are at £50 or above.

Show E is the ideal price distribution, with lots of price bands, most tickets sat in the middle, and a handful at the upper and lower ends tapering off to each side for the smaller niches of the market.

Weeks Out

Use case: A birds-eye view of how future performance weeks are selling in comparison to past weeks; a tracker to expose when future weeks are tracking behind trajectory; and a forecast of how sales will grow moving forwards.

Audience: Sales and marketing teams, producers.

Construction: The Weeks Out is the first report I request when working on a show because it communicates so much about how a show is selling and what its future looks like.

Weeks Out is amongst the most daunting charts which a sales manager will encounter, but you'll come to see that it is in fact is the most incredible resource at your disposal, with a density of insight that allows you to understand the show through a number of lenses out of a single page. Once you understand it, it isn't actually too difficult to build or update. It has been adopted by thousands of shows because of its strength and versatility.

Each week, say on a Monday, input the latest total gross sales for each week of performances into the sheet, arranged by the number of weeks until performance. Hence last week's performances will go in the cell furthest top-right, followed by this week's performances one cell down and to the left, then next week's performances down and to the left of that, and so forth. It produces a cross-tab matrix where the X axis is the number of weeks until performance and Y is the performance week commencing. Then apply conditional formatting to the vertical columns where green is the highest number and red the lowest.

Zero weeks out represents the week commencing the Monday of the week of performances. One week out represents the week commencing one Monday before that, and so forth.

Gross Advance

Performances	Week Commencing	12	11	10	9	8	7	6	5	4	3	2	1	0	Mature
8	7/1/2019	£ 85,731	£ 93,563	£ 103,553	£ 112,604	£ 120,242	£ 129,741	£ 144,511	£ 161,018	£ 174,908	£ 196,325	£ 222,239	£ 254,449	£ 316,995	£ 377,224
8	14/1/2019	£ 96,348	£ 109,881	£ 116,807	£ 125,893	£ 134,086	£ 149,105	£ 163,340	£ 179,128	£ 195,812	£ 218,560	£ 234,908	£ 250,376	£ 305,354	£ 351,157
8	21/1/2019	£ 64,007	£ 71,379	£ 77,013	£ 91,418	£ 104,484	£ 114,994	£ 130,288	£ 146,391	£ 163,024	£ 184,154	£ 205,487	£ 244,598	£ 330,786	£ 383,712
8	28/1/2019	£ 65,590	£ 72,736	£ 84,340	£ 93,849	£ 103,302	£ 115,392	£ 129,374	£ 143,627	£ 160,122	£ 181,891	£ 207,656	£ 238,339	£ 310,344	£ 384,827
8	4/2/2019	£ 53,473	£ 62,831	£ 70,820	£ 79,964	£ 89,502	£ 102,960	£ 119,020	£ 132,391	£ 143,675	£ 162,434	£ 184,001	£ 210,306	£ 298,174	£ 369,736
8	11/2/2019	£ 54,472	£ 60,745	£ 67,617	£ 74,567	£ 86,709	£ 97,886	£ 106,641	£ 118,359	£ 136,193	£ 155,260	£ 173,851	£ 202,209	£ 316,617	£ 399,439
8	18/2/2019	£ 57,818	£ 63,627	£ 70,850	£ 79,492	£ 89,659	£ 104,127	£ 116,945	£ 135,594	£ 154,540	£ 169,780	£ 186,226	£ 236,031	£ 354,405	£ 426,730
8	25/2/2019	£ 58,648	£ 62,858	£ 69,287	£ 77,078	£ 90,645	£ 98,589	£ 115,963	£ 128,683	£ 141,665	£ 157,445	£ 189,087	£ 236,012	£ 328,958	£ 379,991
8	4/3/2019	£ 63,624	£ 72,886	£ 80,303	£ 89,630	£ 98,980	£ 116,816	£ 127,587	£ 141,239	£ 155,238	£ 174,609	£ 210,101	£ 241,178	£ 331,658	£ 386,340
8	11/3/2019	£ 51,698	£ 56,013	£ 64,580	£ 71,003	£ 84,432	£ 92,803	£ 100,894	£ 114,407	£ 134,459	£ 164,785	£ 185,550	£ 220,940	£ 332,422	£ 390,458
8	18/3/2019	£ 58,088	£ 64,404	£ 71,887	£ 78,080	£ 87,625	£ 98,024	£ 104,437	£ 124,002	£ 142,362	£ 160,718	£ 185,344	£ 234,812	£ 347,147	£ 426,991
8	25/3/2019	£ 73,439	£ 79,270	£ 89,786	£ 97,696	£ 105,539	£ 117,238	£ 135,210	£ 150,285	£ 166,039	£ 183,849	£ 213,588	£ 263,352	£ 342,783	
8	1/4/2019	£ 72,934	£ 80,863	£ 88,256	£ 101,580	£ 109,805	£ 125,210	£ 139,143	£ 155,573	£ 176,591	£ 201,711	£ 227,816	£ 263,838		
8	8/4/2019	£ 73,514	£ 80,287	£ 90,079	£ 98,005	£ 112,441	£ 122,685	£ 139,570	£ 155,290	£ 182,331	£ 213,443	£ 248,050			
8	15/4/2019	£ 66,183	£ 70,788	£ 78,425	£ 91,266	£ 99,744	£ 115,366	£ 128,074	£ 153,191	£ 181,989	£ 213,789				
8	22/4/2019	£ 73,244	£ 76,151	£ 84,607	£ 94,841	£ 105,757	£ 115,117	£ 135,286	£ 160,285	£ 184,078					
8	29/4/2019	£ 70,110	£ 77,279	£ 87,346	£ 94,277	£ 107,665	£ 119,225	£ 138,104	£ 161,538						
8	6/5/2019	£ 55,841	£ 65,234	£ 71,846	£ 79,513	£ 90,755	£ 108,571	£ 130,573							
8	13/5/2019	£ 55,704	£ 61,697	£ 66,950	£ 76,296	£ 89,821	£ 110,889								
8	20/5/2019	£ 57,566	£ 63,210	£ 72,246	£ 83,254	£ 99,322									
8	27/5/2019	£ 56,626	£ 65,299	£ 77,814	£ 96,857										
8	3/6/2019	£ 85,120	£ 94,460	£ 104,791											
8	10/6/2019	£ 98,684	£ 107,948												
8	17/6/2019	£ 97,867													
	Average gross	£ 64,500	£ 71,902	£ 79,732	£ 88,507	£ 99,061	£ 110,949	£ 123,545	£ 138,622	£ 154,727	£ 175,087	£ 198,586	£ 233,568	£ 324,805	£ 388,782
	Average % of mature	17%	18%	21%	23%	25%	29%	32%	36%	40%	45%	51%	60%	84%	100%

Comprehension: There are a number of ways to read the weeks out.

1. Eyeing down the matured sales column shows how historic weeks have finished, which is useful to benchmark where sales usually get to. Looking at the furthest right (i.e. the most up-to-date) numbers for each row shows what the load-in for each week currently is, and gives a top-level view of how the advance is distributed, useful for knowing which weeks are problem-areas and where you may have opportunity to increase prices. Use this top-level information about weeks which are doing well and poorly as a jumping-off point for more granular investigation into performances.

2. The colour-coding shows which performance weeks are comparatively tracking behind others. The way this works is to look at a particular number of weeks out (e.g. five weeks out) and compare how a given performance week is currently loaded-in, compared to other weeks at the same number of weeks out. The reason why this is helpful is because, whilst you might know what a performance week needs to finish on, you won't instinctively know what is a good or bad advance at five weeks out, and this helps to direct your attention. The beauty is that you can even do this before you've had any performances mature, because there will already be another four weeks of benchmarking data available.

3. Reading across each row of performance weeks horizontally shows how they have built. Turning from red to amber is good, as it shows that a week which had previously been underperforming has now caught up the lost ground. Turning from green to amber is bad, as it shows that sales have comparatively slowed over time.

Nuances: Colour coding purely by gross advance can be skewed by weeks which have more or fewer performances than usual. To mitigate this, instead apply colouring based on average advance per performance. You'd do this by dividing the total advance for the week by the number of performances in the week, and using this figure for your colour-scale. It is particularly useful around holidays where extra performances are played, and in the first week which often has a different schedule with fewer performances due to the rehearsal schedule.

As well as the basic revenue advance table, you can also create variations for ticket advance, average revenue per performance, week-to-week movement.

It's possible to see the impact of promotions within a weeks out as they appear as a highlighted diagonal line. In the example gross movement report below, the promotion which ran on 11/2/19 is clear because the wraps are higher at week 0 for 11/2/19, at week 1 for 18/2/19 and at week 3 for 25/2/19.

Forecasting is straightforward using the weeks out. Take the average week-to-week movement at zero weeks out, and it will give you an estimate of how much you should expect to move in the current week. Add it to your current advance for this week's performances, and you have an estimate of where the current week will mature. Expand on this basis to all future weeks and you can immediately tell where you are currently tracking to mature at, and where you need to concentrate efforts to boost sales. I put historical actuals in grey, and forecasts in black as a way to see where sales are tracking to end up. Columns at the right hand side show what the target is, what the latest forecast is, and the delta. This is useful for highlighting any weeks which are unlikely to make target and encourages preemptive action to bring them back on course before the problem worsens.

In these examples I have shown a 12-weeks out, however if you have a show with a longer consideration period, and where the average weeks out is greater than about five, then you may choose to produce a 24-weeks out table. It makes for a larger document but the logic in creating it is exactly the same — you just include more historic data.

Gross Movement

Performances	Week Commencing	12	11	10	9	8	7	6	5	4	3	2	1	0	Mature
8	7/1/2019		£ 7,832	£ 9,990	£ 9,051	£ 7,638	£ 9,499	£ 14,770	£ 16,507	£ 13,890	£ 21,417	£ 25,914	£ 32,210	£ 62,546	£ 60,229
8	14/1/2019		£ 13,533	£ 6,926	£ 9,086	£ 8,193	£ 15,019	£ 14,235	£ 15,788	£ 16,684	£ 22,748	£ 16,348	£ 15,468	£ 54,978	£ 45,803
8	21/1/2019		£ 7,372	£ 5,634	£ 14,405	£ 13,066	£ 10,510	£ 15,294	£ 16,103	£ 16,633	£ 21,130	£ 21,333	£ 39,111	£ 86,188	£ 52,926
8	28/1/2019		£ 7,146	£ 11,604	£ 9,509	£ 9,453	£ 12,090	£ 13,982	£ 14,253	£ 16,495	£ 21,769	£ 25,765	£ 30,683	£ 72,005	£ 74,483
8	4/2/2019		£ 9,358	£ 7,989	£ 9,144	£ 9,538	£ 13,458	£ 16,060	£ 13,371	£ 11,284	£ 18,759	£ 21,567	£ 26,305	£ 87,868	£ 71,562
8	11/2/2019		£ 6,273	£ 6,872	£ 6,950	£ 12,142	£ 11,177	£ 8,755	£ 11,718	£ 17,834	£ 19,067	£ 18,591	£ 28,358	£ 114,408	£ 82,822
8	18/2/2019		£ 5,809	£ 7,223	£ 8,642	£ 10,167	£ 14,468	£ 12,818	£ 18,649	£ 18,946	£ 15,240	£ 16,446	£ 49,805	£ 118,374	£ 72,325
8	25/2/2019		£ 4,210	£ 6,429	£ 7,791	£ 13,567	£ 7,944	£ 17,374	£ 12,720	£ 12,982	£ 15,780	£ 31,642	£ 46,925	£ 92,946	£ 51,033
8	4/3/2019		£ 9,262	£ 7,417	£ 9,327	£ 9,350	£ 17,836	£ 10,771	£ 13,652	£ 13,999	£ 19,371	£ 35,492	£ 31,077	£ 90,480	£ 54,682
7	11/3/2019		£ 4,315	£ 8,567	£ 6,423	£ 13,429	£ 8,371	£ 8,091	£ 13,513	£ 20,052	£ 30,326	£ 20,765	£ 35,390	£ 111,482	£ 58,036
8	18/3/2019		£ 6,316	£ 7,483	£ 6,193	£ 9,545	£ 10,399	£ 6,413	£ 19,565	£ 18,360	£ 18,356	£ 24,626	£ 49,468	£ 112,335	£ 79,844
8	25/3/2019		£ 5,831	£ 10,516	£ 7,910	£ 7,843	£ 11,699	£ 17,972	£ 15,075	£ 15,754	£ 17,810	£ 29,739	£ 49,764	£ 79,431	
7	1/4/2019		£ 7,929	£ 7,393	£ 13,324	£ 8,225	£ 15,405	£ 13,933	£ 16,430	£ 21,018	£ 25,120	£ 26,105	£ 36,022		
8	8/4/2019		£ 6,773	£ 9,792	£ 7,926	£ 14,436	£ 10,244	£ 16,885	£ 15,720	£ 27,041	£ 31,112	£ 34,607			
8	15/4/2019		£ 4,605	£ 7,637	£ 12,841	£ 8,478	£ 15,622	£ 12,708	£ 25,117	£ 28,798	£ 31,800				
8	22/4/2019		£ 2,907	£ 8,456	£ 10,234	£ 10,916	£ 9,360	£ 20,169	£ 24,999	£ 23,793					
8	29/4/2019		£ 7,169	£ 10,067	£ 6,931	£ 13,388	£ 11,560	£ 18,879	£ 23,434						
8	6/5/2019		£ 9,393	£ 6,612	£ 7,667	£ 11,242	£ 17,816	£ 22,002							
8	13/5/2019		£ 5,993	£ 5,253	£ 9,346	£ 13,525	£ 21,068								
8	20/5/2019		£ 5,644	£ 9,036	£ 11,008	£ 16,068									
8	27/5/2019		£ 8,673	£ 12,515	£ 19,043										
8	3/6/2019		£ 9,340	£ 10,331											
8	10/6/2019		£ 9,264												
8	17/6/2019														
Average Movement			£ 7,172	£ 8,352	£ 9,655	£ 11,010	£ 12,818	£ 14,506	£ 16,860	£ 18,348	£ 21,987	£ 24,924	£ 36,199	£ 90,253	£ 63,977

Forecasting

Performances	Week Commencing	12	11	10	9	8	7	6	5	4	3	2	1	0	Mature	Target	Latest Projection - Target
8	7/1/2019	£ 85,731	£ 93,563	£ 103,553	£ 112,604	£ 120,242	£ 129,741	£ 144,511	£ 161,018	£ 174,908	£ 196,325	£ 222,239	£ 254,449	£ 316,995	£ 377,224		
8	14/1/2019	£ 96,348	£ 109,881	£ 116,807	£ 125,893	£ 134,086	£ 149,105	£ 163,340	£ 179,128	£ 195,812	£ 218,560	£ 234,908	£ 250,376	£ 305,354	£ 351,157		
8	21/1/2019	£ 64,007	£ 71,379	£ 77,013	£ 91,418	£ 104,484	£ 114,994	£ 130,288	£ 146,391	£ 163,024	£ 184,154	£ 205,487	£ 244,598	£ 330,786	£ 383,712		
8	28/1/2019	£ 65,590	£ 72,736	£ 84,340	£ 93,849	£ 103,302	£ 115,392	£ 129,374	£ 143,627	£ 160,122	£ 181,891	£ 207,656	£ 238,339	£ 310,344	£ 384,827		
8	4/2/2019	£ 53,473	£ 62,831	£ 70,820	£ 79,964	£ 89,502	£ 102,960	£ 119,020	£ 132,391	£ 143,675	£ 162,434	£ 184,001	£ 210,306	£ 298,174	£ 369,736		
8	11/2/2019	£ 54,472	£ 60,745	£ 67,617	£ 74,567	£ 86,709	£ 97,886	£ 106,641	£ 118,359	£ 136,193	£ 155,260	£ 173,851	£ 202,209	£ 316,617	£ 389,439		
8	18/2/2019	£ 57,818	£ 63,627	£ 70,850	£ 79,492	£ 89,659	£ 104,127	£ 116,945	£ 135,594	£ 154,540	£ 169,780	£ 186,226	£ 236,031	£ 344,405	£ 416,730		
8	25/2/2019	£ 58,648	£ 62,858	£ 69,287	£ 77,078	£ 90,645	£ 98,589	£ 115,963	£ 128,683	£ 141,665	£ 157,445	£ 189,087	£ 226,012	£ 318,958	£ 369,991		
8	4/3/2019	£ 63,624	£ 72,886	£ 80,303	£ 89,630	£ 98,980	£ 116,816	£ 127,587	£ 141,239	£ 155,238	£ 174,609	£ 199,101	£ 231,178	£ 321,658	£ 376,340		
8	11/3/2019	£ 51,698	£ 56,013	£ 64,580	£ 71,003	£ 84,432	£ 92,803	£ 100,894	£ 114,407	£ 134,459	£ 154,785	£ 175,550	£ 210,940	£ 322,422	£ 380,458		
8	18/3/2019	£ 58,088	£ 64,404	£ 71,887	£ 78,080	£ 87,625	£ 98,024	£ 104,437	£ 124,002	£ 142,362	£ 160,718	£ 185,344	£ 234,812	£ 347,147	£ 426,991		
8	25/3/2019	£ 73,439	£ 79,270	£ 89,786	£ 97,696	£ 105,539	£ 117,238	£ 135,210	£ 150,285	£ 166,039	£ 183,849	£ 213,588	£ 263,352	£ 342,783	£ 342,783	£ 380,000	-£ 37,217
8	1/4/2019	£ 72,934	£ 80,863	£ 88,256	£ 101,580	£ 109,805	£ 125,210	£ 139,143	£ 155,573	£ 176,591	£ 201,711	£ 227,816	£ 263,838	£ 263,838	£ 263,838	£ 390,000	-£ 126,162
8	8/4/2019	£ 73,514	£ 80,287	£ 90,079	£ 98,005	£ 112,441	£ 122,685	£ 139,570	£ 155,290	£ 182,331	£ 213,443	£ 248,050	£ 248,050	£ 248,050	£ 248,050	£ 390,000	-£ 141,950
8	15/4/2019	£ 66,183	£ 70,788	£ 78,425	£ 91,266	£ 99,744	£ 115,366	£ 128,074	£ 153,191	£ 181,989	£ 213,789	£ 213,789	£ 213,789	£ 213,789	£ 213,789	£ 400,000	-£ 186,211
8	22/4/2019	£ 73,244	£ 76,151	£ 84,607	£ 94,841	£ 105,757	£ 115,117	£ 135,286	£ 160,285	£ 184,078	£ 184,078	£ 184,078	£ 184,078	£ 184,078	£ 184,078	£ 400,000	-£ 215,922
8	29/4/2019	£ 70,110	£ 77,279	£ 87,346	£ 94,277	£ 107,665	£ 119,225	£ 138,104	£ 161,538	£ 161,538	£ 161,538	£ 161,538	£ 161,538	£ 161,538	£ 161,538	£ 400,000	-£ 238,462
8	6/5/2019	£ 55,841	£ 65,234	£ 71,846	£ 79,513	£ 90,755	£ 108,571	£ 130,573	£ 130,573	£ 130,573	£ 130,573	£ 130,573	£ 130,573	£ 130,573	£ 130,573	£ 400,000	-£ 269,427
8	13/5/2019	£ 55,704	£ 61,697	£ 66,950	£ 76,296	£ 89,821	£ 110,889	£ 110,889	£ 110,889	£ 110,889	£ 110,889	£ 110,889	£ 110,889	£ 110,889	£ 110,889	£ 400,000	-£ 289,111
8	20/5/2019	£ 57,566	£ 63,210	£ 72,246	£ 83,254	£ 99,322	£ 99,322	£ 99,322	£ 99,322	£ 99,322	£ 99,322	£ 99,322	£ 99,322	£ 99,322	£ 99,322	£ 400,000	-£ 300,678
8	27/5/2019	£ 56,626	£ 65,299	£ 77,814	£ 96,857	£ 96,857	£ 96,857	£ 96,857	£ 96,857	£ 96,857	£ 96,857	£ 96,857	£ 96,857	£ 96,857	£ 96,857	£ 400,000	-£ 303,143
8	3/6/2019	£ 85,120	£ 94,460	£ 104,791	£ 104,791	£ 104,791	£ 104,791	£ 104,791	£ 104,791	£ 104,791	£ 104,791	£ 104,791	£ 104,791	£ 104,791	£ 104,791	£ 400,000	-£ 295,209
8	10/6/2019	£ 98,684	£ 107,948	£ 107,948	£ 107,948	£ 107,948	£ 107,948	£ 107,948	£ 107,948	£ 107,948	£ 107,948	£ 107,948	£ 107,948	£ 107,948	£ 107,948	£ 400,000	-£ 292,052
8	17/6/2019	£ 97,867	£ 97,867	£ 97,867	£ 97,867	£ 97,867	£ 97,867	£ 97,867	£ 97,867	£ 97,867	£ 97,867	£ 97,867	£ 97,867	£ 97,867	£ 97,867	£ 400,000	-£ 302,133

Ticket Advance

Performances	Week Commencing	12	11	10	9	8	7	6	5	4	3	2	1	0	Mature
8	7/1/2019	1,649	1,800	1,954	2,125	2,227	2,317	2,581	3,157	3,200	3,385	4,116	4,626	5,661	7,397
8	14/1/2019	1,633	2,073	2,204	2,375	2,438	2,616	2,970	3,036	3,497	3,903	4,517	4,900	5,872	6,753
8	21/1/2019	1,143	1,373	1,481	1,793	2,009	2,100	2,208	2,524	3,076	3,348	3,543	4,704	6,241	7,524
8	28/1/2019	1,238	1,276	1,506	1,676	1,878	1,990	2,193	2,762	3,079	3,083	3,993	4,497	5,542	7,546
8	4/2/2019	1,048	1,083	1,336	1,428	1,570	2,019	2,052	2,546	2,612	3,124	3,472	4,124	5,626	6,722
8	11/2/2019	956	1,104	1,252	1,434	1,636	1,748	1,871	2,321	2,670	3,044	3,219	3,427	5,555	8,212
8	18/2/2019	1,071	1,248	1,300	1,529	1,546	1,893	2,207	2,421	3,030	3,329	3,600	4,215	7,378	8,311
8	25/2/2019	1,150	1,200	1,260	1,306	1,619	1,700	1,965	2,340	2,401	3,087	3,317	4,965	6,799	7,271
8	4/3/2019	1,097	1,302	1,575	1,660	1,678	2,049	2,162	2,716	2,772	3,358	4,493	5,362	7,307	7,602
7	11/3/2019	940	949	1,095	1,315	1,564	1,751	1,978	2,200	2,586	3,814	4,251	5,136	6,758	7,675
8	18/3/2019	1,117	1,130	1,218	1,346	1,565	1,815	1,899	2,138	2,498	2,820	3,141	4,604	6,429	7,362
8	25/3/2019	1,245	1,468	1,575	1,776	1,885	2,171	2,651	2,947	2,965	3,405	3,955	4,788	5,910	
7	1/4/2019	1,302	1,555	1,605	1,881	2,153	2,362	2,676	2,829	3,045	3,735	4,142	5,074		
8	8/4/2019	1,387	1,409	1,553	1,849	1,906	2,231	2,737	2,773	3,440	4,185	4,510			
8	15/4/2019	1,298	1,300	1,538	1,601	1,956	2,098	2,247	2,736	3,309	3,686				
8	22/4/2019	1,285	1,410	1,659	1,700	1,923	2,214	2,553	3,082	3,540					
8	29/4/2019	1,298	1,332	1,680	1,700	1,889	2,056	2,511	3,167						
8	6/5/2019	1,095	1,208	1,239	1,371	1,780	1,840	2,560							
8	13/5/2019	960	1,210	1,300	1,413	1,727	1,945								
8	20/5/2019	1,047	1,129	1,246	1,514	1,874									
8	27/5/2019	1,089	1,126	1,415	1,794										
8	3/6/2019	1,443	1,817	1,871											
8	10/6/2019	1,762	2,076												
8	17/6/2019	1,847													

Ticket Movement

Performances	Week Commencing	12	11	10	9	8	7	6	5	4	3	2	1	0	Mature
8	7/1/2019		151	154	171	102	90	264	577	43	185	731	511	1,034	1,736
8	14/1/2019		440	131	171	63	178	354	66	461	406	615	383	972	881
8	21/1/2019		230	108	311	217	91	108	316	552	272	195	1,161	1,537	1,283
8	28/1/2019		39	230	170	202	111	203	569	317	4	910	504	1,045	2,004
8	4/2/2019		35	253	92	142	449	33	494	66	511	348	652	1,502	1,097
8	11/2/2019		149	148	182	202	112	123	450	350	374	175	208	2,127	2,657
8	18/2/2019		177	52	229	17	347	313	215	609	299	271	615	3,163	933
8	25/2/2019		50	60	47	312	81	266	374	61	686	230	1,648	1,834	472
8	4/3/2019		205	273	85	18	372	113	554	56	586	1,135	869	1,945	295
7	11/3/2019		9	145	220	249	187	227	222	386	1,229	437	885	1,621	917
8	18/3/2019		13	89	128	219	251	84	239	360	322	322	1,463	1,824	933
8	25/3/2019		223	107	201	108	286	480	296	18	440	551	833	1,122	
7	1/4/2019		253	50	276	272	209	313	153	216	691	407	932		
8	8/4/2019		21	145	296	57	325	506	36	667	745	325			
8	15/4/2019		2	238	63	355	142	149	489	573	377				
8	22/4/2019		125	249	41	223	291	339	530	458					
8	29/4/2019		34	347	20	189	167	455	656						
8	6/5/2019		113	31	132	409	61	720							
8	13/5/2019		249	90	113	314	218								
8	20/5/2019		82	117	268	360									
8	27/5/2019		37	289	379										
8	3/6/2019		374	55											
8	10/6/2019		314												
8	17/6/2019														
	Average Movement		145	153	171	201	209	281	367	325	475	475	820	1,644	1,201

Lead time

Use case: Establishing a consistent definition for short-term, medium-term, and long-term. These also form the first part of the "tracking target" chart.

Audience: Sales and marketing teams, producers.

Comprehension: Everyone has their own idea of what constitutes "short-term," so it can be helpful to define it within the context of your show or organisation. This enables you to run more meaningful short-, medium-, and long-term advertising campaigns, and measure their success.

As we are defining something foundational, it isn't a number which we would want to change often — or ever. So it's best to conduct this exercise based on at least six months of data for a single production, or based on several years of data for an organisation. Anything less than that and your data may be skewed by unusual short-term patterns, and you'll forever be chasing an out-of-reach KPI.

Construction: As your data source, use all of the matured weeks on a weeks out report. For each number of weeks out calculate the average percentage of matured gross across all performance weeks. Anything less than 33% is long term, 33% to 66% is medium term, and greater than 66% is short term.

In this example, long-term is any booking made more than six weeks out, medium-term is between two and six weeks, and short-term is either in the week of performance or the week before. Marketing colleagues will use this to help them schedule campaigns which launch at the right time in consumers' consideration period, you will use it for tracking whether sales are on track, and producers will take confidence from it by knowing that your audiences don't usually book thirty weeks before the performance, and advance booking starts at six weeks out.

Nuance: It's also possible to calculate lead time using tickets rather than gross, and you will probably get a slightly different result — most likely because you are consistently selling cheap tickets short-term. I recommend that you choose either tickets or revenue, with a bias towards revenue, as that is what typically matters for a show's success. Don't confuse matters by mixing the two.

Trajectory

Performances	Week Commencing	12	11	10	9	8	7	6	5	4	3	2	1	0	Mature
8	7/1/2019	£ 85,731	£ 93,563	£ 103,553	£ 112,604	£ 120,242	£ 129,741	£ 144,511	£ 161,018	£ 174,908	£ 196,325	£ 222,239	£ 254,449	£ 316,995	£ 377,224
8	14/1/2019	£ 96,348	£ 109,881	£ 116,807	£ 125,893	£ 134,086	£ 149,105	£ 163,340	£ 179,128	£ 195,812	£ 218,560	£ 234,908	£ 250,376	£ 305,354	£ 351,157
8	21/1/2019	£ 64,007	£ 71,379	£ 77,013	£ 91,418	£ 104,484	£ 114,994	£ 130,288	£ 146,391	£ 163,024	£ 184,154	£ 205,487	£ 244,598	£ 330,786	£ 383,712
8	28/1/2019	£ 65,590	£ 72,736	£ 84,340	£ 93,849	£ 103,302	£ 115,392	£ 129,374	£ 143,627	£ 160,122	£ 181,891	£ 207,656	£ 238,339	£ 310,344	£ 384,827
8	4/2/2019	£ 53,473	£ 62,831	£ 70,820	£ 79,964	£ 89,502	£ 102,960	£ 119,020	£ 132,391	£ 143,675	£ 162,434	£ 184,001	£ 210,306	£ 298,174	£ 369,736
8	11/2/2019	£ 54,472	£ 60,745	£ 67,617	£ 74,567	£ 86,709	£ 97,886	£ 106,641	£ 118,359	£ 136,193	£ 155,260	£ 173,851	£ 202,209	£ 316,617	£ 389,439
8	18/2/2019	£ 57,818	£ 63,627	£ 70,850	£ 79,492	£ 89,659	£ 104,127	£ 116,945	£ 135,594	£ 154,540	£ 169,780	£ 186,226	£ 236,031	£ 344,405	£ 416,730
8	25/2/2019	£ 58,648	£ 62,858	£ 69,287	£ 77,078	£ 90,645	£ 98,589	£ 115,963	£ 128,683	£ 141,665	£ 157,445	£ 189,087	£ 226,012	£ 318,958	£ 369,991
8	4/3/2019	£ 63,624	£ 72,886	£ 80,303	£ 89,630	£ 98,980	£ 116,816	£ 127,587	£ 141,239	£ 155,238	£ 174,609	£ 199,101	£ 231,178	£ 321,658	£ 376,340
8	11/3/2019	£ 51,698	£ 56,013	£ 64,580	£ 71,003	£ 84,432	£ 92,803	£ 100,894	£ 114,407	£ 134,459	£ 154,785	£ 175,550	£ 210,940	£ 322,422	£ 380,458
8	18/3/2019	£ 58,088	£ 64,404	£ 71,887	£ 78,080	£ 87,625	£ 98,024	£ 104,437	£ 124,002	£ 142,362	£ 160,718	£ 185,344	£ 234,812	£ 347,147	£ 426,991
Average gross		£ 64,500	£ 71,902	£ 79,732	£ 88,507	£ 99,061	£ 110,949	£ 123,545	£ 138,622	£ 154,727	£ 174,178	£ 196,677	£ 230,841	£ 321,169	£ 384,237
Average % of mature		17%	19%	21%	23%	26%	29%	32%	36%	40%	45%	51%	60%	84%	100%
Weeks		13	12	11	10	9	8	7	6	5	4	3	2	1	0
Category		Long term							Medium term					Short term	

Tracking targets

Use case: Understanding whether future performances are on track to meet their targets. Tracking targets bear resemblance to other analyses but has discrete differences. Whereas the Weeks Out is looking at matured weeks, the tracking targets are focused on advance weeks. Whilst the lead time table provides overall definitions for "long term" and "short term", the tracking targets put these into place by quantifying how many tickets are required to be sold each week, in order to reach target.

Audience: Marketing and sales teams, producers.

Comprehension: The trouble with having targets for performance weeks is that it is difficult to know which weeks are on track to make target, and which are falling behind. This is especially true when targets vary between one performance week and the next.

What this chart does is to take your mature target for each performance week, and then apply a "tracking target" of where it should be at right now, given the number of weeks to go.

For example, your target for performances in the week after next may be £410k, but if the historical data shows that performances at two weeks out should be 60% towards their target, then it only needs to be at £246k right now. We can then compare the actual advance right now (£248k) and establish that the performances are tracking £2k up so far.

The purpose of the chart, therefore, is to gauge whether the trajectory of upcoming performances shows that they are likely to meet their targets, and to quantify how much remedial action is necessary to reset their course if not. It acts as an early-warning system so that you are not surprised by a performance week that doesn't meet its goals.

With a row for each performance week, you can see what the target is for the gross when it matures, what the tracking target is at this point in time, the actual gross right now, and the delta between the actual gross and its tracking target.

Construction: If you have already completed the "lead time" table, you can use this for part one. Otherwise, follow the instructions for the lead time chart to calculate this now.

Then, estimate your sales trajectory. Trajectories tend to be fairly consistent within the same venue and genre, so it is fine to take a weeks out or sales figures from a previous show as a guide here. It doesn't have to be overly accurate, it is simply your best guess for when you expect the sales to come in. If in doubt, the conservative approach is to put higher numbers at more weeks out (eg. 50% sold by 12 weeks out, rather than 10%) as this avoids any misplaced over-confidence.

The "Mature" row is the final figure once all performances from the week have been played.

Week zero is the Monday of the performance week so, if you have performances on Sundays, then there are seven days' worth of sales to be made between week zero and maturing.

Week 1 is the Monday before the Monday of performance week.

You can adjust these figures during the run if they prove to be consistently inaccurate, but the expectation is that that you can forget about these once they are set.

Weeks out	Percentage of target
Mature	100%
0	70%
1	65%
2	60%
3	55%
4	50%
5	45%
6	40%
7	35%
8	30%
9	25%
10	20%
11	15%
12	10%

Once you have the basic table above with your percentage targets for each week, you can construct your full tracking table with real data.

This should be a table with the performance dates down the left side (I have used relative dates in the illustration for clarity), as well as the target mature figure (which never changes). Then, calculate the tracking target by multiplying your mature target for the week, in gross, by the percentage from the basic table above. Next to this, put the actual gross as of today, and in the final column put the tracking target less the actual. Use conditional formatting to emphasise the weeks which are tracking furthest behind target.

In this example, the next two weeks are tracking far above target. Then there is a medium-term problem for weeks 6 to 10, with each performance week around £30k behind where it should be right now. Whilst the the long-term targets are much lower, they are currently on track for where they need to be at this stage. So the marketing team can focus their efforts on the medium-term performances.

You can also plot this table in a chart, with gross on the Y axis and week on the X axis. Plot two sets of data: bars for the actual gross, with a line for the target gross. Wherever the bars end below the line, you know you are tracking behind.

Nuance: The strength of this approach is that it frees you to have wildly varying mature targets with peak- and off-peak weeks, and these numbers will clearly show you which weeks are falling behind.

There may be some times in the year where you feel that the trajectory will differ. My advice is to not vary the trajectory numbers because it can create too much uncertainty with colleagues. Instead, clearly illustrate that numbers are tracking above or behind target, and give a commentary to explain why you think this is - seasonal factors, for example - and that it should return to it's normal level afterwards. You likely have special mature targets for seasonal weeks anyway, so creating special tracking targets as well is an unnecessary level of complexity which does more to befuddle than to assure. You should pay particular attention to weeks where prices or booking patterns deviate from the norm, as you won't be able to count on the usual short-term trends and so proactive action is always preferable if things are not going to plan.

In this example we have looked only at gross revenue, but you can also replicate exactly the same in terms of tickets. It can get a little overwhelming for some colleagues with lots of numbers, so I tend to focus on either gross or tickets.

	Week	Target Mature Gross		Tracking Target Gross	Actual Gross	Target - Actual Gross	Date
Last week	7 Jan 2019	£	400,000	£400,000	£426,991	£26,991	07/01/2019
This week	14 Jan 2019	£	400,000	£280,000	£342,783	£62,783	14/01/2019
Next week	21 Jan 2019	£	400,000	£260,000	£263,838	£3,838	21/01/2019
Week after next	28 Jan 2019	£	410,000	£246,000	£248,050	£2,050	28/01/2019
Etc	4 Feb 2019	£	410,000	£225,500	£213,789	-£11,711	04/02/2019
	11 Feb 2019	£	410,000	£205,000	£184,078	-£20,922	11/02/2019
	18 Feb 2019	£	410,000	£184,500	£161,538	-£22,962	18/02/2019
	25 Feb 2019	£	410,000	£164,000	£130,573	-£33,427	25/02/2019
	4 Mar 2019	£	420,000	£147,000	£110,889	-£36,111	04/03/2019
	11 Mar 2019	£	420,000	£126,000	£99,322	-£26,678	11/03/2019
	18 Mar 2019	£	420,000	£105,000	£96,857	-£8,143	18/03/2019
	25 Mar 2019	£	420,000	£84,000	£104,791	£20,791	25/03/2019
	1 Apr 2019	£	420,000	£63,000	£107,948	£44,948	01/04/2019
	8 Apr 2019	£	420,000	£42,000	£97,867	£55,867	08/04/2019

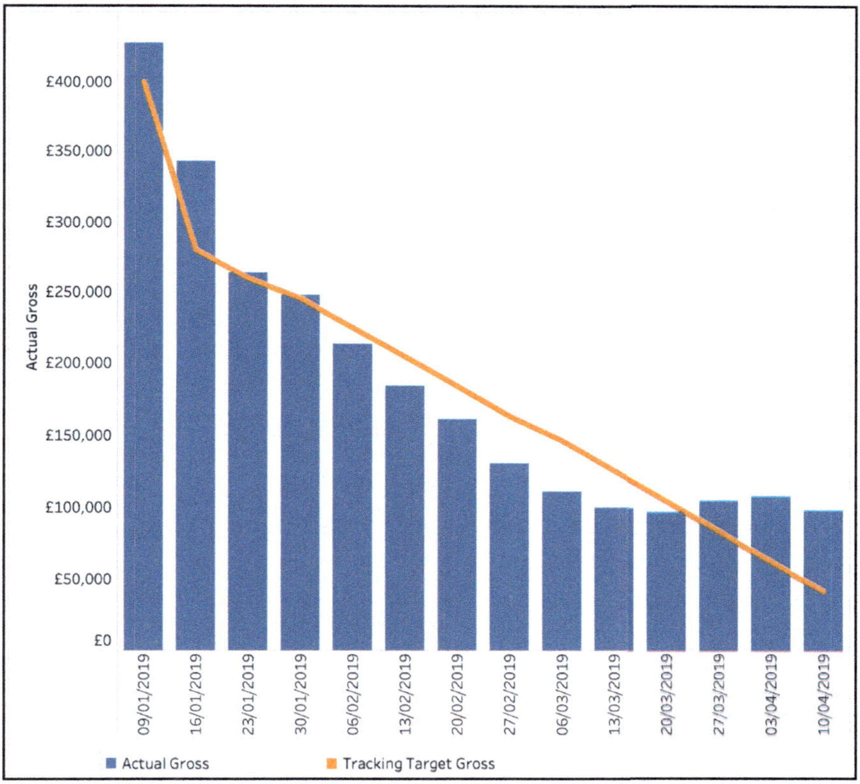

Returning customers by year

Use case: A fantastic high-level view of how well the organisation is engaging the audience to return.

Audience: Marketing teams, senior leadership.

Construction: Using your ticketing database, count the number of customers who booked in each year, and the number of those who were new-to-file versus those who had made a previous booking.

Plot this with the year on the X axis and the percentage of returning visitors on the Y axis. We are looking at percentages of returning customers, rather than absolute numbers.

Comprehension: The graph will start at 0% for the first year where you have data available, and will then shoot up as you re-engage visitors year-on-year. Most likely, it will eventually flatline, and this represents a baseline from which you can set yourself a target to grow.

Nuance: There are inexpensive agencies who will clean and de-dupe your database before the analysis, and this is worth doing, both for this exercise and to reduce costs on your CRM efforts. They will identify customers who have multiple accounts in your database, which is very common when customers forget their passwords or move house, and then merge the accounts together. Generally it brings into stark relief that the size of the database isn't actually as great as first thought, and further motivates staff to work on loyalty.

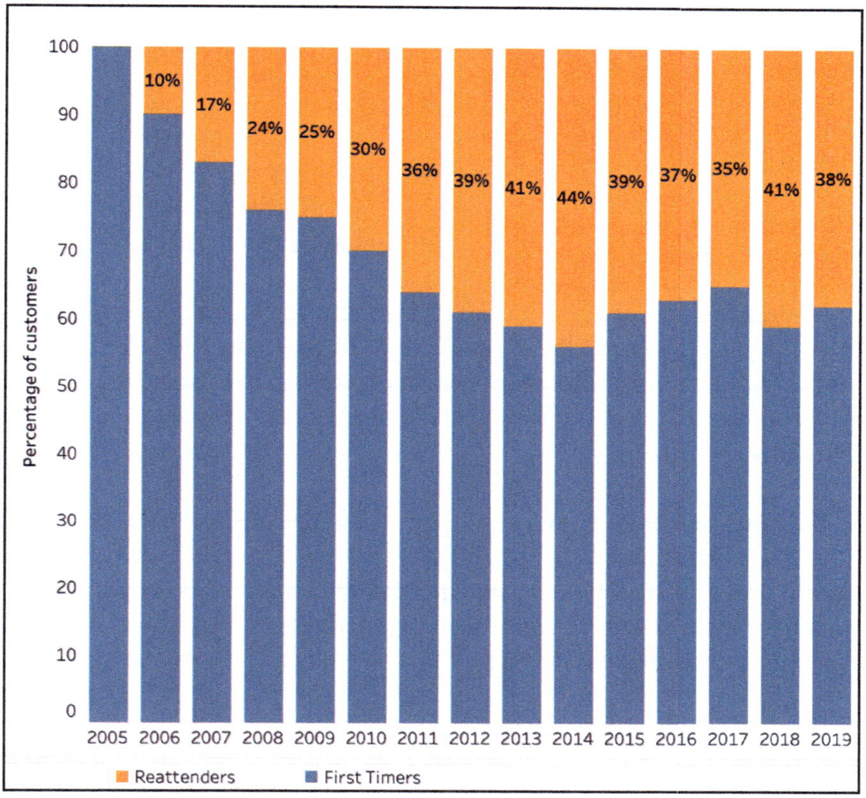

52

---

52 Loyalty at this venue peaked in 2014, when 44% of customers were returning. In the years since 2014, loyalty has been on the decline and new customers have been a larger proportion of the audience — something which the venue should take action to fix, because acquisition is costly.

Dynamic pricing and inventory management

You've toiled to craft the perfect pricing strategy, all the right seats are on sale at all the right prices, and tickets are selling well. So why change the prices now? Two reasons: optimisation and maximisation.

Optimisation is where you were on the right track with a £50 ticket but discover you could actually sell more stock by repricing them to £49. Maximisation is where tickets are selling better than expected and there is opportunity to earn more by increasing the prices of the remaining inventory.

We must recognise the need to adapt when pricing strategies don't yield their desired results. Not all pricing strategies will be successful, and so we should proactively respond to unexpected outcomes. Market dynamics, consumer behaviour and unforeseen external factors can all prompt an adjustment to the original pricing.

Definitions

The key forces which interplay in this chapter are availability, price and demand. They counterbalance one another, so any change made to the supply side will affect the demand side, and vice versa.

Dynamic pricing simply means a change to the advertised price. Contrary to some common misunderstandings, it does not necessitate computer-driven changes, or changes that only move prices upwards. Dynamic pricing can be done every minute or every week, manually or automatically, on one performance or several, and with prices moving up or down. When we refer to dynamic pricing, we simply mean that we alter the price of one ticket from what was previously advertised for sale.

Inventory management is a sibling of dynamic pricing and is concerned with the availability of tickets. The options available with inventory management are to hold off some tickets from sale, to release some previously held tickets, or (in consultation with the producer) to add extra performances on sale. Because they are so closely related, there should be a shared strategy to dynamic pricing and inventory management.

Dynamic pricing and inventory management are always driven by pursuit of a goal. If you've followed the advice in this book so far, that goal will be the one you set before you even went on sale, and will require increasing either occupancy, per-seat yield or per-performance revenue. Measuring progress against this goal will determine whether to move the prices of remaining tickets up or down, or to keep them as they are.

The first step in dynamic pricing is to understand whether prices need to be adjusted, and which ones. The following pages explore the key concepts which can be used to understand whether or not there is room for repricing.

Demand curves

A demand curve is used to show how many tickets consumers want to buy at different prices. When drawn on a graph, the horizontal X axis shows price, and the vertical Y axis shows quantity (how many tickets customers buy).

Usually, the demand curve slopes downward. So as prices increase, the quantity of tickets sold goes down and conversely, as prices go down, the quantity sold increases. If tickets are expensive then fewer people will buy them. But if prices are low, more people will make a purchase.

We can create a demand curve by plotting the actual number of tickets sold at each price point. If the curve is steep (inelastic demand), this means that customers will still buy tickets even if the prices increase. So there may be opportunity to increase revenues by raising ticket prices. If the demand curve is flat (elastic demand), this means that people will buy fewer tickets if prices go up. So, it may be preferable to avoid price rises in case it leads to a drop in sales.

In the diagram, the steep line of the musical shows that its has inelastic demand and so consumers will buy tickets even if prices increase. However the play has a relatively flat line, showing that fewer tickets would be sold if all prices rise.

The demand curve can also help identify optimal pricing points. For instance, if the curve shows that a slight decrease in price could significantly increase the number of tickets sold then it might be worthwhile to lower the price to sell more tickets, and increase overall revenue.

Comparing curves across performance types can help to reveal areas of opportunity. For example, if weekend performances have more inelastic demand then there may be more headroom for higher prices. Whilst midweek matinees might have a flatter curve and therefore need lower prices.

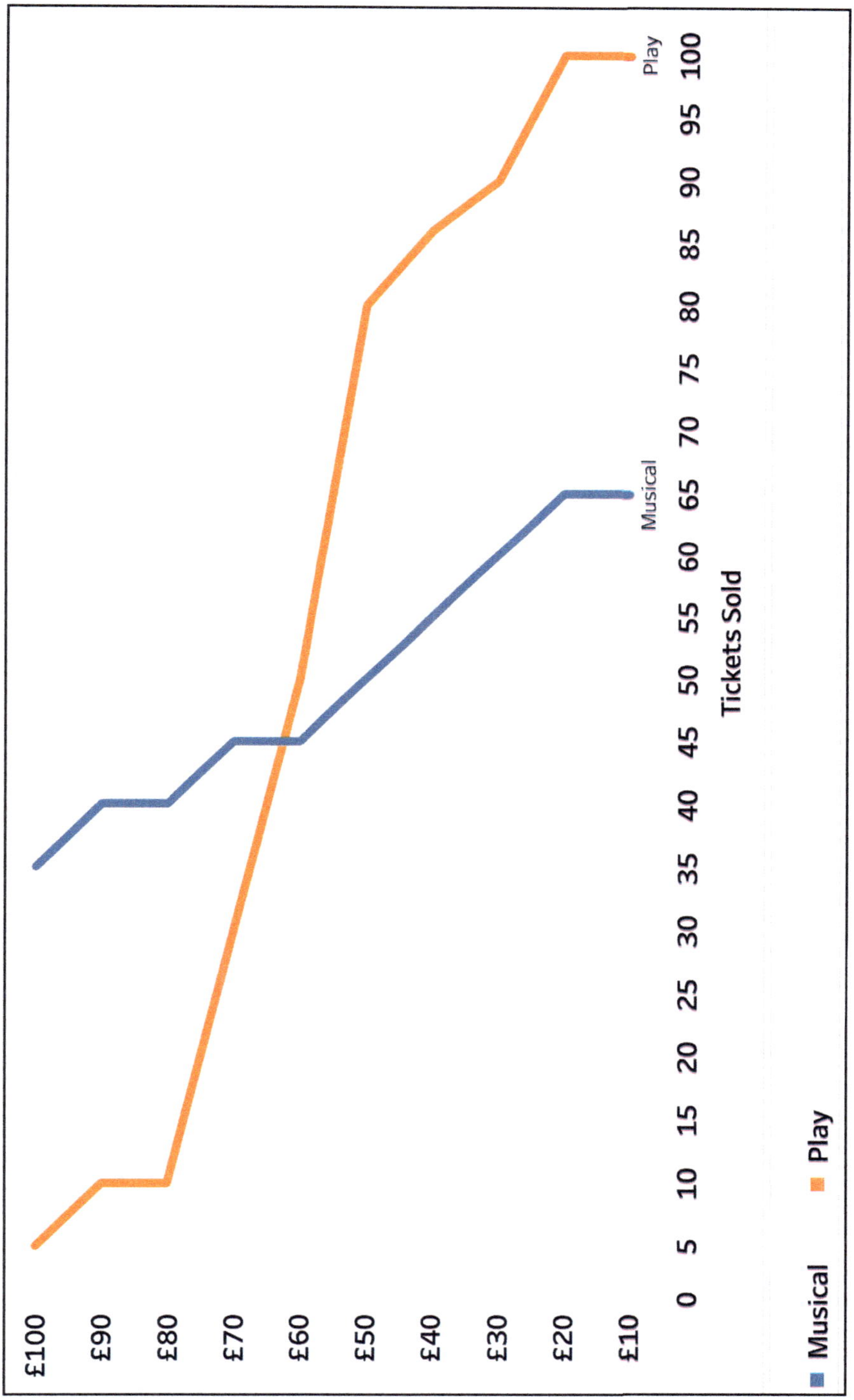
£100
£90
£80
£70
£60
£50
£40
£30
£20
£10
0
5
10
15
20
25
30
35
40
45
50
55
60
65
70
75
80
85
90
95
100
Tickets Sold
Musical
Play
Musical
Play

Consumer price resistance

Price resistance is the threshold at which customers feel the price of a ticket is no longer worth the value they perceive in your product. This point, which is unique to the pairing of each consumer, seat, and performance, means they will decide not to make a purchase. If you're lucky, they will instead seek out a different seat or performance at a price they're willing to pay. If you're unlucky, they will seek out one of your competitors, or decide not to see a show at all.

This can be visualised as the point on the demand curve where a even a small price increase would lead to a substantial drop in quantity purchased. It represents the maximum price most consumers are willing to pay before they start to forgo the purchase.

When tickets are priced too high, we feel the impact of consumer price resistance, as they choose not to buy a ticket at all. Hence there is a need firstly to communicate the value proposition through marketing, and secondly to price tickets within the bounds of how consumers perceive that value.

Homo economicus

We can set out our stall with an expensive weekend tickets and presume that some savvy customers will fill out the otherwise-empty cheaper weekday performances, but it ain't necessarily so. Homo economicus is the theory that humans act perfectly rationally and make buying decisions which maximise the benefits to them[53]. But the reality is that our audiences are Homo Sapiens, not Homo economicus, and they do not behave in perfectly rational ways.

Instead, they may have predetermined that they want to attend on Saturday night because it suits their family's schedule, and when they see Saturday is out of their price range they call it a day, without so much as looking at other performances or realising that advance tickets are cheaper. This is simply too much detail for one simple human to deal with, and so we lose a potential sale.

---

53 Pareto, Vilfredo (1906). "Manual of political economy"

Worse, any nuance is lost when they tell their friends that "the show is too expensive," and after that a whole group of people never looks at our website again.Hence, when pricing, we should always have part of our mind on what a Homo Sapiens' two-second conclusion could be, even whilst we try playing to the logic of Homo economicus.

Implementing dynamic pricing

I think that the paradigm shift from old-school poster advertising to modern-day 24/7 social media advertising is comparable to the change productions feel when moving from "set and forget" pricing to dynamic pricing. Like Dorothy stepping out from black-and-white Kansas into colourful Oz for the first time, this is a whole new world that can be startling for colleagues and producers to handle, so treat it with the same sincerity that all change management deserves.

Impress on colleagues that a willingness to adjust pricing strategies based on realtime feedback and market conditions is needed if you are to make the most from opportunities and achieve your overarching goals. This will require a proactive mindset and much more day-to-day attention than non-dynamic pricing.

Some of the most thorough case studies for dynamic pricing are transparent about the fact that it took several years of trial and error, during which the hours invested were greater than the profit returned, before dynamic pricing started to be a net positive for the organisation. It will be hard, intense work, and require proper buy-in from venue management, producers, marketing and ticketing teams.

A core tenet of dynamic pricing is that the changes should generally be almost imperceptibly small to the consumer, but made so frequently and with such breadth that the aggregate earnings from lots of small marginal gains adds up to something significant. If the changes are large (such as increasing the price of a ticket by 50%) then that is probably a sign that the pricing was wrong in the first place, and should cause you to reconsider your prices more holistically.

You may want to set some parameters, or internal rules of the road, for how dynamic pricing will work. This is so that producers have confidence that the ticketing team is working to an approved standard, and to give the ticketing team day-to-day autonomy in making changes. Done effectively, dynamic pricing moves so quickly that there wouldn't be time to seek approval in the same way as a pricing review dictates, so agreeing parameters upfront allows the ticketing manager to take advantage of fast-moving situations whilst producers are assured that they know the limits of what can happen.

Popular rules of the road to consider are: What is the highest price you would ever want to charge for any ticket? What is the highest price you would want to charge for the seat with the poorest view? What is the lowest price you would ever advertise a ticket for? What size of increment will you move ticket prices by? How frequently will you make dynamic pricing changes? If a seat has been increased in price, is it acceptable to then decrease the price later? How would you deal with an enquiry from a customer who bought seats for more than they are now priced?

The answers here will vary based on the values of your organisation and the commercial goals of the production. My only advice is that the fewer rules you put in place, the greater autonomy it will give the ticketing manager, and hence the greater potential upside which can be earned.

You may also set upon some cosmetic decisions, such as prices always needing to be a whole number (eg. £50 rather than £49.97), or each price level needing to be separated at least £5 away from the next nearest price (so tickets advertised on the same plan at £50 and £55 would be acceptable, but not £50 and £52). You may set a limit on the number of distinct price levels which are ever in use on one plan at a time. Each of these rules acknowledge consumer psychology and ensure that customers have the same great booking process when dynamic prices are in play as they would have with your original, thoroughly thought-out pricing structure.

Dynamic pricing should be led by the realities of actual and forecasted demand for your product, so avoid the pitfall of being overly reactive to competitors. Discussing dynamic pricing among airlines, Robert G. Cross describes a situation where airlines moved prices counter-productively based on what their competitors were doing, rather than on actual consumer demand. He notes that "these weren't strategies at all but knee-jerk reactions to competitors' movements. Now, instead of the CEO controlling prices, [the airline] had its competitors controlling its prices"[54]. Keep an eye on market trends and what competitors are offering, but don't be hoodwinked into an expensive price war. Consumers don't always

---

[54] Cross, R.G. (1998) Revenue management: Hard-core tactics for market domination. New York: Broadway Books.

compare the value of attending one show to another, so don't feel that being undercut by a competitor means that swathes of your audience will leave you. If someone wants to see *Hamilton*, they're not going to buy tickets for *Lion King* simply because they're a few pounds cheaper.

For the same reason, it's also important not to hand over pricing completely to an algorithm. Robert Cross explains that "one of the first questions we had to answer was whether we should give the decision-making function to managers or computers. We decided to use both. The computer would provide the data, and the managers would make the decisions." At the time of writing, artificial intelligence (AI) is making enormous progress each day, but it still remains the case that ticketing managers feel a benefit from supervising the algorithms rather than them being totally self-servicing. There is enough money at stake to make it sensible to have a human backstop, even if the machines are much smarter than us. Based on data alone, algorithms might quite reasonably price up a super-premium ticket for a sold-out show into the high three figures, or even more — a price that a human ticketing manager knows will cause more harm than good.

Dynamic pricing mechanics

Firstly, decide what level of granularity you can work with operationally — the ticketing team must be able to implement whatever you settle on, so remanding every seat four times a day won't work. Common approaches are to look at a week of performances and adjust them all together, or to look at individual performances, or to look at groups of contiguous seats within a performance, or, at the most granular, to look on a seat-by-seat basis. When getting started with dynamic pricing, it can be best to start at a higher level of granularity (like per-week or per-performance) so as to reduce the number of decisions which you have to make and build up confidence around the process.

Then define thresholds which will trigger repricing. For example, if a performance reaches 50% capacity then you may raise all prices by £5, once it gets to 70% you may increase by a further £5, and once it is at 90% you may increase by £5 again. If you auditorium has 1,000 seats, this simple process would generate £7,500 of incremental revenue. (Even with only one hundred seats, it would be an extra £750. Depending on your starting ticket prices, this could be quite a large percentage increase.) It is easy to setup a basic tracking spreadsheet which lays out the current sales by performance and the thresholds at which you'll make changes, and that automatically highlights any which require repricing.

The thresholds exist so that tickets are only increased once there is a base layer of sales and demand has been qualified. This gives assurance that the performance will earn income, and the dynamic pricing uplift is only earned once the base sales have been made.

One downside of this approach is that the uplift is only earned on 50% of tickets, and the first half of a sell-out performance are sold without any uplift. For that reason, I propose two nuances.

Firstly, you should set thresholds which are a matrix of both sales made and days until performance. For example, if there are one hundred days to performance and sales are already at 10%, then increase prices, whereas if there are twenty days to the performance and sales are only at 10%, then decrease prices. This approach acknowledges that sales alone do not define the demand for a performance; they need to be arbitrated alongside the lead-in time. I used this methodology on one long-running musical with a well-defined sales curve, and as a result we were able to make uplifts on

90% of the tickets by spotting a small uptick in demand months ahead of the performance.

If you are working on a smaller show with only one or two performances, spotting these upticks early is more challenging – but you also have much more to gain because you're effectively earning extra income on your entire season, so monitor your sales figures carefully and compare them to similar shows for which you have data.

Performance	Current sales	Price table
1/3/2021 19:30	267	P2
2/3/2021 19:30	96	P1
3/3/2021 19:30	453	P3
4/3/2021 19:30	333	P2
5/3/2021 19:30	623	P4
6/3/2021 19:30	870	P5
7/3/2021 19:30	900	P5
8/3/2021 19:30	928	P5
9/3/2021 19:30	494	P3
10/3/2021 19:30	195	P1
11/3/2021 19:30	150	P1
12/3/2021 19:30	300	P2
13/3/2021 19:30	368	P2
14/3/2021 19:30	250	P2

Price Tables	Threshold
P1 (lowest prices)	< 20% sold
P2	20% : 40% sold
P3	40% : 60% sold
P4	60%: 80% sold
P5 (highest prices)	80%+ sold

Secondly, I suggest that demand does not need to be defined only by sales earned. Indeed, the higher up the marketing funnel you can identify an increase in demand, the more sales you can make with the incremental uplift. For example, more people engaging with your digital advertising than usual, or more people visiting the production webpage, are both early indicators that demand is increasing – even if that demand hasn't yet converted into sales. If you are able to reactively respond to these peaks by increasing pricing rapidly, you can earn incremental revenue when the customers return hours or days later to complete their purchase. This is the equivalent of putting prices up when you see lots of customers walking down the street and heading for your shop, rather than waiting until half a dozen of the new customers have bought a product before repricing. If the signs are there, then you can take action.

Similarly, if you can anticipate that planned marketing activity is due to drive an increase in demand, such as press reviews being published or above-the-line advertising starting, then you can reprice ahead of the sales tracker telling you to.

As a rule of thumb, there is a spurt of demand when a show is announced, which quickly dies down. Then demand for a show increases again once advertising begins and you get closer to first performance, and finally there is heightened demand shortly after opening night due to a combination of a surge in advertising, word of mouth from the early adopters who see it first, and release of production photography, trailers etc. People who had been considering the show are collectively given impetus to book by seeing all of these new marketing assets.

Demand then continues at a relatively stable pace, in line with marketing spend, occasional PR moments and seasonality, before tapering off as the pool of prospects dwindles. In the context of this general framework, at a macro level we would expect ticket prices to increase from on-sale until a while after opening night, and then be gently pulled down to meet dwindling demand. There will of course be smaller adjustments along the way, but this is the broad shape of things.

One exception that I'd like to call out is if the promise of the show is not matched by its execution. One way I've seen this happen was when a title was announced which looked to be the hot ticket of the season — a new play with Hollywood stars and an ace director. Without knowing anything about what the play would be, audiences rushed to book for this title and prices were quickly raised. However, audiences were swiftly disappointed when the play turned out to be a one-star stinker; reviews were terrible, word of mouth was off-putting, and wraps halved overnight.

Another example was when early marketing materials were vague, and only upon release of post-opening photography did customers realise that the show wasn't what they'd imagined it to be.

Both of these shows were able to withstand their sudden decline in wraps because the advances were so strong, but it quickly curtailed any hopes of an extension. For this reason, it's worth remembering that circumstance may force you to bring prices down even once they have reached a lofty height. The fact that you have had strong demand up to opening night does not necessarily mean that it will continue forever, because the customer who buys sight-unseen is not the same as the one who has read the disastrous reviews and seen the photos of the shoddy set.

Finally, per my earlier chapter about being honest with your audiences, this is not an excuse to withhold production photographs or prevent reviewers from visiting. The productions which I mentioned sold tickets in good faith for shows which, on paper, should have been superb, and they were right to show more of the show post-opening in the normal way. It's right to give our customers all of the information which we have at the time to help inform their booking — even when this means that they will choose not to buy. Otherwise they may never return to our theatre.

Rebanding

Rebanding is more granular than uplifting a whole performance, but still relatively straightforward to carry out in most modern ticketing systems. Here, each ticket within a performance increases to the next price band or level, so a ticket which had been advertised as Band C becomes Band B, Band B seats are rebanded to Band A, and so forth. The increments here are usually larger than with true dynamic pricing, so there is a greater risk of reaching consumers' price ceiling and experiencing a sudden drop-off from price resistance. However it can be easy to implement, retains the neatness of the original price structure, and means that you can honour any literature which has been printed with a list of prices (such as a poster that specifies "tickets at £10, £20, £30, £40").

An even more granular way of approaching rebanding is to adjust the bands which individual seats belong to. For example if Band A seats are selling well, then the front row of Band B seats could be rebranded into Band A, whilst leaving the remainder at their original price. This is a more subtle action that will have less impact on the potential uplift, but can delicately cover any smaller changes observed in the demand curve.

Micro-zones

One challenge in rebanding is that it wrongly assumes that all tickets in the same band — or zone — sell equally well. For example, you may have put the first three rows of the circle on at the same price, but the sides of the third row are sure to be less desirable than the centre of the front row. Hence, micro-zones can be created which divide up the primary bands into a smaller granularity. This allows a ticketing manager to then increase the front centre by a small amount — say £2 — whilst retaining the rest of the Band A at its original price. It is a clever balance between the upside of incremental revenue earned from greater granularity, and the minimal effort that comes from rebanding.

Seat-by-seat

This is where a ticketing manager or algorithm will review every seat for every performance, and make adjustments to each one. When done correctly, the upside here is the greatest, because one can leverage highly specific learnings about the demand for individual prices and seats on specific performances at this point in time. For example, your data might show that one seat usually has middling demand but that price resistance is lower than usual for this performance, and hence the seat can be increased in price. This requires a large amount of data, can be time-intensive, and sometimes pushes the technical limits of ticketing systems, but it is the most agile and profitable way to carry out dynamic pricing.

Seat-by-seat is the most practical approach to use for a one-night show or limited season, because there is less historic data to call back on, and a human can rationally make sense of the demand patterns. For a limited-run seasonal show, it can be worthwhile to have a member of staff dedicated to inventory management as they can observe small changes in demand based on the timing of Christmas Day, times of day, and sections of the house — and so make every seat earn its way.

Price wars

Thomas Nagle[55] introduces his concept of "price skimming" with an example of a company facing a new competitor which has no sales, and thus nothing to lose by lowering the price of the generic product. In this hypothetical example, the huge research and development investment the new competitor had made was entirely sunk, but their the manufacturing cost was small — therefore winning sales even at a low price would be a gain for the new company.

Nagle suggests that it would be unwise for the existing company to defend their sales by lowering their own prices to match, as the new entrant could simply keep lowering their price too. As Nagle puts it, "if [the incumbent] were ultimately going to let the competitor have a price advantage, it was better to let them have it at a high price than at a low one. Once the competitor gained some sales, it too would have something to lose from a downward price spiral."

If a company decides to respond to a competitor's price cut, it must consider whether the competitor is willing and able to cut the price again to reestablish the price difference. He advises companies to consider the total cost of a price war, not just the cost of the first shot, before concluding that the cost is worth bearing to defend the sales at risk.

The relevance for putting on shows is that there will always be another new show around the corner which poses some threat to us, but that we should think carefully about our value proposition before diving into price reductions. An established show has more at stake with its longevity than the untested new kid has with its opening splash.

---

[55] Nagle, T., Hogan, J. and Zale, J. (2016) The strategy and tactics of pricing, 5th Edition. Routledge.

Managing risk

Dynamic pricing comes with an added level of risk over "set and forget" pricing. Every time you change a price, you are making a gamble that this will yield better results than your previous approach. When we increase prices, we are trying to get closer to the ceiling of consumer price resistance, but in doing so we always face a threat that we will break the ceiling and consumers will walk away. If we misjudge, then the effects of dynamic pricing can be that fewer tickets are sold and less revenue is earned than would have been by using the original plan from setup.

Customer complaints are more likely with dynamic pricing too, and typical gripes include feeling that the venue is running a "bait and switch" scam where prices start low but are increased when a customer wants to buy, or that it is a deceitful policy to charge customers more who are sat next to one another, or that it is an underhand business practice to change a price once a product is already on sale.

Most of the time, a customer complaint can be easily quelled by a calm conversation with the house manager and a complimentary ice cream, but the worst case is demands for refunds, cancellations of subscription packages, and social media campaigns. Retention is crucial for a venue to thrive, and anything which causes customers to stop coming back will need serious evaluation.

So if one in ten regular audience members stopped attending because of dynamic pricing, then you'd need to be earning at least 10% incremental revenue in order to break even. In fact, that number will be even higher, because the kind of people who re-attend are your most valuable ambassadors, whose reach in promoting the venue and bringing others extends much further than just the tickets they pay for.

One London play, which I wasn't involved in, captured newspaper front pages when it increased its ticket prices from £70 to £400. An outrageous media storm ensued: breakfast TV had interviews with people on the street complaining about how out of touch and unaffordable the West End had become, and how they wouldn't be booking to see the play.

The reality of this story was very different. The play was led by four celebrities at a tiny venue, had virtually sold-out due to incredible reviews, had very accessibly priced tickets at first (which had all sold), and was in its final weeks of performances. As a result, a very, very small number of tickets were put on sale at £400.

Regardless of fact, the incident clearly inflamed the public and gave the wrong impression about Theatreland pricing, forcing the producer to back down — not because consumer demand wasn't there, but because the PR pushback was too great. As a sector, we are grateful to the producer for reverting, because we all need the public to perceive theatre tickets as affordable and accessible, or else we'll all have a harder time filling our auditoria. Even now, £400 is seen as an invisible line in the sand which no play producer in London would dare to cross, and it will be fascinating to see who does so first.

The point of this story is that you must watch out for the early warning signs of resistance to dynamic pricing. After making any changes, closely monitor statistics around intent-to-buy such as calendar page views, conversion rates, and which prices are being purchased. Create a tracker for customer complaints, and log any uptick in those related to pricing or dynamic pricing. If sales do decline then look carefully for the root cause before jumping to assumptions or cancelling the whole project. A decline in sales shouldn't be seen as failure, simply one step within a cycle of test-and-learn. Timely intervention can bring things back on track.

Dynamic pricing can fail when it is misaligned with customer expectations, so be sure that when you are pricing upwards, this is against a bedrock of a successful product. It's dangerous to try increasing prices on a title which isn't already in demand. As we did when creating the setup prices, the dynamic prices should be based on sound market analysis and recognised as valuable by consumers.

Risk in dynamic pricing can be mitigated by piloting a trial on one production within a season, or a couple of performances within a run of a production. It is straightforward to measure the conversion rate from each performance page into a sale, so a cohort analysis where some performances are changed and others kept the same will soon quantify any drop in volume or potential increase in revenues. This can give you confidence and rationale for moving forward with a wider scheme.

Most often, I think that customers who complain have misunderstood either what the venue's dynamic pricing strategy is, how it is carried out in practice, or how other businesses operate. Most of the organisations who I have worked with tend to use dynamic pricing as a means to optimise revenue in peak performances to subsidise their more artistic work. They favour conservative dynamic pricing which rarely goes more than 20% over the original price. Meanwhile other industries such as airlines, hotels, energy companies, and so forth, change prices drastically with huge frequency.

For that reason, transparency with customers is essential, and can go a long way to avoiding the most common headaches associated with dynamic pricing. The best arguments to make are about why you are doing dynamic pricing in the first place, how many accessible tickets you actually sell, and the many ways in which customers can purchase tickets at the lowest price.

Most customer complaints relate to ethics, and hence you also need to decide how you will deal with other people's ethical views. If your organisation is a charity, then is it acceptable to earn extra income from dynamic pricing, if that income can be used to support education activities?

Whatever you decide, make sure you prepare your communications well in advance of any dynamic pricing initiative, in consultation with your whole team — producers, marketing, press, box office, and so forth — rather than having to rush to put together a response the first time someone does complain.

Regrettably, once a customer decides to leave your shop then it is very difficult to ever attract them back. They simply have better things to do in life than to check whether your prices have come down. So treat departing customers with reverence, do all you can to make them stay, capture their data so you can contact them in future with a cheaper offer if one emerges, and learn all you can about their level of price resistance to avoid any other customers walking away. The ecosystem of theatregoers is small and fragile so tread carefully.

Finally, to those who say that it is unethical to charge more to people who buy last minute, I point them to an advert I saw recently for the annual Marxist conference in London. Its poster loudly proclaimed:"Book today — advance tickets are cheaper than on the door." Well, if dynamic pricing is good enough for the Marxists, then it's good enough for me!

Marketing initiatives

I spent a year leading the marketing team at a regional theatre, and another four as a head of department in an advertising agency — but I've never thought of myself as a traditional marketer. Yet even if we are not the ones designing posters and distributing flyers, everyone involved in the selling of tickets is in fact a marketer, and our ultimate mission is to promote the show. It's simply that we deal in the world of Excel and ticketing systems.

There are many comprehensive books on arts marketing available to inclined readers, including Liz Hill's excellent work[56], which is why I've restrained myself from commenting on wider marketing efforts up to now, and offer just a few thoughts in this chapter on how it can be done.

Ticketing is marketing, and it's important that our work isn't carried out in isolation. It should be seen in the context of a wider marketing strategy and needs to be aligned with the objectives and initiatives of the wider advertising campaign, otherwise it will be ineffective or worse, counterproductive. So it's essential to maintain very close working relationships with the rest of the marketing team and treat marketing and ticketing as a two-way street with mutual collaboration.

---

[56] Hill, L. et al. (2018) Creative Arts Marketing. London: Routledge, Taylor & Francis Group.

Lead generation

There is a trend for running marketing activity ahead of tickets going on sale, which I would be cautious of. On the one hand, it seems smart to build buzz in anticipation, planting the seeds of a fanbase. However, we are marketing a one-time purchase and so have a strict cost-per-acquisition (CPA) threshold. My concern about activities like social media advertising that encourages people to sign up to a priority on-sale list, or a podcast series about the making of the show, is that these are very expensive cost-per-acquisition activities that come very early in the sales cycle. In both examples, we are forcing a two-step process where we first advertise for people to join our list (or listen to our podcast), and then may have to spend more again later to re-activate them into buying once tickets are on sale.

More curious, still, is the double-opt-in. Recently I received an email from a theatre whose mailing list I have already subscribed to, informing me that they will soon be running an unexciting promotion, and that I should sign up now for early access. Assuming I did this, it would be the second opt-in I had given them before getting a link to buy these particular tickets.

I think we are doing our audiences a disservice in assuming that they have enthusiasm to jump through three hoops in order to make a purchase. Surely, my being on a core newsletter is signal enough that I might be in the market to purchase tickets from this venue. This campaign is increasing the chances of consumers failing to buy a ticket, by actively putting extra steps and time in the way of a purchase. We should get out of the way and reduce barriers to purchase - not create new hurdles in the way of our customers.

There is unnecessary wastage in customers signing up to a list, who then need to be re-activated another day into buying a ticket. Instead, direct your efforts into building a frictionless checkout where customers can buy a ticket within minutes of first seeing your show advertised. Optimise your advertising towards purchases in order to achieve the lowest possible cost per acquisition.

If you do run a sign-up list where people can enter their email to get early access to tickets, then keep in touch with them regularly before the on-sale. If people sign up, hear nothing for a few weeks, and then get a message out of the blue which announces the priority on-sale is about to begin, they may not be able to secure tickets because they have scheduled a meeting, or gone to the gym, or failed to save up the necessary money to actually purchase the tickets. If these are supposedly your die-hard fans, keep them warm and give them a countdown to on-sale so that they are prepared for tickets to drop.

Some people observe that they get the highest return on investment (ROI) from the conversion stage, and so spend increasingly large marketing sums trying to address customers in this part of the funnel. This is also a mistake. The reason why ROI is so high at the bottom is because you are dealing with a smaller number of people, and conversion rates always move inversely to the number of prospects. By definition, the people in the bottom of the funnel are most likely to purchase, or they would have dropped out by now.

However that doesn't mean you should divert all of your marketing spend to them, because the reality is that most of them will buy a ticket anyway if you have done the work of educating, informing and exciting them about the show. Instead, your biggest investment should go in the biggest part of the funnel: awareness and consideration. If there aren't people in the top, then no customers will ever fall out the bottom.

A colleague once observed that conversion rates were higher from people visiting the "About the venue" webpage than the "Buy tickets" web page, and wondered what information on the venue page was so compelling that customers were more likely to book tickets. They suggested that we copy the venue information onto the ticket homepage, so that this fairy dust can work its conversion magic on more visitors.

Regrettably, this is an example of conversion rates being inversely correlated with prospects — there were magnitudes fewer prospects visiting the venue page than the tickets page, and they inevitably had higher intent-to-buy because they were seeking out more information. It wasn't that the venue page was inspiring them to buy, its that their choice to visit the venue page marked them out as being people with a higher intent than the masses on the tickets page.

Comps

I abhor comps and would prefer to never give out another one. Comps are sometimes requested close to the time of performance for a show which has many empty seats. The rationale is usually that it will be a poor experience for the paying audience to feel that they are surrounded by empty seats, that the actors will have a poor experience looking out to an empty auditorium, and that any visiting reviewers need to get a perception that the show is popular and thriving. Hence, tickets are distributed through networks of friends and the auditorium fills up.

Comps are damaging because word spreads very quickly that free tickets exist and suddenly you have created a problem for yourself where people no longer want to pay for tickets because they've heard that free tickets are circulating. This perpetuates the problem, so you have more empty seats for the following performance. Shows which look to comp are rarely solid-gold blockbusters with one performance that needs help; there is usually a deeper issue, and it is short sighted to expect that a Band-Aid of papering will make things better.

An argument is sometimes made that comped audiences will come back, if they like the show, and bring their friends, but the reality is that less than 5% of audiences ever return to the same production. More to the point, any positive word of mouth they do spread will usually begin with "I got these free tickets to a great show..."

In short, comps do no good whatsoever for your revenue, they bring down the average ticket price, they devalue the show in the minds of prospective consumers, and they shrink the size of your addressable market for tomorrow's performance. Yet when you're looking at an auditorium that's only 10% full, it can be hard to resist calls to give seats away.

So how do you avoid ending up in that difficult situation? By following the principles discussed throughout this book. By the time you are looking at comping, it is already too late to try alternative strategies, so avoiding it requires proactive work. Keep a close eye on sales trajectories and estimate how many tickets each performance is likely to get to. That way, you can speak up early if the number will make for a poor audience or actor experience. Have an honest conversation with the producer and marketing colleagues about the bare minimum acceptable attendance, and run tactical initiatives to move the dial, such as reduced-price "bring a friend" for that performance, or a half-price offer for friends and family of the cast/crew/ venue staff to attend on that performance. In truth, these are comps by another name — but as with any marketing initiative, presentation matters. Someone who pays for one ticket and fills two seats is better than someone who gets in for free and brings nobody.

Another tactic to avoid having to comp a poorly sold auditorium is "dressing the house," or the art of moving people's tickets so that the auditorium looks fuller than it is. Moving everyone further forward, closing the balconies, and covering large central holes, all improve the appearance of the room, for both the audience and the cast.

Closing upper levels should be done as soon as you identify that the performance won't reach its necessary levels. Take whatever cheap prices you had on sale up there and make seats available downstairs at that price. You can always open up the circle again later but, most likely, if you are in the territory of potential comping, then the performance needs all the help it can get.

Dressing the house can be done on the morning of the performance, and ushers can inform patrons of their newly upgraded seats when they check tickets at incoming. The curtain may go up a few minutes late, but it's easier to move people in person on the night than trying to explain it over phone or email. Customers are invariably delighted to be told that they have been "upgraded" to a better seat, and rarely turn their heads to see the rows of empty seats behind them.

Trade nights are another good way to avoid making comps available to the public. On a trade night, you invite B2B industry colleagues see the show so that they can spread the word to their customers, and a quiet performance is a great way to get them in without losing a sellable seat. This is another reason to monitor a performance by performance report regularly and identify weak sales well in advance. If you call up a B2B guest on the day of performance and offer them a free ticket, they will see it for what it is, and no one likes to feel like a filler at a party. So give them the courtesy of an invitation in advance, build that professional relationship, and it'll be doubly beneficial.

When to spend on marketing

Answer: when the going is good, and also when the going is not good.

Obviously, if things are going poorly, they won't turn around on their own. In these cases, it's not groundbreaking advice to find the root cause, try something to fix it — like changing the messaging/creative/pricing/target audience — and then advertise your new initiative.

Yet if things are going well, then you should also be spending on advertising, and this is a lesson which is both less obvious and evidently, for some producers, difficult to learn.

I remember one tour of a musical which played to 60% capacity everywhere it went. Yet at one big venue, sales were at 70% with months to go. The venue director asked the producer how much more they were planning to invest in order for the show to sell-out, but the reply came that they were in fact pulling all investment back early, because the show had already exceeded their target.

Sure, they had recouped their investment on this venue, but they were leaving money on the table. They were effectively saying that they'd rather save their marketing budget for more challenging cities to prop up those performances, rather than earn cream on the successful venue which had clearly demonstrated a highly effective marketing machine already.

Faced with this choice, I would also advise it's better to put the investment into the venue which delivers the higher return on advertising spend and earn near-guaranteed sales, rather than the uphill battle of a sticky venue. As in physics, it takes more energy to get a ball rolling than to keep it rolling — so harness the momentum you already have. Once the hit venue has sold out, you'll have more money to work with than if you did what the touring producer did and let it sit 30% empty. Either way, when a show is a success, invest more and get it to sold out, because you'll need it to tide you through the rainy days.

Ten to one

An important consideration when setting a strategy is your commercial goals for once this production is over. Are you trying to sell one thing to ten people or ten things to one person?

If one product represents the majority of your anticipated sales (like a ticket to your long-running show that you plan to tour nationally or internationally), then remove distractions. Focus on that one product and how to sell it as best you can for the next several years — quite possibly by taking sales from other productions or venues.

On the other hand, if you are trying to establish a local venue with a changing program and a loyal audience which keep returning, then consider what they need to keep coming back. An all-out strategy to aggressively sell out a single production is unlikely to help you in this scenario. Instead, you might be better off considering how you can sell today's production in such a way as to incentivise bookers to return for tomorrow's.

Beyond the ticket

Though we're ticketing managers, selling the ticket is not the end of our job: revenue diversification is also essential in making the show or venue commercially resilient. Selling a drink and a ticket to the next show, or bundling in an item of show merchandise, could increase your per-customer revenue by 50%, so it's worth more than an afterthought.

Spend-per-head is a metric of how much additional income audience members bring to the venue, besides the ticket purchase. It can simply be calculated by summing all of the evening's ancillary revenue (from the venue bar, restaurant, merchandise stand, bookshop, car park, etc.) and dividing it by the total attendance. This gives a monetary figure for the average ancillary spend per customer, and makes for a helpful target which you can set about increasing.

Note that different genres inherently have different spend-per-head, with children's shows at the bottom end, followed by plays, then musicals, and at the top end broad entertainment events where drinking is encouraged, like comedy and sports. We broke the theatre's record for spend-per-head when we hosted a darts evening which brought a crowd of heavy drinkers.

In setting targets to increase your spend-per-head, do so within the context of what each genre can achieve, because a show for the under-fives is never going to be going through kegs of beer like a late-night comedy event.

Are there packages or add-ons which can transform a passive viewing a performance into a luxury experience? Customers delight in having relevant, timely recommendations which can elevate their evenings and take the thinking out of where to eat, drink, or find a quiet spot for a pre-show date. The more intuitively you can place these ancillary spend options in the booking flow, the greater your customer satisfaction and conversion rates.

One venue told me that customers didn't need a pre-show upsell, because the were already satisfied with pre-ordering an interval drink at the bar before the show. After some cajoling, they agreed to try adding a simple option in the booking flow for customers to add a gin and tonic — the venue's most popular seller. Drink sales increased, and more importantly it was all incremental revenue: there was no decline in pre-orders made in-person.

We then tried sending an email to customers in the days leading up the show, asking if they'd like to pre-order a gin and tonic. Again, overall sales increased with no reduction to either the booking flow upsells or the in-person sales.

What had happened was that each of the three touchpoints was connecting with a different customer segment: people who like to plan ahead, people who need a chase, and impulse buyers. There were no complaints about us pestering audiences with the upsell because it was self evidently relevant and of value to them.

The booking flow is also a good opportunity to seek donations from customers whilst they have credit card in hand. In 'Nudge'[57], the authors point to card machines that ask customers to choose between a tip of 15%, 20%, 25%, and "choose your own amount". The result was that tip income increased from the level that customers had previously paid in cash. There were several reasons for this "tipflation". First, the options are skewed higher than what customers might choose for themselves; second, because most customers elect for the middle option, which is 20%; and third, because "choose your own amount" is comparatively hard work when in a hurry. You can apply the same logic in asking for donations.

Another way to increase ancillary spend is experiences such as meet-and-greets, or exclusive merchandise items like signed programmes. (Recall my anecdote about the football team in the pricing chapter, who were more than happy to pay for add-ons like this.) Opportunities to interact with the cast or obtain exclusive memorabilia are especially popular with cult audiences, but you need to think about it early; the very type of audience who will be interested are also the audiences who will be at the first performance, so you need to action it quickly before they've all seen the show and it's too late.

For a broader audience, merchandise (plush toys, keyrings, apparel, imitation props, etc.) are a great way for them to take home a piece of the show. The exclusivity of the item means that you can command a higher price than, say, a keyring would cost in a high street shop.

---

[57] Thaler, R.H. and Sunstein, C.R. (2022) Nudge: The final edition. London: Penguin Books.

For small or regional venues, workshops and behind-the-scenes tours are a great way to engage the community and show audiences all the work that goes into raising the curtain, while earning a little ancillary income from daytime activities in the venue.

That being said, beware the ticketing flow which becomes weighed down with good ideas, such that the offering is now quite cumbersome for the passing consumer to make sense of. The sign that this is occurring is that customers spend a long amount of time on the website when evaluating the options they can book for, but often leave without purchasing.

When this happens, it's worth stepping back and focusing on the hero product. For a first-timer, what is the one thing which you want them to buy? Re-structure your booking flow around this, and save the diversified offering for a more discrete page which fans can seek out.

Once customers are within the booking flow, you can upsell them with add-ons. Once a customer has made a transaction, you can tell them about your other offerings. But generally the confusion which is sowed through trying to present multiple options to first-time audiences just sees too many customers dropping out before purchasing, undoing any gain you make from customers booking into these niche products.

Digital content is increasingly prevalent in the post-Covid world, although there appears to be a stark ceiling on how much audiences are willing to pay for something which is neither a film nor a live event. If you're considering charging for digital content, you need an incentive for people to pay for it — as opposed to coming in person or not engaging with you at all. So if you have an original piece of work, an A-list cast, a limited season with overflowing demand, or a geographically broad audience, you'll have more success selling it than if it's just another production of *Macbeth*. These are the shows where it's worth investing in filming the event and distributing it digitally. Plenty of websites have sprung up in recent years which make the hosting, monetisation and streaming elements very easy, if you can capture the content and get word out to your audience.

Gift cards are highly desirable by consumers for birthdays and holiday seasons. Here, a customer might buy a £100 voucher which their friend can redeem against theatre tickets within the next year. It serves many benefits because it's a thoughtful gift that also allows the recipient the flexibility to choose their own production, dates and seats.

More importantly, for you, it is cashflow-positive. If the recipient's desired tickets come to £110 total, you effectively get two transactions when they "top up" the card — and then there is "wastage" from customers who never redeem their vouchers at all. (Starbucks proudly hold over $1 billion in unused gift cards.[58]) Clearly you need to design terms and conditions which are not predatory and give people a reasonable length of time to make their booking, and perhaps also proactive email reminders that they have a voucher to use. But after a year or two when vouchers are unredeemed, or there is some value still left on the card, the venue has done very well by not actually needing to fulfil any booking.

To sell gift cards well, promote them widely across your website, brochure and social media. The biggest anxiety of these consumers is that their friend won't be able to make use of the card, so give clear messaging that it can be used for all shows online and in person. If your gift cards are part of a scheme which can be used across a chain of venues or nationwide, then promote that hook as well so the voucher feels as good as cash. Asking consumers to choose their own value of gift voucher can cause indecision paralysis, so give a recommended value which is enough to cover two Band A tickets, and then the option to adjust if desired.

One final way to earn extra revenue comes not from customers at all but from corporate sponsorship. A company might write a check that supports the production, in exchange for their corporate logo on the ticket stock, or access to tickets for their staff or customers. These companies can be local or multi-national, and generally support the arts in this way either for corporate social responsibility, to offset their own toxic brand with something more cuddly, to get in front of affluent audiences with disposable income, or to give a perk to their clients.

Whatever their motives, be sure their support won't also come with hidden costs to you. Carefully consider whether the values of your theatre match those of the sponsor, and whether your audience will object to having the Marlboro Man attending the performance. Sponsors may want early access to tickets, last-minute access for sold out shows or exclusive seats reserved especially for them. Their requirements can be exacting and often push the limitations of ticketing systems, so work with them early to define exactly what is needed and create a smooth process.

---

58 Starbucks Earnings Call Q2 2022: https://www.fool.com/earnings/call-transcripts/2022/05/04/starbucks-sbux-q2-2022-earnings-call-transcript/

Venue apps

There has been a post-pandemic trend for venues to launch their own mobile apps, which store e-tickets and facilitate food and drink purchases.

The reality is that consumers do not want this bloatware on their phone for a venue which they attend once or twice a year. Far from being a convenience, having to download and log into an app is actually more work than just collecting a paper ticket from the box office – and many times customers would prefer to stretch their legs with a walk to the bar at the interval, rather than hope that an usher brings a pre-ordered drink on time. Besides, internet connection is often patchy in venues due to their construction and the number of users trying to get online simultaneously, so invariably your app won't work anyway at the time when it might actually be useful.

Similarly, any consideration of keeping audiences informed about the show ahead of time (traffic updates, running times etc.) are better delivered in a software-agnostic way (such as email or SMS), where you can be assured that 100% of the audience have received the message. Meanwhile, the primary user benefit of a venue app – being able to buy tickets – is only of use to someone if they do in fact attend multiple times per year, and I would wager that if they're attending your theatre multiple times a year they are probably attending others just as often. In that case, they probably prefer buying tickets in a web browser or an aggregator app, rather than downloading a separate piece of software for each venue.

For all these reasons, I suggest putting resources elsewhere rather than pursuing a venue app which doesn't actual service customer needs.

Ideas for the future

In this chapter I will discuss some new innovations in the field of ticketing, some which are happening at a small scale already, some which are on the cusp of happening, and some wholly new ideas.

Not showing all available seats

Showing the whole seating plan increases cognitive load for customers and gives them hundreds of redundant options which obstruct their decision-making process.

Instead, we could just show them the two or three best options within each price band. Once they know that the front centre seats of the circle are available, and so are the front aisle seats, then it serves no purpose to display seats in the row behind which are at the same price — because customers will 99% of the time not choose to sit there. It is also a benefit to the venue as it would increase conversion rate and perception of scarcity.

Overbooking

Airlines have been doing this for years but I have so far been unsuccessful at persuading any producers to follow suit — even though it feels like a natural fit for a sold-out performance. The basic principle is that there are always some people who have booked for a performance but don't attend, and for venues which scan tickets or tear off ticket stubs, you can calculate this number of "no shows" based on historical data and work out a reliable minimum number per performance.

The concept would be that performances are then purposely oversold by this number of known no-shows, perhaps at a discounted rate where the customer understands that they will only learn where they are sat at curtain up — and that there is a small risk that they won't get to see the performance (perhaps offset by a free drink and guarantee to see the next performance). The benefit would be reliably 100% full auditoria, a neat way to fill holes in sensitive parts of the house, and incremental revenue from the extra tickets sold.

Buying presale tickets sight-unseen

Presale customers could be offered the chance to name their own price when buying tickets. Then, once all the presale bookings have been made, the customers are allocated to the best available seats within the auditorium based on price. So whoever chose to spend the most would get placed in objectively the best seat, followed by the second-highest paying customer, and so on.

The rationale here is that, like a blind auction, it may result in customers paying a higher price than they would have done by selecting from a plan. As a result, you may end up selling more premium tickets that you would have planned to put on the seating plan. Indeed, the entire performance could be sold at premium rate if that is what customers believe it is worth.

It also adds some element of democracy, because there is no risk that a high-paying presale customer will be usurped by a last-minute customer who bags a discount and ends up sitting next to them — there is an inherent fairness that whoever pays the most, gets the best experience.

Once the presale is over, any remaining seats would go on sale in the conventional way with customers selecting from a plan, but obviously all subsequent customers would be sat behind anyone who purchased in the presale.

Waitlist

When I worked at the ticket office of a successful theatre, I would field half a dozen calls a day from customers who would like to be added to the waitlist for a sold-out performance. I would reply that we had no such facility, and that they should call back later in case one was added.

Years later, it is curious that, to my knowledge, this feature isn't mainstream.I suggest a simple feature where customers name the upper price of ticket which they'd like to buy, pre-authorise their card details and automatically have tickets reserved for them if they become available. A combination of email and SMS alerts could immediately notify them that they've been successful, giving them an hour to confirm before automatically cascading through the next name on the list. This would effectively sell every ticket for very popular shows, remove the stress of customers constantly checking the website, and liberate hours of time from box office staff trying to do this themselves at busy times.

At the very least, it makes sense to capture data on these customers who have gone out of their way to enquire about a show which they probably know is sold out. They will be exactly the kind of people who your marketing team would love to advertise the next show to.

We've already saved you a seat

I'm fascinated by removing psychological barriers to the process of booking tickets, the biggest of which is deciding upon a performance date and where to sit.

In reality, I suspect that most customers can accommodate their plans if given two months' notice, and are generally quite happy to sit in the same seats that they did last time.

Hence I suggest that, when a new play goes on sale, you simply reserve seats for all customers who attended the last play, in the same seats and at the same equivalent performance (i.e. the audience from the first Saturday in the previous season's run would attend on the first Saturday for this new play). Then, email them announcing the play, inform them that the hard work has been done for them because seats are already reserved, and that they simply need to confirm that their credit card on file should be charged.

There's an urgency because you'll require them to pay before the imminent general on sale, when all tickets go on sale to the public, and there's an element of flattery because you make them feel recognised as part of the theatre's community. We know that people value losing things twice as much as they value gaining things, so this language will spur them on to "keep" their reserved ticket before someone else takes it.

It's no problem of course if that can't make that date or would prefer another seat, because you'll allow them to book anywhere in the usual way — but it has gone some way to getting them through the door and bringing down barriers for more customers, as well as helping with that ever-illusive challenge of getting the second booking.

Customer centricity

Tech businesses have pursued a strategy of orientating their business around customer needs at any cost. For example, you can happily return any item to Amazon with no questions asked — well beyond any statutory requirement — purely because they believe that customer satisfaction is one of the most important drivers of growth.

Certainly this is a costly approach, and most of the businesses which evangelise it have yet to turn a profit[59], but it does two things very well: it ensures that business functions are aligned with customer needs, and that the company dominates their chosen vertical. Customer centricity elevates the importance of customer lifetime value rather than that of a single transaction, empowers employees to make proactive decisions, and continually acts on feedback to improve the customer experience.

Ticket selling is traditionally quite rigid, looking after customers until the point that they've bought a ticket and then making few post-sale accommodations. Some areas where we could improve are a WhatsApp number where customers can ask questions, or more lenient booking policies — such as full refunds permitted within 24 hours after booking. Some in the industry understandably worry that such lenient policies would be too costly overall, but I suspect customer-centric policies like this would give more people confidence to book and so would end up as a net positive.

---

59 https://www.cnbc.com/2018/08/29/no-profits-no-problem-the-economy-has-a-growing-appetite-for-unprofitable-companies.html

Conclusion

Theatre should be dead by now. We live in the era of 24-7 television, Hollywood films at home, of 3D, metaverse, on-demand, gamified everything, where the best entertainment in the world is available instantly in the palm of everyone's hands.

Yet, in a world where staying in is the new going out, theatres are packed. Sophocles' two-and-a-half-thousand-year-old play, *Oedipus*, will have two star-led London productions this year, and an adaptation of *The Merchant of Venice* will return to the West End after a national tour, resident in a theatre only a few miles from where it was first performed for King James in 1605. The 150-year old Scandinavian play, *An Enemy of the People,* will have separate star-led productions mounted in both New York and London. All five shows will surely play to packed houses, be profitable for their producers and delight audiences with classic stories told on stage.

Despite everything which the modern world has to offer, customers will open their wallets and buy tickets for experiences which can only be enjoyed live. Together they'll sit in darkness and get swept away to the far-away worlds of their imaginations, in the same way which theatre has been doing for millennia.

Thriving theatres means that the need for passionate, well-informed, experienced ticketing managers is greater than ever. It's up to us to use and continue evolving the principles in these pages to ensure that another 3,000 years from now Sophocles is still being staged — and that those of us who want to make a decent living working in the arts can still do so. If we put the audience first, create sound strategies and are led by the data, then I am optimistic that we'll keep selling out.

Acknowledgements

"Everyone has a book in them, but in most cases that's where it should stay." — Christopher Hitchens [60]

Thank you, the reader, for making it to the end and giving consideration to the ideas I've laid out.

With grateful thanks also to my colleagues at TodayTix Group, AKA, HQ Theatres, Purple Seven, and the National Theatre, who taught me so much and patiently went along with my hare-brained schemes.

With appreciation to all of the clients and producers who have trusted me with their shows, let me experiment with their money, and allowed me to fail so that we could all learn.

Thank you to Derek Walker whose infectious passion for theatre is an inspiration, and to Liam Wright, who has been my steadfast collaborator and brought so many of these ideas to life.

I wouldn't have finished this project without the generosity and expertise of my editorial consultant, Andrew Ladd.

With gratitude to everyone who I have met along the way that has inspired, mentored, nurtured and listened.

Thank you to my friends who never tire of hear me talk about theatre ticketing.

60 C-SPAN discussion 'About Books', 1997

Glossary

Advance
The amount of tickets sold for performances in the future, or the gross income associated with those tickets.

Agents
Third party companies who sell legitimate tickets.

API
Programming interface between the primary venue box office and third party ticket agents. Allows agents to sell tickets live 'off the plan'.

Booking Fee
A cost charged to the customer for buying a ticket. Revenue goes entirely to the ticket seller.

Break-even
The net revenue required for a performance to cover its costs, not making a profit or a loss.

Daily Wrap
Tickets transacted on a particular day, and the gross associated with those tickets.

Doors
Tickets sold on the day of performance.

Dynamic Pricing
Changing the price of a ticket once it is on sale.

Entry Price
The lowest advertised price at which tickets are on sale.

Gross
Short for gross revenue. All revenue taken by a show in a particular period, including VAT and any inside commissions. Excludes restoration levy.

Gross potential (GP)
The maximum potential income if every seat is sold at full price.

House

The number of tickets sold for a particular performance.

Can also refer to the capacity of the auditorium, or all of the physical space in front of the curtain.

Inside Commission

Fee charged to the production for an agent to promote a show.

Matured

Performances that have already occurred, or the income/tickets associated with them.

Net

Short for net revenue. The gross, less VAT and all commissions.

On-sales (Priority and General)

A priority on-sale is selling tickets to a select group (for example fans, members of a specific mailing list, customers of a sponsor or preferred ticket agent). A general on-sale is when tickets are first made available for the public at large to buy.

Open potential

The potential revenue of remaining open seats; how much opportunity is there is if you sold all seats which are currently unsold.

Premiums and super premiums

The highest priced tickets in the best seating position. Premiums are > 20% higher than Band A, and super premiums are higher still.

Price band

Seats at the same price. Band A will be better and higher-priced than Band B, which will be preferable to Band C, and so forth.

Price type

A modification to the price band made on a per-transaction basis. Could be due to a particular type of customer (student, senior, member) or an advertised promotion (two for one in June, book early and save).

Reserve

Tickets which have been booked but not paid for, typically for a group or school.

Restoration Levy

A fee charged to the customer towards a theatre's investment in maintaining their historic buildings.

Sales Channel

The means by a which a ticket has been sold, for example a ticket agent, the show's website, telephone sales via the box office.

Printed in Great Britain
by Amazon

39611157R00149